HAIL TO THE ORANGE AND BLUE!

100 Years of Illinois Football Tradition

LINDA YOUNG

SAGAMORE PUBLISHING INC.
CHAMPAIGN, IL 61824-0673

Production Coordinator: Susan M. Williams
Cover and photo insert design: Michelle R. Dressen
Cover illustration: Jack W. Davis
Production Assistant: Brian J. Moore
Editors: Joyce D. Meyer and Lisa A. Busjahn
Proofreader: Phyllis L. Bannon

10   9   8   7   6   5   4   3   2   1

Library of Congress Catalog Card Number: 90-61018
ISBN: 0-915611-31-7

We have made every effort to trace the ownership of all copyrighted material and to appropriately acknowledge such ownership. In the event of any question arising as to the use of any material, we will be pleased to make the necessary changes in future printings.

Photo credits: Pages 45, 179, Champaign News-Gazette; pages 61 bottom, 191 top, 192, 193, 197, 199, 211, Mark Jones; pages 93, 150, 152 bottom, 154, 155, 201, Brian J. Moore; page 110, Lester Nehamkin; page 137, Curt Beamer; pages 159, 165, 179, 189, 194, Gary Anderson; pages 170, 175, Mike Smeltzer. All other photos courtesy of the University of Illinois Athletic Department.

Sagamore Publishing Inc.
PO Box 673
Champaign, IL 61824-0673
Printed in the United States of America

To Scott Williams,
for having the vision—and perseverance—to get the whole thing started

CONTENTS

PART IV: FROM ELIOT TO ELLIOTT

PART V: THE MODERN ERA

ACKNOWLEDGMENTS

Digging through 100 years of anything is, I found, a major undertaking and could not be accomplished without the cooperation—usually cheerful—of a number of people. There's hardly a person involved with the Division of Intercollegiate Athletics who hasn't offered an encouraging word during the course of this project. They have no idea how much I appreciate their support.

My thanks first and foremost to the University of Illinois sports information staff. Mike Pearson, Dick Barnes, Kent Brown, Dave Johnson, graduate assistants Frank Reed and Kevin Nordquist and office manager Janice Revell were always more than willing to help me dig through volumes of records to find something. All I had to do was ask, and believe me, I asked.

Thanks also to athletic director-football coach John Mackovic and his staffs who always found time from their busy schedules to help me out. Also to Dike Eddleman, Bill Butkovich, Stan Wallace, Sam Rebecca, Loren Tate, and LaVere L. Astroth, who were among those taking time to share the history they lived.

To all my friends and family who have graciously promised to buy the book, especially those of you with little or no interest in football. Thanks, guys, that's a great boost to the ego.

Finally, special thanks to Alice Cozad for insisting simply, yes, you can.

Linda Young

The often-sung phrase, "We're loyal to you Illinois," raises several fond thoughts for me.

First and foremost, the University of Illinois itself, truly one of the great educational institutions in the world. Implicit in that thought is the recognition of its superb faculty—past and present—who expand their daily opportunities of teaching and research to make our world a better place.

Secondly and not surprisingly, I think of Illini football. From its humble and tentative beginnings, University of Illinois football has witnessed the creation of traditions, the achievement of greatness, and the greatness of true sportsmanship. To have been part of one of the golden eras of Illinois football is a memory that grows sweeter with each passing day. Like the many players whose names you will encounter in the following pages, I recognize that success is not singular. The success we enjoyed was also built by the contributions of many players whose names you may not recall. But they are nonetheless a part of the greatness of the Illinois football tradition. I shall not forget them.

It goes without saying that the coaches, assistant coaches, the Athletic Association staff members, and the fans who supported us through the good years and the lean also shared the hope, inspired the same dedication, and worked just as diligently and energetically as Bob Zuppke, Ray Eliot, Pete Elliott, and John Mackovic. They all helped build the Illinois football tradition. On a more personal note, I must not forget Assistant Coach Bill Taylor, who helped teach me to be a winner.

Those of us who had the great honor to wear the Orange and Blue as part of the University of Illinois and its football tradition owe a great deal to many. I have found that my "Illinois loyalty" has grown through the years as its meaning and value continue to unfold. My memories of players and coaches and former teammates, watching my nephew play with the 1980-83 Fighting Illini, all serve as strong bonds to the University.

Like all of those with special ties to Illinois, I am delighted to be able to relive some of my memories in the pages of this book. I'm sure it will bring back equally meaningful memories for all Illini—friends, fans, and family. The tradition will undoubtedly continue because together, "We're loyal to you Illinois."

Dick Butkus

Dick Butkus
1990

PART I: THE EARLY ILLINI

ILLINOIS
1890
1990
FOOTBALL
100 YEARS OF TRADITION
®

"Football was a swashbuckling, inventive game at Illinois and elsewhere in the pioneer days of the Gay Nineties."

Lon Eubanks

"There ain't no such animal."

—An unidentified upperclassman's reply when questioned about the 1889 University of Illinois football team.

All Scott Williams intended to do was keep a promise.

Before entering the University of Illinois in 1889, Williams played as a back for the State Normal University high school team. Williams was going to enter the University of Illinois as a prep. His teammates planned to play football at nearby Illinois Wesleyan University. They assured him he was a cinch to make the Illinois team, and Williams promised that if he did, he and his teammates would set up a game with Wesleyan.

What he didn't know was that few of the 519 students and 39 faculty members on the Champaign-Urbana campus had ever heard, nor did they care to hear, of a college football game, even though the first one had been played between Princeton and Rutgers in 1869, two years after the University of Illinois opened its doors.

"When I inquired about the football team at the university, an upperclassman gruffly replied, 'there ain't no such animal,' " Williams would later recall. "Imagine that if you can. Here [I] was a player from a high school less than fifty miles away. . . and neither I nor anyone else at Normal or Wesleyan knew there wasn't a football team at Illinois. . . Probably nothing could better illustrate the absolute disorganization of intercollegiate athletics at that time."

Scott Williams' First Team

Nevertheless, when Williams noticed a bulletin board card advertising that anyone interested in football should report to campus that afternoon, he did just that. That afternoon he saw ". . . about a dozen fellows chasing a sort of portable bath tub inflated by lung power, kicking it in any direction whenever they got a chance to." He watched them until they sat down to rest. When he approached and bashfully asked to play when they were ready to start the game, they replied that the game was over and he could play some other day.

Scott Williams didn't take no for an answer. He recalled his feelings at the time: "That made me sore, and I gave that outfit a lecture on football, trying to circle the big tub with my arms and show how the ball was carried, passed and kicked, also explaining the scrimmage and the points in scoring. The boys lined up and we played a few minutes in a funny kind of a way, but they liked it and agreed to come out again some other time."

Few others on the Illinois campus shared their enthusiasm. When word got out that someone on campus knew how to play football, student leaders denounced the sport as a "brutal Indian game." Williams recalled, "The upperclassman who pinned the football notice on the bulletin board was 'bawled out' good and plenty and I was told that it wasn't healthy for preps to butt in and start any rough stuff."

By the next year much of the initial upperclassmen antagonism subsided. Unfortunately, it was replaced with little enthusiasm. Nevertheless, Williams and a handful of other would-be football players went to the athletic powers-that-be with an impassioned plea and a promise to pay their own expenses to let them play Wesleyan in Bloomington. Finally, with the assurance that Williams and his teammates would foot the bill themselves for uniforms and train fare, the university gave its approval for a football team to represent the University of Illinois at the Illinois Oratorical Association meeting in Bloomington. In those days athletics was commonly piggybacked to oratorical meets.

On October 2, 1890, with Scott Williams serving as coach, captain, and quarterback, the University of Illinois lost to Wesleyan, 16-0, but Illini football had its foot in the door.

A Challenge From Purdue

What little momentum had been generated might never have been sustained had not Purdue president John Henry Smart invited the 12 Illinois players over for a game in West Lafayette, Indiana.

"He [Smart] said our university beat his in some ways, but if we would bring our football team over to Lafayette, they would beat the everlasting daylights out of us," Williams said. That invitation apparently touched the pride of many of Illinois' best athletes, including that of an upperclassman named George Huff, who would eventually become the driving force in building Illinois athletics.

For the next eight weeks, learning everything they could from Williams and a rulebook, the Illinois team prepared for Purdue. Williams joked during the train ride to the game that the husky Illinois upperclassmen should take care not to kill any of the Indiana boys. No fear of that. Purdue, which had already been playing the game for three seasons, won 62-0.

The *Daily Illini* put it this way: "The Purdue eleven had been training under a coach at Indianapolis and could show our boys more tricks in five minutes than our boys ever knew about football. They had a faculty of appropriating the ball to their own use and only allowed their opponents to get possession of it about a dozen times during the game. This accounts for the nothing on our side of the score.

Action from the first U of I football game vs. Illinois Wesleyan in 1890

Game ball from first U of I football victory, November 27, 1890

"However, our boys learned a lot more about football than they would have if they had not gone, so they have that for a consolation."

On the way home Williams feared it might be he whom the husky upperclassmen would want to squash.

"I would probably have begged and pleaded with them not to kill me if I hadn't had a sneaking sort of wish that they would put me out of my misery before I had to face the university crowd again," he said. None of the players expected what they saw upon their return to Champaign-Urbana.

"If anyone thinks that Illinois loyalty is a development of later days, let them look at the picture of that broken and beaten team playing even then an all-but-despised game, feeling keenly the disgrace they felt they had brought upon the school they loved," Williams said. "Then look at the team as they got off of the cars, meeting instead of curses and imprecations, the cheers of a bunch of students down to welcome them home. They were grabbed and slapped on the back, and heavy hearts beat high again when told with oaths of emphasis

that 'you had the nerve to tackle them at their own game. Never mind the score, we'll even that up later. We're proud of you and we'll stay by you till the cows come home.' "

In defeat, Illinois' first great football rivalry was born. Fans were getting hooked on the game. So, too, were the players.

Player Commitment, Fan Loyalty

"Some fine things have happened in the history of Illinois athletics," Williams said, "but I know of nothing finer than the loyalty that made the prominent athletes of their day submit to the orders of a freshman captain and punish themselves physically and mentally by playing a game that they then despised."

George Huff, who would be known simply as "G" to his many friends during his long career as an Illinois athlete, coach, and athletic director, showed the first sign of his tremendous devotion to Illinois. Said Williams, "George Huff played for a long time from sheer loyalty . . . But he fell for it as they all do sooner or later."

George Huff, Athletic Director, 1901-1936

The first season ended on a high note. Five days after the Purdue debacle, Illinois beat Wesleyan at the Illini's first home football game. The game was played at the Champaign County Fairgrounds in Urbana. Admission was 25 cents for men, and the ladies got in free. Nearly 300 spectators attended.

The Illinois team had been practicing a few of the tricks they learned at Purdue to show Wesleyan, but they couldn't do it without a boost. Illinois wasn't blessed with many substitutes and near the end of the game the home team was exhausted, prompting the call for help from the spectators. Robert Humphrey Forbes, an agricultural engineering student, class of '92, loosened his tie, but kept his derby hat on as he leaped into the fray.

These men were the original Illini:William A. Furber, left tackle; Herbert Bowen, left end; Ralph Hart and Walter Shattuck, left guards; George Huff, center; Andrew Gates, right guard; James Steele, right tackle; Fred Clark, right end; Scott Williams, quarterback; Arthur Pillsbury, William F. Slater,and Royal Wright, halfbacks; Ed Clark and Albert Higgins, fullbacks; Arthur Bush, substitute; and, of course,a special tip of the derby to Robert Humphrey Forbes.

The original Illinois football team

HAIL TO THE ORANGE AND BLUE !

The first uniforms may not have been regulation, but they were memorable. Wrote Robert Lackey, who played for Purdue in that 62-0 shellacking, and later coached the Illini in 1891, "The Illini uniforms were wonderful to look at. They were made by a harness maker out of white canvas with a cap made of pasteboard to resemble a Turkish fez with a black rosette on the side."

2 CONTROVERSIES AND RIVALRIES

"The style of play at the start resembled basketball in its open formation."

—Scott Williams, first
Illini captain, quarterback, and coach

By 1891, Scott Williams no longer needed to serve as the Illini's head coach, nor did he quarterback or always captain the team. Football was becoming well established in Champaign-Urbana and Williams could play any position where he was needed. He had time to teach other players the finer points of their positions. Before he left for Cornell in 1893, Williams played every position except guard and center for Illinois.

Robert Lackey, who had captained the Purdue team that had beaten Illinois a year earlier, became the new coach and part-time halfback. Illinois joined its first league, the Illinois Intercollegiate League, with Knox, Eureka, and Illinois Wesleyan. Illinois' only loss was 8-0 to Lake Forest in the season opener. Lake Forest later forfeited that game for using ineligible players. College football was starting to resemble the modern game in both style and controversy.

Illinois won the league championship cup, but not without a few detours on the way. After Lake Forest forfeited to Illinois, giving the Illini five points toward the championship cup, Knox College, which was to have played Lake Forest later in the season, also claimed five points. At this juncture, the league committee decided the Galesburg school had to play a game in Champaign.

Illinois Field, site of early U of I football games

The October 6 *Daily Illini* reported what followed this way: "When our boys appeared for the game, the gates of the park were closed. The reason given was 'that the owners had been informed that for the past three days and a half, betting had been practiced within the enclosures of that park.' Queer though it may seem, not half of the Knox football team came out of the park after dinner, and yet they should have had no knowledge of the park being closed. If their team had put in its appearance, we might have adjourned to the fairgrounds or some neighboring pasture and played the game anyway. As they didn't, nothing was left for us to do but come home. The points for the entire contest stood Knox 31 [including the Lake Forest game they didn't play], Illinois 30."

Knox and Illinois did play later in the season and Illinois' 12-0 victory assured the Illini the championship cup.

Refining the Game

By then the game, as played by the Illini, had already made great strides. Said Williams, "The style of play at the start resembled basketball in its open formation. Linemen stood an easy distance apart, the ends playing in with the line. There was no interference. The center rolled the ball back with his foot, the quarter tossed it to a halfback some five or 10 yards behind the line, and the half started out upon an unknown course with high hopes and the determination to do the best he could.

"Before the first season ended, we had caught up on several years' advancement made by other teams, were playing closer together, had some sort of interference, had cut off the 'snap back' at center and were tackling at the knees instead of riding opponents around the waist or neck. We even had acquired a double pass behind the line. Next year we developed the 'V' and under the tutelage of [E.K.] 'Boss' Hall of Dartmouth in '92 and '93, Illinois developed a class of football second to none in the west."

In 1892 Hall put the Illini in green uniforms, a color that would be abandoned two years later when Illinois settled permanently on orange

and blue. He also put Illinois through perhaps the most demanding schedule ever foisted on a college football team. The Illini, 18 players strong, played six games in eight days, in three states.

Hall's Ironman Trip

October 21 at St. Louis: Illinois 22, Washington University 0

October 22 at Omaha: Illinois 20, Doane College 0

October 24 at Lincoln: Nebraska 6, Illinois 0

October 26 at Baldwin, KS: Illinois 26, Baker University 10

October 27 at Lawrence, KS: Kansas 26, Illinois 4

October 29 at Kansas City: Illinois 42, Kansas City Athletic Club 0

E.K. "Boss" Hall

After the trip, the Illini still had six games to go in what ended as a 9-3-2 season. The Illini played Northwestern (16-16) for the first time and they renewed their increasingly bitter rivalry with Purdue that year. In those days it was not uncommon for a coach to step off the sidelines and into the game. Purdue's Ben Donnelly did just that, replacing one of his ends. Hall, refusing to be outdone, lined up opposite Donnelly, and the two glared at each other as the ball was snapped. Purdue won the game 12-6.

Even though Illinois played 14 games that season, Lake Forest refused to play, Wisconsin forfeited, and the Beloit and Iowa games never materialized. The loosely run Northwestern Intercollegiate Football League, to which Illinois belonged, soon folded.

Intercollegiate Controversy

In the early years, an Illinois season was considered pretty dull if it didn't produce a bitter squawk.

In 1893 Northwestern had a 12-10 lead when the game was called because of darkness with just ten minutes remaining and the Illini within 12 yards of Northwestern's end zone. The referee decided the halftime score would be the official score and it went down as a 0-0 tie. Illinois came close to beating Purdue later that year, but had to settle for a 26-26 tie.

Louis D. Vail became coach in 1894, a season that produced such lopsided victories as 54-6 over Lake Forest and 66-0 over Northwestern. The season also produced a disappointing 22-2 loss to despised Purdue.

Controversies continued, but now with new complaints. The first came on November 21 in a game against Chicago. The *Daily Illini* put it this way: "Hotchkiss [Illinois] carried the ball 90 yards for a touchdown. Captain Allen [Chicago] yelled time, but the referee would not give it. [Robert] Gaut kicked a goal and the score stood 12 to 10 in favor of Illinois. The umpire asked Chicago to play ball and they refused.

"Vail offered to retire from the game. Captain Allen refused to talk to him and called his men from the field, refusing to play. The umpire waited the time limit allowed for a team to resume play and then gave Illinois the game 6-0.

"As to the propriety of Mr. Vail playing [it

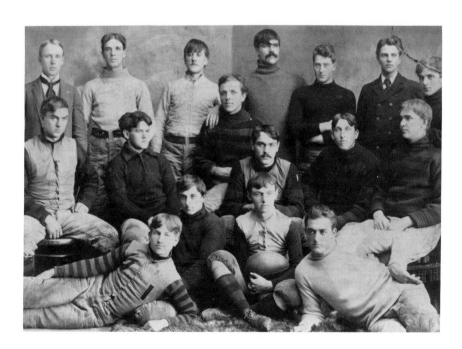

The 1893 Fighting Illini

Illini in action against Purdue, 1894

can be pointed out that] Mr. Stagg for two successive years played with his team. Even this year he has participated in one game."

Three days later it was the orange and blue's turn to beef when the Illini met Indianapolis Light Artillery.

Again, the *Daily Illini*: "Time and again the visitors were held to four downs, but instead of giving the [Illinois] varsity the ball, it was given to ILA to try again. Time and again did they fumble the ball, and someone of the home team [Illinois] fell on it, only to have the satisfaction and temper, as well, rudely shattered by having the ball being taken from them and returned to the ILA. . .With the score Illinois 14 and ILA 12, the linesman called 'time' but the referee thought the wheels in his cranium kept better time than the stop watch and ordered the play to go on. ILA tried a touchdown, fumbling the ball, and when the players got up the gathering twilight revealed [Illinois'] Sconce and Chester holding the ball. Referee announced 'Artillery touchdown'!"

It was an 18-14 Illinois loss with a season record of 5-3-0.

The Beginnings of the Big 10

In 1895, "G" Huff, who first graced the Illinois campus as a prep at age 15, returned to

Illinois as head coach after spending two years at Dartmouth. Ben Donnelly, no longer glaring across the line of scrimmage, signed on as an assistant. Except for a new wrinkle to the Purdue rivalry, it was a fairly uneventful year.

But off the field, this year produced an event of lasting implications. On January 11, Illinois President Andrew Sloan Draper met with the presidents of Chicago, Michigan, Northwestern, Wisconsin, and Purdue at the Palmer House in Chicago. That meeting produced an agreement among the universities to form the Intercollegiate Conference of Faculty Representatives, an unglamorous title that would become popularly known as the Western Athletic Conference and, ultimately, the Big 10.

Illinois, 4-1-1 going into its final game of the season, invaded Purdue with hopes of finally besting the Boilermakers. They came home with both a 6-2 loss and bitter feelings that would echo for years. It seems heavy rain hit the Lafayette area before the game and the Illini's "pony" backs, Harry Baum and Harvey Sconce, spent much of the afternoon stuck in the mud. For years Illinois partisans complained that Purdue had done nothing to drain the water from the field in order to slow down its fleet rival.

For the first time, the university faculty and administration recognized the football team with the school's first post-season banquet, and the first Varsity "I"s were awarded.

Huff coached his second season in 1896, later giving up football duties to concentrate on his first love, baseball. He would also later assume the duties of athletic director, a post he would hold until his death in 1936. The Illini went 4-2-1, the tie being 4-4 with Purdue.

On November 20, 1897, Illinois played its first night game, and the only indoor game it would play for more than 80 years, against the Carlisle Indians.

There was no turf on the Chicago Coliseum floor; instead the field was covered with tanbark, the same kind of surface used for the

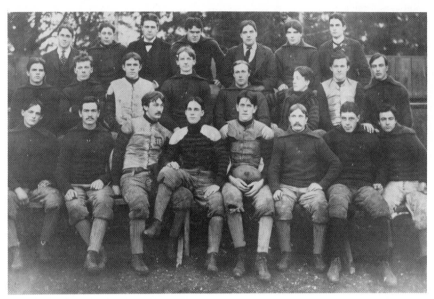

The 1896 Illinois football team

In 1897, the Illini had a pair of firsts. One was that, on October 23, Illinois finally beat Purdue, 34-4 on Illinois Field.

During the Purdue game, Arthur Hall, a substitute runningback, was injured and Illinois coaches rushed to help him from the field. Hall, who would later coach the Illini from 1907 to 1912, broke free from his would-be helpers to return to the game. On the next play, Hall ran for a touchdown.

Illinois' bitter rivalry with Purdue began to fade after the Illini finally posted a victory, but that rivalry was to be replaced by a long and spirited one against Chicago.

Clarence Herschberger, an All-American, was Chicago's star halfback; Arthur Johnston was Illinois' most adept runner. Both had to be carried from the field, having sustained broken collarbones after colliding with each other. Herschberger's replacement would run for the winning touchdown in Chicago's 18-12 victory.

circus. There were also 10,000 people in the stands, an unheard-of number, including 700 who boarded a pair of special trains from Champaign. The Illini led that historical game 6-5 at halftime, but the Indians' superior stamina wore Illinois down in the second half en route to a 23-6 victory.

Both Michigan and Notre Dame appeared on Illinois' schedule for the first time in 1898. Both games were Illinois losses. The Illini also played Minnesota for the first time and got their first taste of November weather in Minnesota. The Illini had to wear mittens, but they warmed up with an 11-10 victory. The season record was 4-5.

During this season, the Athletic Association altered its procedure of awarding the Varsity "I", giving it out only when Illinois beat teams from Chicago, Michigan, Wisconsin, or Minnesota. The policy came into play the next year when Illinois didn't win any of those games.

Zuppke on Huff:

"I went to Illinois because of George Huff and I remained there because of him. Down through the years we had our differences—entirely of honest opinion—but I respected him more than any man I have ever known. His friendship had the solidity and durability of a rock. He protected his coaches, gave them a free hand and expected them to do their jobs."

3

REGULATIONS AND INNOVATIONS

"No one was able to count the hordes of alumni who flocked to theTwin Cities. . ."

—*Daily Illini'*s description
of the first Homecoming

In the waning days of 1899, Indiana and Iowa were admitted to the conference, making what had been the Big 7 the Big 9, but in 1900 the Illini, coached by Fred Smith, didn't have much to do with the confused and confusing conference championship.

Illinois finished with a 7-3-2 record, but except for its 17-5 victory over Purdue, that record was fashioned against primarily lightweight opposition. There was no clear-cut champion that year and nobody quite figured the whole thing out. The *Chicago Tribune* reported, "The championship race in 1900 is a hopeless muddle. Iowa and Minnesota finished without a defeat but Iowa played only three games and Minnesota only four. Wisconsin had also a good showing but played only three games, while Chicago and Illinois played six games."

Edgar Holt's 1901 Illinois team's losses in an 8-2 season came only to Northwestern and Minnesota. Chicago, which the Illini had not played in three previous seasons, was a 24-0 victim in a game that made Garland "Jake" Stahl, who later went on to manage the Boston Red Sox, famous.

News accounts relate that Stahl "was continually drawn back from his guard position to carry the ball, and he smashed his way through the Maroons like a battering ram."

Captain of that team was tackle Justa Lindgren, a good football player who would later become an even better Illinois coach and academic man.

Holt's team in 1902 finished 10-2-1, but could do no better than fifth in the conference. Nevertheless, the Illini recorded eight shutouts, and scores included such lopsided victories as 80-0 over Iowa and 47-0 over Indiana.

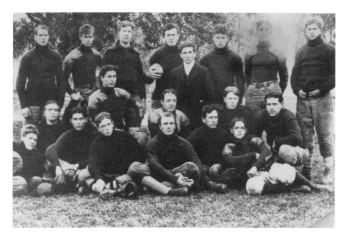

1899 Illini football team

George Huff, Illinois athletic director

Huff hired George Woodruff, who had coached the University of Pennsylvania to great success, for the 1903 season. The idea looked brilliant as Illinois rolled over its first eight foes, including 24-0 over Purdue, but the Illini lost their last four games and didn't score a point in the final three losses to Minnesota, Iowa, and Nebraska. As soon as that 8-6 season ended, Woodruff got on a train headed east. He never came back.

The College of Coaches

That disaster convinced Huff to try a new coaching philosophy. The Illini went to a "college of coaches" concept, a system that lasted nine seasons. Justa Lindgren, Arthur Hall, Fred Lowenthal, and Clyde Mathews were in charge of the first team, one that went 9-2-1 and put center John Haselwood, guard Charles Fairweather, and end Claude Rothgeb on the *Chicago Tribune* All-Western Team.

Rothgeb was one of the swiftest men ever seen on the field to date. He once equalled the world record for the indoor 40-yard dash and, against heavily favored Chicago in his senior season, Rothgeb got loose on a long end-around that helped the Illini fashion a 6-6 tie.

Lowenthal acted as head coach in 1905, Lindgren in 1906, and Hall would finish out the era, beginning in 1907. Those first three teams

were anything but outstanding. But tackle Fred Wham, whose final season was in 1908, was long considered one of the finest linemen Illinois ever produced. Charles Fairweather and guard Forest Van Hook were the other major stars of the early 1900s.

Justa Lindgren, member of the "College of Coaches"

The New Forward Pass

By 1907, the future of football itself was under heavy fire because the rough-and-tumble game produced a large number of serious injuries. Had not President Theodore Roosevelt personally stepped in and forced changes in some of the most dangerous aspects of the game, college football might not have survived. The Illini went 3-2 that season.

In 1908 rumblings were growing louder by the day to open up the game. Nothing opened it more than the newfangled forward pass, a weapon that Hall, who had just the guy to throw the football, was quick to install in the Illini playbook.

Pomery "Pom" Sinnock weighed 130 pounds and stood just about tall enough to see over the top of his bent-over linemen, but he could throw the ball while running full speed with tremendous accuracy. Against Northwestern in 1908, Sinnock threw often enough to complete 25 passes in a 64-8 Illinois victory. The team finished 5-1-1.

In 1909, Illinois made its first trip to the East, winning at Syracuse 17-8. It was a young team, with men like guard Glenn Butzer, end Chauncy Oliver, and center John Twist, a fast, agile man despite his 230 pounds, gaining experience in front of a sophomore quarterback-kicker named Otto Seiler. This 1909 team finished 5-2 and although they lost to Chicago

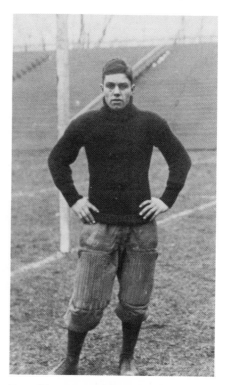

Pom Sinnock, 1908 quarterback

14-8, they laid the groundwork for 1910.

With a talented line blocking, Seiler dropkicking field goals at will, and a defensive wall that refused to crumble, Illinois outscored its seven foes 89-0 in 1910.

Three times—against Chicago, Indiana, and Syracuse—Seiler dropkicked the Illini to 3-0 victories. The last-minute kick he drilled to beat Indiana provided the only points that the

The 1910 Fighting Illini—unbeaten, untied, unscored upon

Regulations and Innovations

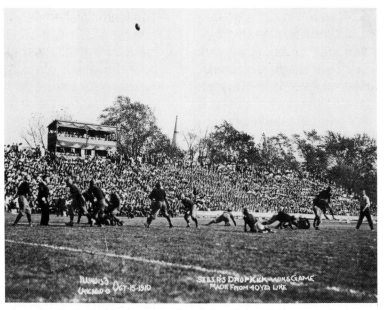

First homecoming game, against Chicago

Hoosiers surrendered that season, but even that kick was not so dramatic as the one that beat Chicago on October 15.

Seiler had been so ill that week that he was hospitalized, but he left his hospital bed Saturday morning in plenty of time to dropkick the 38-yard field goal that triggered one of the first of many wild celebrations on the Illinois campus.

America's First Homecoming

The first Homecoming on any campus was celebrated by the Illini on October 15 and 16, 1910. Homecoming was the brainchild of the just-graduated W. Elmer Ekblaw and C.F. Williams. The two sat on the steps of the YMCA that year, pondering what it would be like to be old grads.

From that conversation sprang the idea to plan an annual weekend of reunion for the alumni. Unlike Scott Williams' proposal to start a football team 20 years before, this idea to have a Homecoming met instant enthusiastic approval from faculty, students, and alumni.

The two honorary societies then on campus, the Shield and Trident and the Phoenix, took up the plan and presented it in the form of a petition to the Council of Administration. The

petition was granted and plans were laid for the first Homecoming.

Almost as soon as alumni received their notices, thrilled acceptances were returned. When the big weekend finally came, revelers began reaching the campus as early as Thursday morning by train, automobile, and every other means of transportation available.

The *Daily Illini* reported that even without Seiler's heroic dropkick against Chicago, the celebration would have been a success: "No one was able to count the hordes of alumni who flocked to the Twin Cities, congregated in hilarious groups on the street corners, hurried through the campus looking up old landmarks, roaming the old buildings and gazing in awe at the new additions to ground and architecture."

Scores that year also included Illinois 13, Millikin 0; Illinois 29, Drake 0; Illinois 11, Purdue 0; and Illinois 27, Northwestern 0.

A Taste for National Prominence

Nineteen ten was the year of Illinois' first Western Conference championship. The Illini shared that title with Minnesota. Seiler gave credit for the championship to his blockers.

"There may have been better lines in the history of American football, but I doubt it,"

Seiler once said. "I feel like I am in a position to judge the character of that line because I did the kicking most of the time, and I could have sat down and enjoyed a cup of tea and then kicked the ball. No one would have been in the way or had a chance to block that kick."

Seiler, Twist, and Butzer made Walter Eckersall's first-team all-conference list. Left guard Charles Belting and end Oliver were second-team selections.

Seiler would fully appreciate the value of their blocking, for while he returned for the 1911 season, most of that powerful front line did not.

The team finished 4-2-1 and lacked the defensive grit that had made the previous squad so fearful. The Illini lost to Chicago 24-0 and to powerful Minnesota 11-0; they played Indiana to a scoreless tie.

By the next season, 1912, Illinois wasn't crossing the goal often at all and its 3-3-1 conference record had the fans in a lather. They still reveled in the power that Illinois had shown two seasons earlier, and they let "G" Huff know that they wanted Illinois to achieve a national prominence similar to what was then enjoyed by Wisconsin, Minnesota, and Michigan.

Illinois homecoming pins through the years

"Homecoming is a thrilling time, when the fraternities and sororities start to decorate, the band is practicing, alumni arrive. There is a thrill in the air as the "Fighting Illini" spirit builds to a higher and higher pitch before Saturday afternoon. What a university! What a campus! What a wonderful group of alumni! Oh yes, and we hope, what a football team!"

Wendell S. Wilson, thoughts on Homecoming
Football '27

PART II: THE ZUPPKE ERA

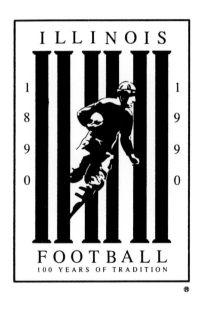

ILLINOIS

1890   1990

FOOTBALL
100 YEARS OF TRADITION

"There are two schools of thought on my painting," Zuppke once laughed. "Some stand in front of my water colors and oils and say, 'Great power. Great technique. Great knowledge of color.' Another group stands in front of one of my canvases and murmurs, 'He must have been a great football coach.'"

4

ZUPPKE: AN ILLINOIS COACHING LEGEND

"I've never regretted the decision to go to Illinois. It is my home, my life."

—Coach Robert Carl Zuppke

The first third of the 20th century was dominated by coaching giants—Michigan's Fielding H. Yost, Chicago's Amos Alonzo Stagg, Notre Dame's Knute Rockne, and Illinois' Robert Carl Zuppke.

Zuppke was a philosopher, humorist, and even an artist of some reputation, but most of all, Bob Zuppke was a football coach who loved to innovate and make winning teams out of eager but inexperienced young college men.

Robert Carl Zuppke was born in Berlin, Germany on July 2, 1879. His family moved to Milwaukee, Wisconsin two years later. He quit school at 13 and went into business painting signs, but it didn't take him long to realize that returning to seventh grade held more potential than his 50 cents a week salary.

Zuppke was still a student in good standing at West Division High School in Milwaukee in 1898 when the high school principal announced that anyone in the mood to "break his neck" should report to football practice. He did, and he was a mainstay in West Division's football opener against Fond du Lac, a game where many of West Division's finest, including Zuppke, were so badly beaten up that the sport was quickly abolished. Zuppke's reward was a broken collarbone.

However, as was to become his style, Zuppke ignored what should have been common sense.

"I was an audacious and enthusiastic young fellow in those days," Zuppke once said, "so I organized a team called the 'West Ends.' Unhindered by eligibility rules, we were able to get a good eleven together. Since I was head man I made the team in a breeze. In fact, I was the star defect." He attended State Normal in Milwaukee for two years and, after teaching in a country school, went to the University of Wisconsin to finish his bachelor's degree.

Zuppke himself had played college football for Wisconsin, and had won the Michigan state championship at Muskegon in 1907, but he really didn't distinguish himself until he coached the 1911 and 1912 Oak Park, Illinois, high school national championship football teams.

Zuppke Takes Charge

After those successes, Northwestern, Lafayette, and Purdue universities approached Zuppke with handsome coaching offers, but Illinois alumnus George Carr persuaded his friend not to sign any contract until he had spoken with Illinois athletic director "G" Huff.

"The thing that really did make a tremendous impression on me was "G" Huff's personality," Zuppke later said. "He told me that Illinois hadn't been doing too well in football and that they needed a football coach with teeth. He didn't paint a glowing picture of the job; he just dealt the facts straight up. He offered me $2,700 a year and I accepted . . .

"I've never regretted the decision to go to Illinois. It is my home, my life."

For 29 seasons and 224 college football games, Illinois was indeed Bob Zuppke's football life. Chuck Flynn, Illinois' long-time director of athletic publicity, wrote of Zuppke:

"Tradition dictated against a high school coach moving to the college rank, but . . . Bob

Zuppke's name [became] synonymous with knowledge of football. . .He blazed many new paths. At Oak Park he had devised the famous 'flea-flicker,' a forward, followed by a lateral pass, so-called because the man who threw the lateral flicked it off his fingers as if the ball were a flea. [Zuppke also pioneered] the screen pass, originated the spiral pass from center and was the first to use the huddle formation for calling plays in 1921. He [developed] spring practice in 1914 . . . [and] was among the first to chart and use strategy maps for quarterbacks . . . [Zuppke also] devised the 'flying trapeze.' "

Harold Pogue: A Zuppke Man

Twenty-six candidates reported for Zuppke's first team in 1913. Among them was Harold Pogue, a slenderly built, 142-pound sophomore back with thick glasses who had been cut from the freshman squad because he was so small.

The tale is told that Zuppke had seen the scholarly looking but speedy Harold Pogue run in an intramural track meet in 1913 and invited him to report to the football team that fall. Pogue quickly became fiercely loyal to Zuppke. Illinois easily won Zuppke's first collegiate game, 21-0 over Kentucky. Fullback Enos Rowe and halfback Eugene Schobinger were the stars that day.

During Illinois' 24-7 win over Missouri, Pogue's star began to rise. Pogue ran for a 20-yard first-half touchdown that tied the score at 7, then scored twice more in the second half. The Illini won their next contest against Northwestern 37-0, raising enthusiasm for the Illini and their former high school coach to a fever pitch. That fever spiked even higher when Illinois slogged through the mud for a 10-0 victory over Indiana, sending them to Chicago to meet the powerful Maroons.

"I was scared to play pastel green," Pogue later said. "I played quarterback that year and was back in the safety position when, on the fourth play of the game, Des Jardiens of the Maroons got off one of his long, spiral punts. While the ball was coming toward me—it seemed to be in the air for hours—I died a dozen deaths.

"Finally it settled in my arms and I started to run. I had no sense of time or space, I was simply impelled by terror and it was fortunate that I was headed in the right direction. Finally I was over the Chicago goal and stood there, blinking, trying to orient myself to my surroundings. If the Illinois crowd was surprised, I was astounded."

That 65-yard dash gave Illinois a 7-0 lead, an advantage that held up until the second half when the veteran Maroons scored four times to post a 28-7 victory. Pogue suffered a shoulder injury and had to miss the Illini's last two games of the season, a scoreless tie with Purdue and a 19-9 loss to Minnesota.

1914: A Championship Season

The next year, 1914, Pogue and Schobinger were ready to go in the backfield, joined by a couple of fellows named George "Potsy" Clark and Bart Macomber. Clark, at 149 pounds, and end Perry Graves, at 146 pounds, were near Pogue's size. George Squier played at left end and Ralph "Slooey" Chapman anchored the line with help from Lennox Armstrong and John Watson. This season not only silenced initial criticism of high school coach Zuppke, but also gave Illinois its first national championship.

Illinois opened the season by beating tiny Christian Brothers College 37-0. Schobinger and Clark each scored two touchdowns and Pogue, who only played about five minutes, scored on a 17-yard pass reception from Macomber.

The next week, Illinois announced to the world that it was serious about winning the Western Conference title. Pogue, Schobinger, and Clark each scored a touchdown in a 51-0 rout of Indiana. A week later, Ohio State fell 37-0 as Pogue scored three touchdowns and Macomber booted three field goals. Then Illinois went to Minnesota and for three quarters the two teams pushed each other up and down the field without a score.

Illinois drove to the Gopher 3-yard line early in the fourth quarter, but again didn't

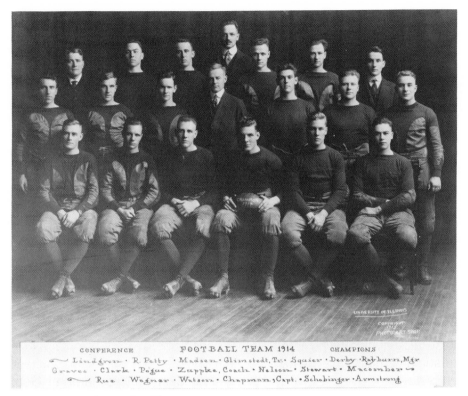

CONFERENCE   FOOTBALL TEAM 1914   CHAMPIONS
Lindgren · R. Petty · Madsen · Glimstedt, Tr · Squier · Derby · Rayburn, Mgr
Graves · Clark · Pogue · Zuppke, Coach · Nelson · Stewart · Macomber
Rue · Wagner · Watson · Chapman, Capt · Schobinger · Armstrong

1914 National Champion Team

score. The Illini got the ball back at midfield and passed to the 1-yard line, where Clark blasted over for a touchdown. The Illini got the next kickoff, returned it to the Minnesota 45 and, on the second play, Harold Pogue raced 35 yards to put Illinois up 14-0. Zuppke began to relax.

Afterwards Zuppke said, "Late in the fourth quarter we had a 14-0 lead and I pulled out nine of the regulars. Minnesota began to throw passes and before you could say 'Bob's your uncle' the Gophers scored. Following the kickoff they began to complete more passes and marched down the field. I didn't waste any time putting our regulars back into the game.

"Pogue usually played the safety position, but before he went back in, I told him to take an 'up' position in the secondary and grab one of those passes."

Pogue paid attention. Minutes later he indeed grabbed one of those passes and zig-zagged 75 yards for a touchdown to seal Illinois' 21-6 win.

Just two games remained between the Illini and a championship. The most important

MACOMBER

Bart Macomber

Zuppke: an Illinois Coaching Legend

was a Homecoming game with Chicago at Illinois Field.

More than 21,000 fans jammed the field, thousands more than it could comfortably accommodate. Stagg's Maroons scored quickly and maintained a 7-0 lead through halftime, but the Illini were on the attack and in the third quarter Potsy Clark broke free for a 40-yard gain. Pogue picked up 25 more, and on fourth down inside the Maroons' 5-yard line, Macomber tossed a game-tying touchdown pass to Pogue.

In the fourth quarter, a Des Jardiens punt travelled only to the Chicago 25. The Illini took advantage. Pogue scored from the 1- yard line. Clark took the next kickoff 95 yards to seal Illinois' 21-7 victory.

The next week Pogue ran two punts 65 yards for touchdowns. Clark ran 70 yards with a punt for a score. The Illini secured a 24-9 victory over Wisconsin and both a conference and a national championship, ending with a 7-0 record.

All that remained for that year were the accolades. Slooey Chapman was the first Illinois player to be named to Walter Camp's All-American first team. Harold Pogue made the third unit. Seven Illini made Walter Eckersall's All-Conference team: Chapman, Squier, Clark, and Pogue were first-team honorees, and Graves, Armstrong, and Schobinger were named to the second unit.

Pain and Determination

Chapman graduated in 1915. Pogue, after scoring twice in an early-season 75-7 win over the Rolla School of Mines, missed much of the rest of the year with a bad ankle. Clark played despite a broken jaw, and several other Illini were injured at key points during the season.

Nevertheless, Illinois came into the Minnesota showdown with the conference lead at stake. That Homecoming game ended in a 6-6 tie and was best noted for a bit of disagreement between Zuppke and Minnesota back Joe "Galloping" Sprafka. Zuppke insisted that Sprafka had gone out of bounds in the course of

a 24-yard touchdown run. Sprafka's reply, according to Zup: "I only had one foot out."

Sprafka's touchdown gave Minnesota a 6-0 lead. That's how the game might have ended if not for the courage of Potsy Clark. When Bernard Halstrom shook free for a 50-yard gain to put Illinois on the Minnesota 12 late in the game, Clark, wearing a special mask to protect his broken jaw, barked signals through the wire and attempted a lateral to Macomber. The play was smothered. The Illini tried virtually the same play again, but with one twist. Macomber took the pass from center and lateralled to Clark, who tiptoed past the surprised visitors for the tying points. Illinois fans may have envisioned taking home a 7-6 victory, but Macomber, usually a deadly accurate kicker, missed the point.

Illinois went on to post victories over Wisconsin (17-3) and Chicago (10-0) to finish 5-0-2 and share the league title with Minnesota. Watson and Macomber made first-team all-

Ralph "Slooey" Chapman, Illinois' first All-American Player

conference, and Macomber became the second Illini player picked for Walter Camp's All-American squad.

A Talent for Upsets

The 1916 Illinois season could have been nondescript. Only Macomber remained from the championship teams, and the Illini finished 3-3-1 and in fifth place in the Big 9. However, Bob Zuppke loved upset-makers, and never did that show more convincingly than on November 4 in Minneapolis when the Illini met the powerful Minnesota team, called by just about everybody the "perfect team."

The Gophers had outscored four opponents 241-14 and had shown South Dakota and Iowa the door by scores of 81-0 and 67-0, respectively. After Illinois, the "perfect team" would outscore Wisconsin and Chicago by a collective 103-0 score. Illinois, on the other hand, was 2-2 and would lose to Chicago and play a scoreless tie with the Badgers. Chicago newspaper columnist Ring Lardner humorously suggested that Zuppke and his players get off the train in Chicago and take in a little big-city culture instead of going on to get mauled in Minnesota.

Minnesota boasted Albert Baston, twice an All-American end, as captain; Clair "Shorty" Long at quarterback; Joe Sprafka and Hal Hansen as halfbacks; and A.D. "Pudge" Wyman at fullback. That backfield was, reports said, the terror of the Midwest.

Minnesota coach Dr. Henry Williams went so far as to have a special booth constructed so that media giants such as Walter Camp, E.C. Patterson of *Collier's*, and other notables could watch the expected rout in splendor.

Zuppke, of course, paid no mind. He'd already broken training tradition by having his team scrimmage hard every day in practice that week. That night before the game, Zuppke broke all rules by encouraging his players to go out for the evening. For those who wanted to stay put, he hired a group of singers to perform comedy songs. He may have done this after watching his players practice that afternoon.

"We began practicing and were so nerv-

ous and upset," Macomber later said, "we could not even hang on to the ball when running signals."

Game day came and Zuppke had the Gophers in his psychological lair. For some reason his watch was fast that day, he would recount with a smile. The Illini were on the field long before the giants from the north came to warm up. When they did arrive, Illini halfback Edward "Dutch" Sternaman turned and remarked for all to hear, "Why Coach, they don't look so big."

That remark broke the tension. Macomber got set to kick off with the help of last-minute instructions from the coach. "This Minnesota outfit is superstitious," Zuppke said, "and they've got a formula they always follow on the first three plays. First Galloping Sprafka will carry the ball, next Wyman will carry it and then Shorty Long will lug it. On the first three plays, tackle those men in that order."

Sure enough, on the first play Sprafka carried for three yards to the Minnesota 10. Wyman and Long had little luck with their turns and the Gophers had to kick to Sternaman, who returned the punt ten yards to the Gopher 45. Macomber passed to Sternaman, who carried it to the Minnesota 25. "I called a spread formation, the first time that this formation had ever been played by anyone," Macomber later said. "This is where the linemen spread 10 yards apart and the backfield men did the same thing making a box formation . . . I passed 20 yards to Sternaman." The Illini kept pushing until Macomber scored on a one-yard run and added the extra point.

Nevertheless, the Gophers thought this Illini lead to be just a temporary setback and Sprafka took the ensuing kickoff to his own 30-yard line. They were on the 45 when Williams brought out his famous passing combination, Wyman to Baston, but Zuppke called for an even more famous passing combination. Wyman passed to Illinois' Reynold "Ren" Kraft, who raced 50 yards for the touchdown. That put the Illini up 14-0 with time left in the first half.

"In between halves, Zuppke told us that Minnesota was not through, but would come back strong," Macomber said. "He also told me to stall and to keep Minnesota bottled up down in their own territory. Stalling was not too noticeable in those days and the officials were more or less reluctant to call this infraction of the rules."

Minnesota scored a touchdown and added a safety to make the score 14-9, but Macomber passed, kicked, punted, and stalled so the Illini could secure one of the most incredible upsets in college football history.

The 11 players who put the fight in the Illini that memorable day were Reynold "Ren" Kraft, left end; Elmer T. "Swede" Rundquist, left tackle; Otis Petty, left guard; Harry Schlaudeman, center; Frank Stewart, right guard; Ross Petty, right tackle; Paul G. Christensen, right end; Bart Macomber, quarterback; Edward C. "Dutch" Sternaman, left halfback; William W. "Bill" Anderson, right halfback; and R.C. "Bob" Knop, fullback.

The World War I Years

World War I took precedence over the next two seasons. The Illini finished 5-2-1 and fifth in the Big 9 in 1917. George Halas, who later made a name for himself with another football team in Illinois, was the centerpiece of one of the most bizarre plays ever. Halas was used that fall as Zuppke's kick return man. Against Wisconsin, he went back to take a kick and then looked up in amazement.

"Suddenly, the ball lost speed and took on an unusual shape," Halas wrote in his autobiography. "I caught it and stood there. The episode caused considerable consternation among officials. The referee called for a new ball and told Wisconsin to kick again. I demote myself every time I think about that event. I should have run for a touchdown while everyone was scratching his head."

With several of their players, including captain Dutch Sternaman, in the military service in 1918, the Illini finished 4-0 in the league, 5-2 overall. Burt Ingwersen, who would serve the University of Illinois for decades as an assistant coach, was acting captain during Sternaman's absence. Illinois was first in the conference, but only the Illini and Chicago played as many as four league games. The Illini played one of their games at Illinois Field in front of an

George Halas: halfback/end for the 1917 Illini

empty house. A flu epidemic raged in October of that year and no spectators were allowed to watch Illinois' 7-0 loss to Great Lakes.

The Vets Return

The 1919 team, with many returning vets, was widely regarded as the national champion, despite a 14-10 loss to Wisconsin. Zuppke's men took on a murderous seven-game schedule that season, all against Big 9 foes.

Illinois travelled to Ohio State with the conference championship on the line. Buckeye followers were so confident of victory that extra newspapers had been printed for quick distribution just in case.

"Ohio State smears Illinois," the headline read. Those papers got out early and one landed in the hands of Bob Zuppke, with Ohio State leading 7-6 and five minutes left in the game.

"It made me mad, so I sent in a substitute to tell [Lawrence] Walquist to throw a pass to [Charles] Carney no matter what signal [quarterback] Bob Fletcher called."

Three times Walquist and Carney hooked up on pass completions until finally the Illini were deep in Ohio State territory. Only eight seconds remained, and place-kicker Ralph Fletcher was out of the game with an ankle injury.

"I'll kick it," Bob Fletcher volunteered. And he did, 25 yards, to win 9-7. What he didn't say

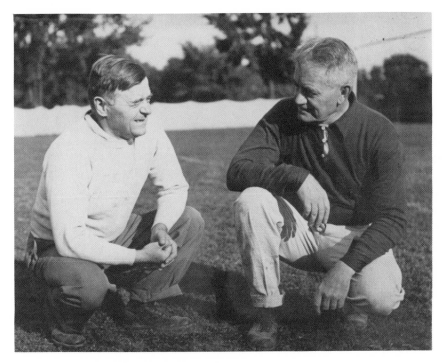

Coaches Bob Zuppke and Justa Lindgren

was that he'd never before tried to kick a field goal.

Sternaman scored a touchdown in that game, noteworthy because it was the only touchdown Ohio State gave up that entire season.

Sternaman, Ingwersen, and all-conference guard Clarence Applegran graduated the next year, but in 1920 Carney was back as were the Fletcher brothers and fullback Jack Crangle. Despite a 14-9 loss to Wisconsin, Illinois again went into the season finale against Ohio State with the conference championship on the line. This time, Ohio State won 7-0. Illinois' 1920 season record was 5-2.

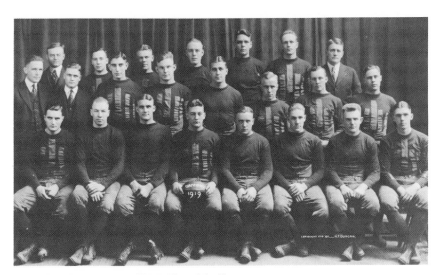

The 1919 Conference Championship Team

Zuppke: an Illinois Coaching Legend

Confusing Ohio State for an Upset

The Ohio State-Illinois rivalry was a great one in those days. In 1921, Illinois lost every game in the conference before going to Columbus for the season finale, and the Buckeyes were undefeated. Illinois had put only eight points on the board in four previous conference games, but Zuppke predicted victory. And, he insisted, he'd use only 11 men to achieve it.

Zuppke had first conceived of the huddle while at Oak Park. He brought it back for the 1921 season and added a new twist for the Buckeyes. Instead of huddling directly behind the ball, the players huddled far to one side. When they broke the huddle, they charged diagonally to their positions, confusing the Buckeyes and making it difficult for them to shift defensively.

Zuppke had scouted the Buckeyes and knew that whenever they were in scoring position and needed short yardage, they almost always relied on the same play: the quarterback carries the ball from a split backfield formation. Zuppke ordered Crangle to watch for that play. He did, and when early in the game Ohio State was facing fourth and two from the Illinois 12-yard line, Crangle squashed Buckeye ballcarrier Pete Stinchcomb.

In the second period, Crangle ran for 20 yards to the Ohio State 40. Don Peden gained four. On the next play, Peden dropped back to pass. The pass was intended for end Dave Wilson, but Wilson fell down. The ball slipped through a Buckeye defender's arms and into the hands of Walquist, who scooted into the end zone for the only score of the day. This upset not only was the highlight of Illinois' football season, but also may have provided the moment that put the fight in the Fighting Illini. Unfortunately for several Illini, it was the last college football game they would ever play.

A Team Riddled by Ineligibility

Eight days after the Ohio State upset, a pair of semipro teams, Taylorville and Carlinville, were to meet on a makeshift field. Locals had money on the game. When word got out that the Carlinville squad would include many Notre Dame players, Taylorville wanted some ringers of their own.

Roy "Dope" Simpson and Vern Mullen, Taylorville boys who played end for the Illini, were summoned to help. They got about ten teammates to come to town, including Harry Gamage who would later coach at Kentucky. Taylorville and the Illini won the game 16-0, and the wagers, estimates of which were as high as $100,000, were paid. It was a costly mistake for the Illini. That winter, Wisconsin questioned Walquist's eligibility when he showed up to play basketball. The ensuing investigation confirmed the unauthorized game.

"We shouldn't have done it," Gamage said. "Of course, in those days kids were hard up ... But there was a rule in the conference that if you played on any team other than your own team during the school year, you're automatically ineligible."

The next year, the Illini had to struggle to win two games. Only a pair of Steve Coutchie field goals allowed Illinois to beat Northwestern 6-3, and one by Robert Clark gave the Illini a 3-0 victory over Wisconsin that knocked the Badgers out of championship contention.

Zuppke loved that overmatched but courageous team; the young Illini, in turn, praised their coach. The freshmen in 1922 did show some promise, especially a speedy halfback whom Zuppke figured might make a pretty good runner. His name? Harold "Red" Grange.

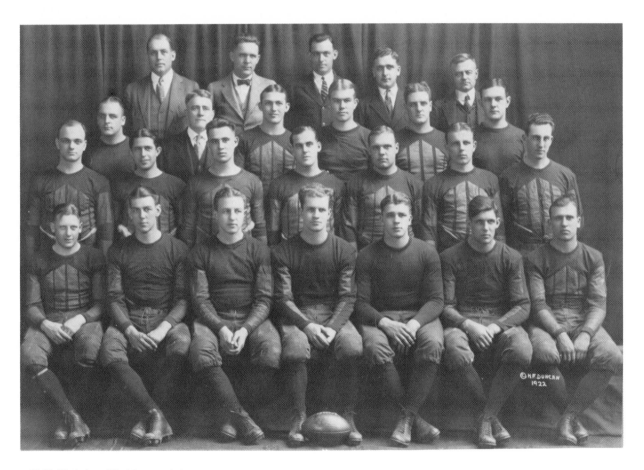

1922 Fighting Illini team picture

Many times Zuppke upsets were crafted with the same 11 players on the field from start to finish. Zuppke told his players before that momentous upset of Ohio State in 1921 that the starters play no matter what. Nobody but a dead man leaves the field, he told them. That phrase became a tradition as he used it often over the next two decades, sometimes to be taken only too literally.

"Several years later we were playing another team," Zuppke said. "I did not have the reserves and once more I said, 'nobody but a dead man comes out.' There were about five minutes left to play and we were going all right with a touchdown but no goal, when I noticed one of our players stretched out on the ground. He was all in.

"I called to a sophomore lineman, told him to report to the referee and take the place of the recumbent regular. The sophomore, reporting to the referee, bent over and peered at the injured player. The sub straightened up and came running back to the bench to my astonishment. I managed to ask him what happened.

" 'Why coach,' he said, 'you said nobody but a dead man comes out, and he's still breathing.' "

5

GEORGE HUFF AND MEMORIAL STADIUM

"The stadium will be many things—a memorial to Illini who have died in the war, a recreational field and an imposing place for our varsity game. But it will also be an unprecedented expression of Illinois spirit."
—Athletic Director
George Huff

Two things "G" Huff could count very, very well were heads and cash. So, when a crowd of more than 20,000, paying upwards of $2 a head, jammed Illinois Field on November 20, 1920, to watch Ohio State defeat Illinois 7-0, Huff hung his head in dismay, and not just because that game gave Ohio State the undisputed conference championship over the Illini. Huff also realized that officially, Illinois Field held 17,000 people in its wooden grandstands. The rest were jammed into the end zones.

Huff believed that on that day and others he could have sold upwards of 50,000 tickets if only he had the seats. Illinois Field could guarantee visiting teams only $15,000, a paltry sum when some schools were already demanding three times that much money.

Ohio State had already broken ground for its million-dollar horseshoe. Harvard and Yale each had magnificent new stadiums, and plans were in the works for playgrounds at Iowa State, Cincinnati, Kansas, Oregon, and Columbia, all schools of lesser prestige than Illinois, which was then the nation's fourth largest university. Huff wanted a treasure more magnificent than any of these others to rise from the Illinois prairies.

Planning a Stadium

During the winter of 1920-21 Huff plotted and planned his strategy for achieving the goal. He had already spent years developing intramural athletics and had originated a coaching school. Now, with many of the 7,000 Illinois students involved with athletics, a spirit of sportsmanship soared at Illinois. The stadium, Huff imagined, would stand as a memorial to the 183 Illini, 182 men and one woman, Gladys Gilpatrick, who died in the recently fought World War. By April 25, 1921, with Bob Zuppke at his side to serve as the chief fund-raiser, Huff was ready to set the wheels in motion. They announced the stadium drive during a pair of mass meetings on campus. Newspaper accounts recall the day:

"The gym annex looked like the Chicago Coliseum during the Republican convention. It was packed with men and girls, seated in orderly rows, with county, state and country standards lifted high.

"First, university president David Kinley spoke to the gatherings, both at the auditorium and at the gym annex, telling them the Memorial Stadium would bring a touch of Greek glory to the prairie. Then Huff rose to speak.

" 'I want to see a great Stadium at the University of Illinois,' Huff said. 'I believe that you will get it. I believe there is great spirit at this university. The Stadium will be many things— a memorial to Illini who have died in the war, a recreational field and an imposing place for our varsity game. But it will also be an unprecedented expression of Illinois spirit.' "

When he finished, Zuppke stepped to the podium, asking who would make the first $1,000 pledge. R.L. Cavalcanti, a Latin American student, was first to stand.

Zuppke and Huff on a stadium fundraising trip to California

"I will give, sir."

Ten minutes later, Zuppke announced that $700,000 had been pledged, twice the expected student quota.

"The meetings were a riot of enthusiasm, each student trying to outdo his neighbor in his demonstrations of loyalty to his alma mater," one account read. "Men and women who came to the meetings with the fullest intention of subscribing $50 came away happy that they had pledged $100 or $150 or $200. They pledged more than they felt, in many cases, that they could afford, but they were willing to make the sacrifices, to deny themselves little luxuries or to shut down on necessities, in order to do their utmost for Illinois and her Stadium."

The Illini Heritage

Shortly thereafter, Huff, Zuppke, Elmer Ekblaw, a father of Homecoming and the campaign's manager, and Frederic A. Russell, a university professor and ardent stadium supporter, fanned out across the nation to seek pledges from Illini clubs everywhere.

In the midst of it all, the spirit of the Fighting Illini became cast in stone. Every alum was reminded of Illinois' Indian heritage, of the tribe's great heart and fighting spirit.

"In every state in the Union, and in foreign countries, college men know about this great Stadium project," Alumni Association president Merle J. Trees wrote in an open letter to all Illinois alums.

"You will make that day.
You have the Illini heart, the Illini spirit.
To that heart and spirit, as President of the Alumni Association, I now appeal.
Let's get together and
Build That Stadium for Fighting Illini!"

Nearly 26,000 contributors, pledging almost $2 million, answered that call. Huff envisioned a $2.5 million palace with the finest football facility in the land, seats for 75,000 that could be expanded to 120,000, and a surrounding track. Under the stands there would be basketball floors, handball courts, wrestling areas, lockers, and showers. There might be room for ice skaters and even some dormitory space.

Outside, he saw a 100-acre recreation field with baseball diamonds, football, hockey, soccer, and lacrosse fields, tennis and archery courts, perhaps even a polo field.

Some, like Robert F. Carr, '93, president of Dearborn Drug and Chemical in Chicago, gave a great deal. "I am buying $10,000 worth of happiness," he said.

Said $1,000 contributor Avery Brundage, an ex-Illini track man who would go on to head the International Olympic Committee, "As a monument to past and an inspiration to present and future teams, I am glad to contribute to the building of the most imposing stadium in the country." Most gave $100 or $200, due in regular payment schedules. Soon the stadium architectural design was complete, with east and west stands that would seat nearly 57,000 between the goal lines, a red brick and Bedford stone exterior, and 100 memorial columns rising from each stand. A few of those columns in the honor court, as it was called, would go unassigned, but most would bear the name and rank of one Illini who did not return from the war.

"The towers will be so high," Zuppke said, "that if a searchlight is placed on top, they will illuminate the name of Illinois from the Statue of Liberty to the Golden Gate."

By the spring of 1922, the Board of Trustees accepted the stadium site recommended by the Campus Plan Commission, the Stadium Committee, and the University Architects. It was 40 acres of what was then a hayfield, west of Mount Hope Cemetery in Champaign.

Construction Begins

Just after 1 p.m. on September 11, 1922, Huff turned the first spadeful of earth and the race was on to complete the playing field and seats in time for the targeted first game in Memorial Stadium, November 3, 1923, Homecoming.

By December, the foundation was in place, but steel shipments came in slowly. Winter lingered into spring, delaying progress, and there was a shortage of workers.

By August, 300 workers had poured the concrete for only 20,000 seats. A month later 37,000 seats were poured, but Homecoming tickets were being sold for seats that did not yet exist. Huff was virtually begging contributors to make good on their pledges.

The transplanted bluegrass that covered

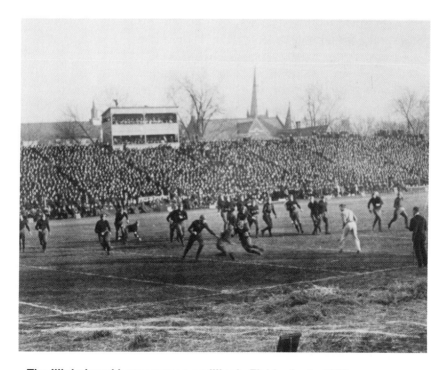

The Illini played home games on Illinois Field prior to 1923

George Huff and Memorial Stadium

Groundbreaking for Memorial Stadium

the field was taking hold. The Athletic Association decided the east side of the stadium, same as in Illinois Field, would be the Illini's side.

High school teams from all over Illinois tried to schedule games with Champaign and Urbana schools on November 3 so they could

finish in time to see Chicago and Illinois in the great stadium. Others simply left the date open. Several colleges in the state moved their games up to Friday so fans could see both games.

Bob Fletcher, whose famous field goal against Ohio State in 1919 gave Illinois the

Bob Zuppke and George Huff inspect digging for the new stadium

HAIL TO THE ORANGE AND BLUE!

The stadium under construction

So too came the rain. All day it poured. And as the stadium was not completed, neither were permanent walkways leading to the entrances. Huff had the foresight to install crushed stone walks from both First and Fourth streets, but the combination of rain and new construction can only equal mud.

The next day Red Grange, who had scored the stadium's first and only touchdown in Illinois' 7-0 victory that Saturday, walked back to the stadium to reflect on it all. There he saw thousands of shoes and boots abandoned to the muck.

Illinois would play two more games in its unfinished stadium that year. The Illini would win the conference championship, and they would be declared national champions.

Finishing Touches

Much work remained before the ramp towers and the memorial colonnades would be in place and the rough stands would be completed. For another year, Huff would plead and cajole to see that pledge money was paid. The stadium would never become quite the regal palace that Huff had hoped.

Nevertheless, by October 18, 1924, the 2,700 tons of steel, 800 tons of reinforcing bars, 4.8 million bricks, 50,000 barrels of cement,

conference championship, would not schedule the Findley, Ohio, high school team he coached for that date. Instead he would bring his school's 15 players to Champaign to see the game.

The First Game

Finally, November 3 arrived. Wrote L.M. Tobin, the school's long-time athletic publicist,

"Majestic, almost overpowering, the stadium stands against the November sky, waiting to welcome the greatest Illinois rallying of all time.

"For the trail already is dotted with the figures of the returning tribe. They know that they will not see the stadium in its definite majesty, for time and time again it has been told to them that only the seats could be completed for Homecoming.

"They will not see the beautiful memorial columns and colonnades until they come back again in 1924—but they will see enough to satisfy them of the certain splendor of the stadium and to make them proud that they have helped to make the Great Dream a glorious reality."

And the tribe did come, 60,636 strong, three times the number ever seen in Illinois Field, and a crowd surpassed in the Midwest only by that which celebrated the opening of Ohio Stadium a year earlier.

The stadium dedication game against Michigan

7,200 tons of cut stones, 404 miles of lumber, and 17 miles of seats covered with 21 acres of paint were in place.

Vaunted Michigan was in town to provide the opposition, and dedication ceremonies began the day before the game.

Said university president Kinley, "It is a pledge that we will manifest in our academic work, in our sports, in all that we do, that fine spirit and idealism which implies the qualities— loyalty, self-sacrifice and belief in our institution—of which the Stadium is a memorial. By our use of this great monument will it be determined from year to year whether we are keeping on the high plane of ethical aspiration and conduct that our beloved and honored dead raised for us; whether we are continuing to honor them by infusing into our life at the University the spirit, the purposes, the faith, the devotion to duty, which inspired them. According as we do this will the Illini spirit live and grow strong and we shall be able to stand, by and by, with unblushing faces, at the judgment bar of our fellow Illini whose memory we honor, and report to them that we have kept the faith; and that honor, truth, and loyalty are still watchwords of all Illini."

Finally, the parades had passed, the speeches had faded, the flag was raised, and Michigan kicked off to Red Grange.

Stadium dedication parade

HAIL TO THE ORANGE AND BLUE!

Columns Dedicated to Those Who Gave Their Lives in WWI

Truman O. Aarvig
Alvin J. Adams
Charles P. Anderson
Michael L. Angarola
Alan N. Ash
John W. Bailey
Harold J. Barnes
Lowell W. Bartlett
Bohuslav Bartos
Frank A Benitz
John S. Bennehoff
Merrill M. Benson
Edward H. Berry
Arthur L. Beyerlein
Benjamin H. Bloebaum
Irwin J. Bluestein
Vinson R. Boardman
Henry H. Boger
Arthur L. Bonner
Marcus H. Branham
George R. Brannon
William E. Brotherton
Bayard Brown
Waldo R. Brown
Harold C. Buchanan
John E. Burroughs
Charles B. Busey
Charles E. Caldwell, Jr.
William J. Callahan
Jay I. Carpenter
Lee S. Cassell
Leslie G. Chandler
Minor J. Chapin
Harry L. Clayton
Paul M. Clendenen
Henry R. Colton
Linn P. Cookson
Charles E. Cooper
Willis H. Cork
Joseph C. Crismore
Bruce N. Culmer
Robert M. Cutter
Homer W. Dahringer
John H. Dallenbach
Theodore F. Demeter
Townsend F. Dodd
James E. Durst
Vincent J. Dushek

William F. Earnest
Adrian C. Edwards
Arthur M. Evans
Emery C. Farver
Arthur W. Freer
Lloyd H. Ghislin
Ralph E. Gifford
Gladys Gilpatrick
Thomas Goodfellow
Algernon D. Gorman
Orlando M. Gochnaur
Isaac V. Goltra
Otto B. Gray
Edward F. Greene
Julius E. Gregory
Charles H. Gundlock
Charles L. Gustafson
George P. Gustafson
Melsor E. Gustafson
Chester G. Hadden
Frederick Hadra
William J. Hamilton
Frank L. Hammerstrand
John C. Hanley
Howard H. Hardy
Tillman H. Harpole
Arthur H. Harris
Everett L. Harshbarger
Gerhard F. Hartwig
Calvin W. Hesse
James B. Hickman
John A. Hirstein
Leonard C. Hoskins
Oscar L. Housel
Allen K. Hyde
Lester H. Ihrig
Ralph Imes
Grant R. Ireland
Robert P. Irvine
Lenton W. James
Frank A. Jarrett
Hubert Jessen
Joseph H. Johnston
Archibald F. Keehner
Curtis E. Kelso
Clinton D. Kendall
James H. Kendall
Elmore A. Kirkland

Robert D. Kirkland
Bayard T. Klotzsche
Lynn E. Knorr
John C. Kromer
Edgar A. Lawrence
Theodore E. Layden
John C. Lee
Raymond G. Leggett
Samuel B. Leiser
Everett R. Leisure
Lester R. Lewis
Wilfred Lewis
Leslie A. Liggett
John R. Lindsey
Robert L. Long
LeCount R. Lovellette
Bernard M. Lyons
Clare P. McCaskey
Isaac F. McCollister
Leo G. McCormack
Joel F. McDavid
John McDonough
William H. Mandeville
Lewis V. Manspeaker
Leo J. Mattingly
Dean E. Memmen
Alexander V. Mercer
Russell Micenheimer
Leo C. Miller
Wayne K. Moore
Alfred T. Morison
Guy E. Morse
Charles S. Narkinsky
Ralph M. Noble
Tomas Olazagasti
Thomas J. Palmer
Raymond W. Parker
Miles M. Parmely
Lloyd M. Parr
Homer C. Parrish
Walter C. Paton
Clyde F. Pendleton
Herbert C. Petersen
William C. Peterson
Louis I. Phillis
Eric F. Pihlgard
Horatio N. Powell
Hugh M. Price

Benjamin J. Prince
George H. Raab
James K. Read
Lawrence S. Riddle
John W. Ruckman
Harold C. Schreiner
Harold S. Seibert
William J. Sense
Philip F. Shaffner
A. Vernon Sheetz
Otis E. Simpson
Clarence W. Smith
Philip O. Smith
William E. Smoot
Reginald G. Squibb
Otto Staeheli
Charles L. Starkel
Harry H. Strauch
Harold H. Sutherland
Dana E. Swift
Alexander S. Tarnoski
John L. Teare
Ralph W. Tippet
Norman J. Tweedie
Charles A. Wagner, Jr.
Elliot P. Walker
Edward Wallace
Burt H. Ward
Manierre B. Ware
William E. Wheeler, Jr.
George E. Wilcox
Lloyd G. Williams
Frederic H. Winslow
Warren C. Woodward
Henry Young
Ashford F. Corbin
Harry M. Gray
Kent D. Hagler
Alfred E. James
Louis R. Kratze
Unknown Illini Dead
Students' Army and
  Navy Training Corps
  Dead
Curtis G. Redden
  University of Michigan
Laurens C. Shull
  University of Chicago

6

RED GRANGE AND GLORY

"If you have the football and 11 guys are after you, if you're smart, you'll run."

—Harold Edward Grange

It is, of course, the immortal Red Grange to whom Zuppke's name will forever be linked. "Grench," Zuppke called him. Zup, with his thick German accent, mispronounced just about everybody's name, but as Grange once said, as long as his coach called him "Grench" he knew he was all right. If he heard "Red"— look out!

Harold Edward "Red" Grange was born the son of a timber camp foreman on June 13, 1903, in Forksville, Pennsylvania. Harold's mother died when he was five. Shortly after his wife's death, Lyle Grange moved his four children to Wheaton, Illinois.

In high school, Harold earned 16 varsity letters in four sports. He averaged five touchdowns a game and kicked 30 straight extra points for a Wheaton football team that lost only one game during his tenure, that loss coming on a day when Grange had to leave the game after being kicked in the head. Yet he was better known as a basketball and track athlete.

Grange first met Bob Zuppke during a high school state track meet. "I won the 100 and the 200 and he came and put his arm around me and said 'If you come down, I think you have a chance of making our team,' " Grange told *Sports Illustrated* in 1985. "That's the only selling job he did. Anything more than that was beneath his dignity.

Bob Zuppke and Harold "Red" Grange, two Illinois legends

The Block "I" salutes the Ghost

"In those days you'd line up and [they would] say, 'What sport are you going out for?' I said, 'Basketball.' I always thought I was a better basketball player than anything. They

Red Grange

said, 'You play four years of football in high school?' 'Yeah.' 'Football's bigger at Illinois than basketball. You go out for football.' "

He did. So did 120 other freshmen, many of them large and most with all-this or all-that credentials. Grange came back to his fraternity house without having checked out a uniform.

"They got out a paddle and made me bend over. And I said, 'Football makes a lot of sense to me.' "

So Grange got back in line. He stood behind the player who got number 76 and in front of the player who would wear number 78.

No other Illinois player would ever wear number 77 again.

The Legend Begins

Harold Grange made his varsity debut October 6, 1923, against powerful Nebraska. Sports writer Damon Runyon said Grange was "three or four men and a horse rolled into one." Paul Gallico called him a "touchdown factory," and colleague Grantland Rice, widely credited with nicknaming Grange the "Galloping Ghost," said this:

HAIL TO THE ORANGE AND BLUE!

The 1923 Fighting Illini

*"A streak of fire, a breath of flame,
Eluding all who reach and clutch;
A gray ghost thrown into the game
That rival hands may rarely touch;
A rubber bounding, blasting soul,
Whose destination is the goal—
Red Grange of Illinois."*

The next week, Grange's totals were 153 yards and one touchdown in a 21-7 win over Butler. Two weeks after that, Grange's fourth-quarter touchdown gave the Illini a 9-6 win over Iowa. In only 19 minutes against Northwestern he rushed for 104 yards and three more touchdowns. Illinois won 29-0. No wonder 60,000 plus slogged through the rain on November 3, 1923, to see Grange and the Illini play for the first time in their magnificent Memorial Stadium.

The crowd roared when Grange ran 42 yards against Amos Alonzo Stagg's University of Chicago powerhouse in the first quarter. It screamed again when he broke free for a 60-yard gain. Yet neither team scored during the first half.

Grange in action

Red Grange and Glory

In the third quarter, Illinois had the ball at its own 37-yard line. Grange gained three yards. Wally McIlwain added five more. Grange ran five more yards before he broke free for 23 yards. After one more run around end and a 15-yard gain, the ball was on Chicago's 7-yard line. McIlwain went into the middle for two before Grange ran straight through the middle and leaped into the end zone from five yards out. The first score ever in Memorial Stadium was the only score of that day.

Grange played in two of the Illini's final three games, all victories. When the season was done, Illinois had a share of the conference title with Michigan, and Grange had 12 touchdowns, 1,260 total yards and All-American status in the eyes of Walter Camp and just about everybody else. Only the *Michigan Daily* placed Grange on its second team, a slight it would regret after the Illini's 1924 Homecoming game.

Three Teams on the Field

After that game the *Big 10 Weekly* would report, "There were three teams on the field—Michigan, Illinois, and Red Grange, and by far the greatest of all three was Red Grange . . ."

Prior to the Homecoming game, Coach Zuppke was in his customary fret. How would the Illini's blockers open holes for his All-American halfback, Red Grange? Frank Rokusek, the captain and end, had a bad leg that Zuppke feared wouldn't hold up. McIlwain had been sent home to bed the night before with the flu.

Detroit newspaper reporter E.A. Batchelor, watching in amazement, wrote this description of the game. "Coming down to plain cases, Mr. Grange, who is the best running back that this writer ever saw—the best backfield for that matter—defeated Michigan by a score of 39 to 14. Mr. Grange seized the opening kickoff and planted the ball behind the Michigan goal line. He caught the ball on his own 10-yard line, ran down the left sideline for about 50 yards, cut back towards midfield and sped across the last chalk mark entirely unattended. The six nearest men to him at the time were Illinois men. Michigan had 11 players somewhere on the field but Harold had no means of knowing it.

"Of course running a kickoff the length of the field is more or less of a fluke. The seven points on the scoreboard hurt Michigan, but she accepted them as just a natural handicap. She felt sure that she would stop Grange when he tried to run from scrimmage. She didn't. Before the first quarter was over, he had sprinted 66 yards for a touchdown, 55 for another and 44 for still another.

"You will notice that Michigan was stopping him gradually, by cutting eleven yards off his runs each time he decided that he needed another six points. All this took place in the first

The 1924 Fighting Illini team

HAIL TO THE ORANGE AND BLUE!

12 minutes of the first quarter. In other words, with one-fifth of the playing time gone, Michigan was 27 points to the bad, as (Earl) Britton had goaled after the first three Grange touchdowns.

"Well, if Michigan couldn't stop Grange, Illinois had a man who could and did. Coach Zuppke stopped him cold by taking him out of the game . . .

"Red remained on the bench throughout the second period and it was all right with Michigan. . . But he came back to work in the third chapter and brought more bad news. After contenting himself with some modest gains, he finally decided that it was time to make another touchdown so he loped 12 yards and made it. Having demonstrated that he was a pretty fair man at carrying the ball, Grange put on a forward passing sketch towards the end of the game. The critics used to say that all he could do was run and it cut him to the quick, so he learned some new tricks. Of course saying that all Grange can do is run with the ball is a good deal like saying that all Caruso could do was sing, or all that Dempsey can do is fight. There would be no real sting in the criticism even if true. Yet it must be admitted that if Grange ever gets the forward passing habit to an incurable degree, he will still be on the first team. He tried seven passes and completed six of them, including one that nestled gracefully into the arms of an Illinois gent who was leaning gracefully on the Michigan goal line in one corner of the field, and who promptly carried it over. That made six touchdowns for which Grange was responsible. Against a team that claimed championship brackets last fall and had hopes of winning an undisputed title this year, that is good enough to earn a journeyman's card in the Touchdown Makers' union."

Batchelor, of course, was not the only observer open-mouthed at Grange's feats. A crowd of 66,609 was stuffed into the newly dedicated Memorial Stadium. The *Daily Illini* chronicled its reaction:

"After the first Grange amble, the crowd sat still and gasped, the gasp changed to a chuckle on the second, a laugh on the third and on the fourth it gasped again."

Michigan coach Fielding Yost purpose-fully put the ball in Grange's hands that day. After all, his Wolverines had given up only 12 points the season before and had yet to surrender a point in two previous 1924 games. Kick the ball to Grange, Yost thought, and the Wolverine defenders would smother him.

That strategy resulted in Grange's 212 net rushing yards and a touchdown pass. Why did Zuppke remove Red from the game for more than a quarter? "Two reasons," he said. "One was fear of injury to Red. The second is that I didn't want to spoil the show. . ."

After Michigan was defeated 39-14, Grange took the next week off, watching his teammates beat DePauw 45-0. He was back the following week to rush for 151 yards and score two touchdowns in a 36-0 pasting of Iowa.

Challenge and Injury

Chicago and Stagg figured not to repeat Michigan's mistakes. The Ghost couldn't score, Stagg reasoned, if he couldn't get his hands on the ball. Chicago won the toss, elected to receive, and methodically drove to the Illinois 4-yard line before fumbling. Illinois couldn't move from there and soon the Maroons were on the march again. This time they drove for the score.

The Maroons took the kickoff and slowly charged the length of the field. Chicago was ahead 14-0 before Grange laid his hands on the football, but there was no way Stagg's men would allow him to run, so he threw five passes good for 86 yards. He caught two passes from Earl Britton for 40 yards. Finally, Grange scored a touchdown, but Chicago countered and was up 21-7. Grange scored again just before halftime. In the third quarter, Grange took off on a run from his 20-yard line, tiptoeing past the bodies at the line of scrimmage and into the clear. Touchdown. Score: 21-21.

That's how it would end because a 51-yard Grange touchdown run was called back for a penalty. Nevertheless, it was a three-touchdown, 196-yard rushing day for Grange, and he threw for 86 more yards, a feat that would no doubt be immortalized if not for what he had done three weeks earlier.

At Minnesota the next week, Grange inter-

Grange and his famous jersey after his last college game

cepted a third-quarter pass. A Gopher player threw him out of bounds, another piled onto him, and Minnesota drew a penalty. It took Grange a long time to get to his feet, but he insisted upon staying in the game. Zuppke, however, soon called him to the sidelines. Grange's right arm was hanging due to strained shoulder ligaments. This injury kept him out of the rest of that 20-7 loss and the next week's season finale, a 7-0 win over Ohio State. Grange finished the season with 13 touchdowns, 1,164 total offensive yards, and nationwide acclamation as the greatest football player in the land.

The Final Illini Season

Red Grange had only one more season of college play, during which every opposition defensive player had his sights set on number 77. To make matters worse, many of the talented players who had run interference for

him had graduated. This 1925 season would be Grange's worst. He would score only six touchdowns. Three of them were scored in the lackluster 1-3 start that included Illinois' first loss in Memorial Stadium, 14-0 to Nebraska, and a 3-0 loss to Michigan.

Eastern writers were skeptical of the Midwestern adulation of Grange. That skepticism melted, though, in the cold mud at Franklin Field when, on October 31, 1925, Illinois travelled east to meet the University of Pennsylvania before a crowd of 63,000. The Eastern skeptics were converted after Grange rushed 237 yards and scored three touchdowns.

Red Grange would not score another touchdown in college football. He played his last college game on November 21, 1925, in front of a record crowd of 85,000 at Ohio Stadium. Though he did not score, his 103 rushing yards and 42 more passing led the Illini to a 14-9 victory over Ohio State.

HAIL TO THE ORANGE AND BLUE!

Turning Pro

After the game, Grange announced he would turn pro, sign with the Chicago Bears, and embark on a barnstorming tour that ultimately would make him wealthy and the National Football League credible. Although their friendship was later mended, Zuppke and Grange wouldn't speak for two years because of Grange's fascination with the pro game.

He left college football with 31 touchdowns, 2,071 rushing yards, and 525 passing yards. In 247 games of high school, college, and professional football, it is believed Grange carried the ball 4,013 times, gained 33,820 yards, which equals 19 and a quarter miles, and scored 2,366 points. More than three quarters of a million people sat in football stadiums to watch Grange run for Illinois.

"They can argue all they want about the greatest football player who ever lived," Zuppke once said. "I was satisfied I had him when I had Red Grange."

Yet the Galloping Ghost never thought of himself in terms of greatness.

"I played football the only way I knew how," he told *Sports Illustrated*. "If you have the football and 11 guys are after you, if you're smart, you'll run. It was no big deal."

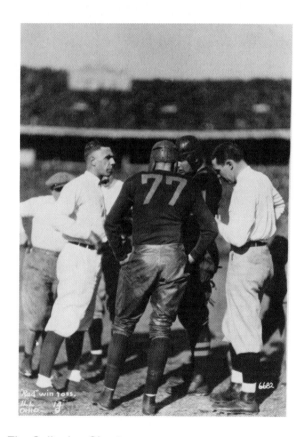

The Galloping Ghost

"There are two shapes now moving
Two ghosts that drift and glide,
And which of them to tackle
Each rival must decide.
They shift with special swiftness
Across the swarded range.
And one of them's a shadow,
And one of them is Grange."

—Grantland Rice

"I doubt if any of his players ever loved the guy, but their respect and affection were tremendous."

—Ernie Lovejoy, former
Illinois player

Red Grange was gone, but in 1926 Zuppke hardly had to ask any aspiring Illinois high school player to come and play where the Ghost had galloped. They came by the dozens to take Grange's place in the Illini backfield. Some became guards, a few became ends, but no one replaced Red Grange. Illinois had a good season, but not a great one.

Bernie Shively was an All-American at guard and the Illini put on another impressive display against Pennsylvania. The Quakers came into the game famous for their hidden ball offense, but Zuppke had a solid defensive strategy and the Illini posted a 3-0 victory on Forrest I. "Frosty" Peters' field goal. The season was most important, however, because many talented young players from that 6-2 team gained valuable experience.

A Team of Nobodies

A year later many of those players would dominate the Big 10. Guys like center Bob Reitsch; guards Russ Crane and Albert "Butch" Nowack; end Garland "Gardie" Grange (Red's brother); tackles Louis Gordon and Lloyd Burdick; and a group of small swift backs, including Doug Mills (who would later become the school's athletic director), Jud Timm, and Fred "Fritz"

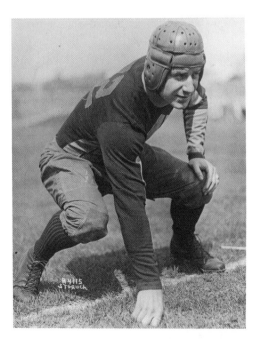

Russ Crane, member of the "Team of Nobodies"

Forrest I. "Frosty" Peters

Humbert. They were called a team of nobodies from out of nowhere, but when it was over, they were 7-0-1, 5-0 in the league, and champions of the Western Conference.

The Illini got it started in the league with a 7-6 upset against Northwestern. Nowack, who could kick as well as he could block, converted after a Walter "Bud" Jolley touchdown to provide the margin of victory. The next week Timm

scored after Gardie Grange recovered a fumble and Ernie Schultz jumped on a blocked punt in the Michigan end zone, leading the Illini to a 14-0 win.

Touchdowns by Humbert and Frank Walker (the latter on a 53-yard run) dispatched Iowa 14-0. Walker scored twice and Nowack blocked a punt for a safety to give the Illini a 15-6 win over Chicago. Finally, the Illini beat Ohio State 13-0 on two touchdown passes, one good for 23 yards from Dwight Stuessy to Humbert, the other from Al French to Timm for 25 yards.

In Grantland Rice's eyes, Crane and Reitsch were All-Americans. Reitsch made Walter Eckersall's third team.

The 1928 Conference Championship

Most of the players were back in 1928 and they were tough. The Illini tuned up for the conference season with wins of 33-6 over Bradley and 31-0 over Coe. They beat Indiana 13-7 and Northwestern 6-0 to run their conference winning streak to seven.

The next week they travelled to Ann Arbor to meet a Michigan team that was going through one of its worst seasons. However, the rival Wolverines' Joe Gembis field goal brought Michigan a 3-0 victory. It was a bitter loss, but it was the last one Illinois would suffer that year. As a matter of fact, Gembis' field goal repre-

1928 Illinois team

HAIL TO THE ORANGE AND BLUE!

sented the last points the Illini would give up in the season. Chicago was dispatched 40-0 and Ohio State beaten 8-0. Butler was defeated 14-0.

Later that season the Wolverines did the Illini a favor. Illinois was leading Ohio State 8-

Bob Zuppke and Butch Nowack

0 in the season finale on a Forrest Peters touchdown and a safety. The crowd in Memorial Stadium rose to its feet with a thunderous roar. The stadium scoreboard flashed good news. Michigan had beaten Iowa 10-7 and Minnesota had topped Wisconsin 6-0. An Illinois win meant an Illinois championship. It was Zuppke's last conference championship, and the Illini wouldn't win another for 18 seasons.

Depression Years

Nineteen twenty-nine wasn't such a bad year even though Peters spent much of the season in the infirmary and injuries decimated the Illinois lineup. Illinois finished 6-1-1, 3-1-1 in the league, and was runner-up to Purdue. Notable moments from that season were a 27-0 win at Ohio State—the last victory Illinois would

achieve at Ohio Stadium until 1947—and a 17-7 win over an outstanding Army team, led by All-American Red Cagle. More than 67,000 fans, the biggest crowd to date at Memorial Stadium, witnessed that game.

The victory was a memory to treasure, in part because the Great Depression was settling over the nation and as well, because Illinois' football fortunes were sinking. Illinois' only conference victory in 1930 was 28-0 over Chicago, a school that was by now beginning to suffer a serious football decline and would abandon the sport before the decade was out. The Illini would go 3-5.

Illinois did have a pretty good halfback in those days named Gilbert Berry. Zuppke claimed Berry would have been legendary had he had the luxury of a strong line working in front of him. Also that year the Illini had a nearsighted, balding tackle named Raymond Nusspickel. (Nusspickel would take his mother's maiden name years later to become Ray Eliot.) Nusspickel wasn't the greatest lineman, although Zuppke used to say he'd be a candidate for All-American honors if only he could see across the line of scrimmage.

So low had Illinois' fortunes sunk in 1931 that days before Illinois was to play Chicago, its sixth game of the season, an exasperated Zuppke told his assistant coaches that he had no clue as to where he could go to find a fullback.

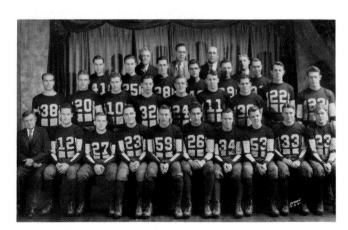

1931 Illinois football squad

Raymond Nusspickel, later Coach Ray Eliot

Johnny Sabo, an Illinois assistant, found a candidate on campus. Edwin Kolfenbach weighed only 156 pounds and knew nothing about the Illini offense, but in the span of less than four days he learned the signals, mastered the offense as best he could, and was in the lineup against the Maroons. Kolfenbach played all the way through the 5-4 1932 season.

Illinois' downhill slide might have been thought of as nothing more than a brief aberration if the Illini could have found a couple of extra points in 1933. Wisconsin fell 21-0, Northwestern 3-0, and Chicago 7-0. But 7-6 losses to both Michigan and Ohio State cost Zuppke's team a chance at the championship.

One Last Season of Greatness

Zuppke's 1934 team, however, turned back the clock for one last season of greatness. It also turned around one-point victories, 7-6 over the Wolverines and 14-13 over Ohio State.

Win or lose, Zuppke still growled about the extra point. "Football needs an appendectomy," he once said. "Removal of the point after touchdown."

Illinois was favored to beat the Wolverines and did, thanks to a John Theodore touchdown and a Lester Lindberg extra point. The Illini were not favored to topple the mighty Buckeyes.

Red Grange was in Champaign for that Ohio State game. He described the action in *Zuppke of Illinois*:

"When the Illinois team came out on the field, they looked like a bunch of high school boys dressed up in their older brothers' football suits. I thought it would be a slaughter of the in-

1934 Illinois football team

HAIL TO THE ORANGE AND BLUE!

nocents. The Ohio State squad looked as though they would chase the Illini right through Exit 12 into the Boneyard! But never sell Zuppke short! The Illini got the jump on the Buckeyes, took the lead, kept scrapping for every inch of ground and staved off the flashy Ohio State backfield.

"Had I been an alumnus of Ohio State, California, Princeton or even Harvard, I would have called the performance of the Illini magnificent, simply from the standpoint of football courage."

Grange also got to watch one of Zuppke's famous trick plays, the "Flying Trapeze." The Illini lateralled the ball back and forth while the Buckeyes tried to figure out where it was going next. The ball finally wound up in Jack Beynon's hands, and he threw it to Eugene Dykstra, who was standing alone in the end zone.

After the Buckeye upset, only Zuppke's alma mater, Wisconsin, separated the Illini from the conference championship. Allen Mahnke picked off an Illinois pass and ran 22 yards for the game's only touchdown in a 7-3 Badger victory.

The following week, Chuck Galbreath caught a 9-yard touchdown pass from Beynon and the Illini held Chicago star Jay Berwanger in check to give the Illini a 6-0 victory and 7-1 season.

Personal Tragedy

Zuppke's Illini wouldn't see such heights again. However, in 1935, they did see California for the first time. Illinois played at Southern Cal and came home a 19-0 winner. The school would win only once more in its final five games that season and finish 3-5 for the year.

Prior to the 1936 season, Zuppke's wife of nearly 30 years, Fanny, had died. Those who knew the coach say much of his zest for life went with her. Five days after Illinois opened the season with a 9-6 win over DePaul, George Huff, the man who hired Zuppke out of the high school ranks, died.

George Huff and Bob Zuppke had been devoted friends and colleagues for 23 years. Zuppke would gladly have postponed or even cancelled that week's game against Washington of St. Louis, but it was always Huff's wish that the Illinois athletic program move forward no matter what. So that game, and indeed the rest of the schedule, went on as planned. Illinois finished 4-3-1 that year and Wendell Wilson succeeded Huff as athletic director.

The Dean of the League

It would be Zuppke's last winning season.

George Huff's tombstone, with Memorial Stadium in background

The End of an Era

Bob Zuppke with Knute Rockne

The next year, 1937, would be Zuppke's 25th at Illinois. When Chicago's coach Stagg retired after 41 seasons, Zup was the dean of his league. With that in mind, one of Wilson's earliest acts as athletic director was to announce that 1937 would be a year of tribute to the Illinois coach.

Zuppke was honored around the league as well. Ohio State presented him with a scroll that read, in part, "To you we dedicate anew the inscription carved high on the tower of our own Ohio Stadium, scene of classic combat with your teams: 'For friendship through contest.' "

And, after more than 30 years, Wisconsin gave one of its most prominent alumni his "W" sweater at a star-studded post-season banquet in Chicago attended by more than 1,200 alumni and friends, including Illinois Governor Henry Horner.

On the field, Illinois compiled a so-so 3-3-2 season. The Illini also stunned Northwestern 6-0 that fall, knocking the Wildcats out of the conference race.

Power Struggles

Zuppke relished the idea of molding ordinary football players into players of considerable usefulness. He also relished the idea of dimming a star's light. However, he did not relish the idea of recruiting. Athletic scholarships were becoming entrenched throughout the nation as the 1930s waned. Not at Illinois. Not with Bob Zuppke.

"Imagine paying someone to play football," Zuppke once said.

It was a high-minded attitude, but not a practical one. Players, who once might have come to Illinois just for the honor of playing for Bob Zuppke, no longer found quite so much honor in that alone. By 1938, the Illini were falling further and further behind in finding quality football players.

Zuppke did not always treat the players he had gently. Harsh words would cross his lips and rough-and-tumble practice sessions were commonplace. Players came to Illinois, but some soon left because of Zuppke's heavy-handed methods. At the same time, Athletic Director Wilson, Professor Fred Russell, chairman of the university's athletic board, and members of the board itself were ready to push Zuppke out. Rumor had it that Wilson himself was preparing to take over the coaching duties.

Zuppke, however, said he would never quit, at least until he had the makings of a competitive football team to leave his successor. Nevertheless, after a 3-5 season, the athletic board asked for and accepted Zuppke's letter of resignation in late November.

This move was quickly and overwhelmingly rejected by the university's board of trustees, which entered its regular meeting that day not knowing it would be asked to approve Zuppke's resignation. When Harold Pogue, Zuppke's one-time star back and current member of the trustees, got wind of the move to purge his old coach, he made an impassioned closed-door plea to the board of trustees on Zuppke's behalf.

Nobody outside those doors ever knew exactly what Pogue said that day. But when the meeting was over, the board had voted 8-1 against accepting any resignation. Board President Oscar Mayer issued this formal statement: "The board of trustees at the University of Illinois disapproves of any change in the status of Coach Zuppke."

Zuppke's power was restored, but the differences between coach and athletic director were far from resolved. Three years later, both Zuppke and Wilson would be out. Wilson would be replaced by Doug Mills.

The 1939 team went 3-4-1 but came up with a major upset in a 16-7 win over Michigan and running back Tom Harmon. The inspiration for the Illini that day was that someone in the Michigan entourage said that Harmon was better than Grange.

In 1940 Illinois beat Bradley 31-0 in its season opener. The Illini didn't beat anybody else, finishing 1-7.

In 1941 the Illini had enough to beat Miami of Ohio 45-0 and Drake 40-0, but didn't have the weapons to stay with Minnesota (34-6), Notre Dame (49-14), Michigan (20-0), Iowa (21-0), and Ohio State (12-7).

A Minnesota newspaper described the Gopher victory like this: "The truth about today's game, if it can be called that, is that Illinois was outweighed, outmanned and overmatched. That the Illini fought bravely is beside the point. They had the same chance to win that they would have had to stop a tank barehanded."

Finally, five days before the Illini were to close the 1941 season at Northwestern and after publicly insisting that he would never resign, Zuppke did just that.

An Illinois Man

On November 22, 1941, in front of 35,000 cheering fans and a barrage of cameramen recording his every move, Zuppke watched Northwestern sophomore Bill De Correvont score three times and the Wildcats post a 27-0 victory.

Harold Pogue was with Zuppke that last day. So were Butch Nowack, Jim McMillen, and Ray Gallivan, all former players. Howard Barry of the *Chicago Tribune* described Zuppke this way:

"Only once—just before the last gun—did Zuppke give any sign that he was thinking of the end. In the final half minute he kept switching his glance from the field to the big electric clock that was running off the seconds. His lips were very straight then as though there were almost too many minutes of great days going through his mind.

Bob Zuppke and Tom Riggs

"Then came the gun. Zuppke got up, thrust his hands into the pockets of his coat and walked out across the field. Later, in the dressing room, more of his former players came to see him. Lou Gordon was there. So were Gil Berry, Jack Beynon, Bob Reitsch, Emil Schultz, and Bob Wehrli.

" 'I'm still an Illinois man,' Zuppke said. 'And I always will be. Often, when people part, they remember the bad things about one another. What I want to remember about Illinois is the thousand kindnesses that were done for me there—not the one or two unpleasant experiences. Illinois did much more for me than I could ever do for Illinois.'

"Then he went out the door through the lane between waiting friends . . . "

Zuppke left with 131 victories, 81 losses, and 13 ties in 29 seasons and was 76-66-8 in the league, including seven conference championships and two undefeated teams.

Although Zuppke never set foot in an Illinois practice session after his retirement, he did attend most of the school's home games. Zuppke turned down numerous coaching offers. He did serve as an adviser to George Halas' Chicago Bears for a brief time.

On December 22, 1957, at the age of 78, Zuppke died.

"When I think of Zup," said Charles "Ernie" Lovejoy, who played for Zuppke during the teens, "I think of a small, tough Dutchman with great talent and imagination and a will to win. No diplomacy, no small talk, contempt for a lazy man and a shoddy job, a certain amount of humor when he told the joke, but an immense teacher and philosopher . . . I doubt if any of his players ever loved the guy, but their respect and affection were tremendous."

"The Little Dutchman"

HAIL TO THE ORANGE AND BLUE!

Zuppke-isms:

- "Nobody but a dead man leaves the field."

- "Definition of an All-American: A fast back, weak opposition, and a poet in the press box."

- "The game of football is to college life what good color is to a painting. It makes college life throb and vibrate."

- "All quitters are good losers."

- "Victory in football is 40 percent ability and 60 percent spirit."

- "The hero of 1,000 perfect plays becomes a bum after one error."

- "Football may be a brutal game; but brutes cannot play it. Courage and initiative are the first requisites."

- "Whenever the ball is snapped, every man should play to excess, even beyond his ability."

- "Theory should lead to practice and practice to more theory."

- "If the team wins all of its games, the alumni are loyal."

- "Never let hope elude you, hang to the ups and downs of the game with the primitive virtue which never says quit."

PART III: THE ELIOT YEARS

ILLINOIS
1890 1990
FOOTBALL
100 YEARS OF TRADITION

"We'll have the will to win, and if we go down, we'll go down fighting . . . hard and clean. That's the Illinois way."

Ray Eliot

A LONG ROAD TO ROSES

"Anything you think you can do, you can do."

—Coach Ray Eliot

Many top coaches, including William and Mary's Carl Marvin Voyles and Washington's Jimmy Phelan, wanted Bob Zuppke's old job. It took athletic director Doug Mills and the athletic board nearly two and a half months to find the coach they wanted.

On January 12, 1942, Mills left his office in Huff Gym and walked down the hall to line coach Ray Eliot's office.

"Congratulations, Ray. The job is yours," he told Eliot.

"With six words [Mills] sent me into a new life . . . I was thrilled at Doug's utterance. I was overwhelmed when the football players, who had been standing in the hallway, broke into my office and hoisted me on their shoulders. I was so stunned that I forgot to grab my coat. No one else remembered. So I was dragged halfway around campus in the middle of winter in my shirt sleeves."

At a speaking engagement just hours after he had accepted the $6,000 one-year contract, Eliot told his audience,

"I'll say to the football players next year 'Anything you think you can do, you can do.' We have a definite goal ahead. I won't concede anything to any team in the Big 10.

"Oh, we'll have our headaches, plenty of them, but we'll guarantee this. Every man who goes on that football field will carry a feeling that we can win. We'll face Minnesota next October with a twinkle in our eye and victory in our hearts."

Of course, nobody except Eliot really believed that. The Illini hadn't won a Big 10 Conference game in two years, the Gophers hadn't lost one.

Ray Eliot, Arthur Hall, and Bob Zuppke

Eliot's First Winning Season

Eliot led the Illini onto the Memorial Stadium turf for the first time against South Dakota on September 26, 1942. "My heart was in my throat as I wondered just what in the world the outcome of the game would be," Eliot told the *Chicago Sun-Times* years later. The outcome was 46-0 in Illinois' favor. It was a 67-0 victory when Butler came calling a week later.

But that was South Dakota and Butler. Put them together and they couldn't begin to equal Minnesota. The Gophers were deep and talented. Tackle Dick Wildung and backs Bill Daley, Herm Frickey, Mike Welch, Vic Kulbitski, and Bill Garnass would be ready to wreak havoc if given half a chance.

The Illini hadn't achieved a win in the league since the final game of 1939. Illinois' talent was mostly unknown and certainly untried. Eliot used 17 players in front of a Homecoming crowd of 24,276.

Ray Eliot leading his team out of the locker room

"I was nervous all morning," Eliot told Lou Engel of the *Champaign-Urbana Courier* 25 years later. "I couldn't sit down. We were trying to convince the players that the boys from Minnesota were just human beings. We tried to sell them on the fact that they could make mistakes like us and the team that made the least mistakes would win.

"All the things you kept telling the boys, you hoped you believed yourself."

The game began with a Gopher touchdown. The Gophers went up 7-0 when Daley scampered 81 yards for a score. Still in the first quarter, Daley swung wide and was hit by Illinois linebacker Ray Florek. At the same time, Alex Agase pulled the ball out of Daley's arms and ran 35 yards for a score.

"That was the first indication for the boys in the press box that Agase would be a good football player," Eliot later told the *Chicago Tribune.*

With the score tied 13-13 late in the fourth quarter, a Gopher snap from center sailed into the end zone. Agase, in hot pursuit, sailed right in with it. That touchdown set off a celebration reminiscent of 26 years earlier and Ray Eliot was named United Press International's Coach of the Week. "Anything you think you can do, you can do," became the catch-phrase of Eliot's 18-year tenure.

A week later, Iowa was dispatched 12-7. The Illini also posted a 14-7 win over Northwestern and a 20-0 victory over Camp Grant. Its losses were 21-14 to Notre Dame, although the Illini twice were stopped inside the Irish 30-yard line late in that game; 28-14 to Michigan; 44-20 to Ohio State, although Tony Butkovich ran 83 yards for a score with a kickoff, and 6-0 to Great Lakes for a remarkable 6-4 season.

It was an astonishing turnaround. Line coach Justa Lindgren had been part of Illinois football for 39 years. He'd never seen anything quite like this.

"[Eliot] took a bunch of boys who lacked faith in themselves, who were defeatists, and he gave them courage," Lindgren told the *Chicago Daily News* near the end of the 1942 season. "He couldn't give them superior playing ability. They weren't great players and they weren't, as a unit, a great team . . . He has talked common sense to these boys, they've believed him and they've acted on that belief."

1943's Disappearing Illini

The Illini believed they would be conference champions in 1943. But there was no military training base on or near the Illinois campus as there was in other places. So Eliot lost Agase, Tony Butkovich, Joe Buscemi, John Genis,

Frank Bauman, Mike Kasap, and Art Dufelmeier. In all, more than 100 eligible athletes were called away between spring drills and the 1943 season. The team became known as "the Disappearing Illini."

Illinois won only three of ten games that year. Its most ironic loss was to its old rival Purdue, where many of Eliot's young athletes were in training. Agase, Butkovich, Buscemi, Genis, Bauman, and Kasap all wore Boilermaker uniforms.

This is how reporter Bill Schmelzle described that day: ". . . It was a crazy battle from the first play. Illinois opened with an elaborate T-formation offense, which was a mere two weeks old, and used it consistently throughout the game. There were touchdown runs of 70 and 80 yards,

ing the former Illinois players' request to cross the field and sit with Eliot.

"All of a sudden, we [Illinois] scored real quick and Burnham was over there on the Purdue sideline waving like crazy," Tony Butkovich said. "We were sitting there laughing at him, they wanted him to think we didn't see him, so they let him wait awhile. Finally they went back over, he put them back in the game and they ended up beating us pretty good."

"I think," said Chuck Flynn, then acting as Illinois' sports information director, "it was indicative of the support Ray had from those players that even though they were playing varsity football for Purdue as Navy V-5s, they were still loyal to their coach."

Alex Agase, one of 1943's "Disappearing Illini"

and three other scores were called back. Two blocked kicks, intercepted passes, 143 yards of penalties and an unbelievable total of 20 fumbles added to the 60 minutes of confusion . . . Even though Purdue won, it was still an Illinois day."

The Boilermakers got ahead so quickly that coach Elmer Burnham figured they were in for an easy day, so he had no qualms about grant-

A Bizarre Defeat

Illinois, 0-3 by this point, would win its next two games, 25-7 over Wisconsin in their first game against fellow civilians, and 33-25 over Pittsburgh when the "scooter" backs, Eddie Bray and Ed McGovern, combined for five touchdowns. Then they were spanked 47-0 by

Notre Dame. The next week, they would give Michigan's team, beefed up by the military addition of Minnesota's Daley and Wisconsin's Elroy Hirsch, fits, but would fall 42-6.

A week later, Illinois won over Iowa 19-10, led by McGovern's 95-yard run in a pouring rain. Then Illinois went to Ohio State for the season's next-to-last game. Neither Eliot's Illini nor Paul Brown's Buckeyes benefited from service programs. Bray averaged nearly 11 yards a carry, McGovern nearly eight, and Don Greenwood more than five yards. The teams returned to their locker rooms after the final gun, tied 26-26.

Or so Eliot thought. Neither he nor anybody else that day saw linesman Paul Gobel throw a flag on the last play after Ohio State's Dean Sensenbaugher had thrown an incomplete pass into the Illinois end zone.

Flynn remembers what happened next: "Some of our players were in the shower when the referee came into the dressing room and said 'Ray, you have to bring your team back on the field, there was an offside penalty on the final play of the game.'"

To avoid forfeiting the game, Eliot took his players—some of whom were without shoes or shoulder pads—back to the field where Ohio State's John Stungis kicked his first collegiate field goal 23 yards and Ohio State secured a bizarre 29-26 victory. Illinois ended that season a week later, losing to Northwestern 53-6. Eddie Bray scored the only Illinois touchdown, running 90 yards on a kickoff return.

Buddy Young: Runner, Receiver

Eliot's 1944 team consisted of 16- and 17-year-old kids. One of them was Buddy Young. Claude "Buddy" Young could run like nobody had seen in Champaign since Red Grange. Buddy Young, at 5-foot-5 and 160 pounds, could run faster than Grange. He once held the American record in the 60-yard dash and won just about every sprint championship in sight for the Illini track team. When he came to Illinois he was a fine track athlete.

"Sprinters are straight runners, and if Young runs that way, he's too small to do any damage in college football," Eliot once said. He soon changed his mind.

Buddy Young

Although Alphonse "Flip" Anders had broken the color barrier at Illinois five years earlier, a black athlete was still an anomaly on college campuses in 1944. Bill Butkovich said of his 1944 teammate, "The stigma of the black athlete at that time didn't seem to affect Buddy

Alphonse "Flip" Anders, first black to play at Illinois

at all. We told people he was coming and we didn't want any embarrassment or anything. And most people cooperated."

Whatever Young's feelings were about being among the few black college athletes of that era, at least he was not alone. Paul Patterson, also a black athlete, played in front of Young. Young got two carries for nine yards and a touchdown in his first game, a 79-6 win over Illinois Normal. Two weeks later, he picked up 120 yards, including a 93-yard touchdown run, in seven carries as Illinois played Great Lakes to a 26-26 tie. The run still stands as the longest run from scrimmage ever by an Illini player.

The next week Young was in the starting lineup. Against Pittsburgh he darted 93 yards for a score, and he galloped 74 yards for a touchdown in a 13-7 loss to Notre Dame. Later, Young was knocked out of that game when he was kicked in the head during a play that provided the source of much controversy. For that 5-4-1 season, Young racked up 841 yards, averaged 8.8 yards per carry, and equalled Grange's single-season record with 13 touchdowns.

If Illini fans thought they would watch Young fly past defenses for three more seasons, they were wrong. In 1945 the Illini won only two of nine games.

Illinois' Heroes Return

Illinois was waiting for their heroes to return in 1946. It would be worth the wait.

Alex Agase came back to the University of Illinois in 1946 with a Purple Heart. Art Dufelmeier came back 60 pounds lighter after spending 11 months in a German prison camp. Buddy Young came back after seriously considering taking his speed to UCLA. Tony Butkovich, killed at Okinawa in 1945, didn't come back at all.

Nevertheless, as many as 300 aspiring Illini, most of them returning from military service, showed up for practice that fall. Holdover Mac Wenskunas, a center-linebacker, served as captain. Everybody knew this team could be the most powerful Illinois team ever assembled, or it could be torn apart by post-war pressures.

Nineteen members of the 1945 football team get their first taste of post-war plane travel

A Long Road to Roses

"The '46 team was a very difficult team for Ray to coach," Chuck Flynn explained. "In the first place, the majority of them now were married, they drank, they caroused, they carried on and they weren't used to the kind of discipline that going to college and observing training rules and so on required."

Dwight "Dike" Eddleman, an established athletic legend from Centralia High School who was a freshman Illini punter and back on that team, said, "You had guys who had been shot at, Alex must have been 26, 27 years old. It was hard to keep guys coming out, being at practice on time. It was a new transition for them to come back to school after they'd been in service. But they met the challenge."

The Illini had little trouble dispatching Pittsburgh 33-7 on the road in their season opener. Illini fans' appetites were whet for the next weekend's home game showdown with powerful Notre Dame.

A clear 80-degree day greeted the record crowd of 75,119. Ticket demand for that day was so heavy that the student supply of Athletic Association cards ran dry. The athletic staff held a hasty meeting and Flynn was dispatched to get 5,000 temporary cards printed for the game.

Those 5,000 wound up in folding chairs lining the track on either sideline. "But as the game progressed, those chairs began to move with the ball as far as possible," Flynn said. The Johnny Lujack-led Irish dominated from the beginning, winning 26-6 to move their record against Illinois to 9-0-1.

Dike Eddleman, the greatest all-around Illinois athlete

Building a Team Effort

The loss to Notre Dame cooled the fans' hopes, but they warmed up again the next week when Illinois opened the Big Nine season with its first victory over Purdue in 27 years, 43-7. Young was held in check, gaining only 40 yards on 12 carries, but Perry Moss, a transfer from

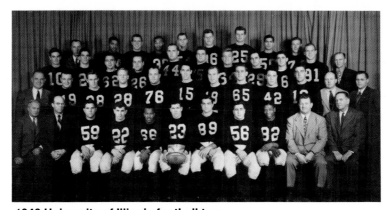

1946 University of Illinois football team

HAIL TO THE ORANGE AND BLUE!

Tulsa, passed to Ike Owens to score on the opening play. Moss also ran for two touchdowns and Eddleman got loose for a 45-yard scoring run.

The following week, the Illini went to Indiana expecting an easy time against the 1945 league champion Hoosiers who did not benefit from returning veterans. Moss and Patterson combined on a 22-yard first-quarter touchdown pass to put Illinois up 7-0. The Hoosiers came back five minutes later and scored a 14-7 upset when Indiana drove 37 yards in the final quarter. Illinois was 2-2. Nobody was happy. The loss triggered waves of soul-searching from both inside and outside the Illinois football family.

Eliot walked into Doug Mills's office offering to resign, an offer that was instantly rejected. The coach was hanged in effigy on campus, and the Monday workout was altered to include a long, and sometimes loud gripe session.

"We had a good defense but at Indiana we were strictly a bunch of individuals," Eliot said years later. "So I laid it on the line that Monday. I proved to them that their way wouldn't work and my way would. From that day we became a team."

Five days later Wisconsin came to Memorial Stadium for Illinois' 36th Homecoming game. The Badgers took a 21-14 lead into the fourth quarter. A Rykovich 19-yard run to the Wisconsin 1-yard line keyed a 54-yard scoring drive early in the quarter. Moss got the final yard to make it 21-20, but Don Maechtle missed the extra point and Illinois' season still hung in the balance.

In the final minutes, Rykovich, a halfback, threw a 31-yard pass to Owens to start a 57-yard drive. Moss added 14 more with a pass to Joe Buscemi. Rykovich carried it into the end zone from three yards out. Maechtle made the extra point and the Illini were 27-21 winners.

The next week Illinois played Michigan and won 13-9. Patterson and Sam Zatkoff scored touchdowns, but it was the Illini line that stopped Michigan three times inside the Illinois 20 in the final period. Alex Agase, Jocko Wrenn, Babe Serpico, Joe Buscemi, Jim Valek, Lou Agase, Bob Cunz, Vern Seliger, Russell Steger, and Ray Florek took turns holding the Wolverines out of the end zone. Steger scored a fourth-quarter touchdown the following week to spark a 7-0 win at Iowa.

On the Way to Pasadena

The next game was a home game with Ohio State. It was 43 degrees and muddy when it started to rain. However, 61,519 spectators were in place that November Saturday.

Ohio State went up 7-0 in the second quarter when powerful fullback Joe Whisler bucked 17 yards. The Illini came back. Zatkoff blocked a punt for a safety and Buddy Young turned a short pass from Art Dufelmeier into a spectacular 34-yard gain, setting up Moss for a 1-yard touchdown plunge to make it 9-7 at the half.

The 1947 Fighting Illini

Whisler, who picked up the bulk of the Buckeyes' 199 rushing yards that day, kept pounding and pounding into the Illinois line. Why he wasn't called to pound one more time from Illinois' 2-yard line with time running out, nobody ever quite figured out. Instead quarterback George Spencer stepped back to pass, looking for end Jameson Crane. The crowd, peering into the fog, wondered what happened next. They still wondered as they saw a muddy figure emerge from the fog, slosh toward the middle of the field and run 98 yards for the touchdown. Illinois' 16-7 victory virtually clinched a berth in the 1947 Rose Bowl. Fans later learned it was Rykovich who stepped in front of Jameson and never broke stride as he made his long journey to the end zone.

Illinois had its first victory over Ohio State since 1934, and sole possession of the league lead. With a victory at Northwestern the following Saturday, it would have an invitation to the Rose Bowl, the first under the newly signed agreement between what are now the Big 10 and Pac-10 conferences. Tom Siler described the Illinois' 20-0 victory at Dyche Stadium in the *Chicago Sun:*

"Actually Northwestern, playing without five regulars, never had a chance. Alex Agase, who played the first 46 minutes of the game without a rest, kept his fellow forwards so fired up for the big test that the Wildcats found it impossible to dent the opposing 25-yard line. The Illini had built up quite a reputation in weeks past for goal-line stands, but they needed no such heroics yesterday."

Dufelmeier ran for 123 yards, including a 53-yard touchdown; Young added 83 more. Moss threw a touchdown pass to Bill Huber and reserve Bert Piggott was credited with the final score.

The Illini were going to Pasadena. Pasadena was less than thrilled.

Frustration, Harassment, and Victory

This was, after all, the first year of the Rose Bowl's conference hookup. UCLA, ranked No. 3, wanted unbeaten Army and California boy Glenn Davis on New Year's Day. This Illinois team, with two losses, would be no match for the mighty Bruins. West Coast newspapers said as much and said so often. Eliot used that to his advantage.

He needed something to spark the Illini, who weren't crazy about spending four weeks and the holiday season in California, far from wives and families. They had spent days riding the Illinois Central Railroad, travelling west via

Alex Agase, Buddy Young, and actor Alan Ladd at the 1947 Rose Bowl

HAIL TO THE ORANGE AND BLUE!

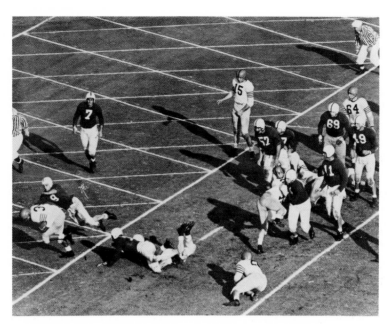

Buddy Young scores a touchdown at the1947 Rose Bowl

New Orleans, thanks to Board of Trustees President Wayne Johnston, who also happened to serve as president of the Illinois Central.

"He decided it would be a good idea if we used the Illinois Central tracks as far as possible," Flynn said. "So we got on a pullman and went to New Orleans, transferred to the Southern Pacific, went across the south part of the United States and arrived almost two days late in Pasadena.

"To make matters worse, it was raining and it continued to rain every day until it quit on New Year's Eve. There weren't many wives or families along, this really was a pioneering trip, so there were a lot of unhappy kids."

They weren't any happier when they were harassed at their Pasadena hotel because of the presence of the black players, an insult that hotel personnel did their best to smooth over. Nor were they pleased when the Rose Bowl committee gave each player $5 and a box of dried fruit for Christmas. Trips to a Hollywood studio helped. The Illini rubbed noses with Bob Hope and Bing Crosby and watched them film one of their famous "Road" movies. Still, players were both bored and rowdy.

Eliot sent two players home because they disappeared for two days. And, of course, the Illini were subjected to almost daily snipes from the Los Angeles-area press. Eliot made those newspaper articles part of his daily reading—to the players. In case they didn't hear him, he made sure the news was posted where the players couldn't miss it.

"I guess you could say that the viciousness of the West Coast press in their remarks about us helped us win a football game that day," Eliot said years later. It helped an 11-point underdog win 45-14, silencing Eliot's critics in California—and in Illinois—forever.

The rain had stopped and New Year's Day, 1947, dawned sunny and 78 degrees in southern California. The game commenced.

On the first play from scrimmage, Rykovich caught a short pass from Moss and ran 44 yards to the UCLA 16-yard line. Young ran to the 10, then to the 3. Three plays later, Rykovich scored. Just like that, Illinois was up 6-0. Maechtle's kick was wide. UCLA, with the help of a 28-yard gain on a fake punt, got its only lead later in the quarter on a quarterback sneak. The Bruins would enjoy another highlight when, late in the first half, Al Hoish dashed 102 yards with a kickoff to score, but by that point the Illini already had 25 points and were well on their way to more.

In the second quarter, Young scored on a quick opener. Patterson squirted around end for a 4-yard score, and after Patterson set up another fancy end run, Moss sneaked over from the 1-yard line. It was 25-14 at halftime and the Illini had only begun.

The third quarter was scoreless, but Illinois had driven inside the UCLA 1-yard line as it ended. Young got the scoring honors to open the final period.

Then the defense got in the scoring act. Seconds after Young's last touchdown, Steger picked off a Bruin pass and rolled 63 yards to the end zone. In the final minutes, tackle Stan Green grabbed a UCLA pass and lumbered 19 yards.

Rykovich and Young each gained 103 yards as Illinois outrushed UCLA 320-62, and Agase beat up the Bruins' center so badly that, in the third quarter, the officials asked him to take it easy.

The Illini were Rose Bowl champions. And finally, five full years after Doug Mills had first stepped into Eliot's office with word of his promotion, Eliot's detractors were convinced that this coach wasn't so bad after all.

"Mr. Illini" with his children

"It's not what he said, it's how he said it," said Sam Rebecca, of Eliot. "He got down to a whisper sometimes. He would quote poetry from time to time. He talked about measuring a man by the size of his heart. He could make you feel like the whole world was focused on you. This is your opportunity, your future, your whole life there for the taking. He was orange and blue all the way, the university was everything to him. He exemplified everything that was said about the Fighting Illini, he helped build that tradition."

"The guy could just get you so wound up and make you feel so intense that he could bring tears to your eyes sometimes."

—Sam Rebecca
Illinois kicker

Many players that Eliot greeted in 1946 had run out of eligibility. Buddy Young, by now married and a father, had given up his senior season in favor of professional football. Stan Green, the tackle who scored Illinois' final Rose Bowl touchdown, quit the team before the 1947 season began. Moss, Eddleman, Steger, Dufelmeier, Owens, Buscemi, Lou Agase, and Lester Bingaman, who was an all-conference performer at guard in 1945, led the Illini to a 5-3-1 season.

Steger ran for 112 yards to lead Illinois to a 14-0 season-opening victory over Pittsburgh. A week later, the Illini came home from Iowa 35-12 winners. They next played Army to a 0-0 tie at Yankee Stadium in New York, and the following week Steger bulled for 103 yards in a 40-13 win over Minnesota.

Back-to-back 14-7 losses to Purdue and Michigan took the Illini out of the title race, but the fun wasn't finished. The next week, Eddleman sprinted to an Illinois-record 92-yard punt return, highlighting a 60-14 non-conference win over Western Michigan. Ohio State fell 28-7 in the mud the following week.

The Illini expected little trouble with cellar-dwelling Northwestern in the season finale at Memorial Stadium. They were wrong. The

Ray Eliot being carried from the field

Wildcats intercepted three Moss passes, including one that Northwestern's Loran Day turned into a 32-yard touchdown late in the first half. That was the key play in Northwestern's 28-13 win. Illinois wouldn't beat the Wildcats again until 1951.

Moss passed for 713 yards that season, nearly 500 more than he'd thrown for a year before. Owens was named All-American at end, and he, Agase, and Steger earned all-conference honors.

A Short Span of Mediocrity

The Illini were headed for a short span of mediocrity in 1948 and '49. They were 3-6 in 1948, only 2-5 in the Big 10, but nothing was more disappointing to Eliot than the 28-20 loss at Michigan.

The Illini led 14-7 when Eddleman and Jack Pierce backed up to wait for a Wolverine kickoff. Eliot had a play where they would criss-cross. If the kick went to Pierce, he would hand the ball to Eddleman. If Dike caught it, he would merely fake the handoff. The kick floated to Eddleman at the 2-yard line.

"They thought Jack was going to get the ball and they just killed Jack and not a guy touched me. It was a pretty good fake, there wasn't a guy within 10 yards of me," Eddleman said.

Unfortunately, when Eddleman reached the Michigan end zone, 98 yards away, he learned the Illini had been called offside on the play.

"Ray Eliot was the maddest I ever saw him after that one. Here it was such a big thrill, then they called it back," Eddleman said. "Here, we would have been ahead 21-7, but we got beat 28-20."

The next week, Eddleman booted an 88-yard punt, still an Illinois record, in the Illini's 14-0 win over Iowa. Illinois didn't win again until the third game of the 1949 season, also against the Hawkeyes.

The 1949 season was a pretty nondescript 3-4-2, but that year marked the debut of a back who got Illini partisans started on the inevitable comparisons with Grange. Johnny Karras rushed for 732 yards in seven conference games and 826 yards in all games. As a sophomore,

Karras set a Big 10 ground-gaining record and was named Most Valuable Player, honors that eluded even Grange in his first season.

The Argo Express

Karras came to Illinois out of Argo High School in Summit in the fall of 1946. He looked around, saw guys like Buddy Young and Paul Patterson in the backfield, and enlisted in the army, but the "Argo Express" came back two years later when the Illini backfield wasn't quite so crowded. In 1949 Johnny Karras was Eliot's starter at right halfback. Except for missing two games in 1950 because of an injury, for the next three seasons he was never anywhere else.

Karras couldn't pass or play much defense, but he could run. In 1950, despite the injury, he ran for 593 yards and four touchdowns for a 7-2 team. Karras made All-Big 10 as a second-teamer in 1950 as did tackle Al Tate. Fullback Dick Raklovits, guard Charles Brown, defensive end Tony Klimek, and center Bill Vohaska were all named to the first team. Raklovits, Vohaska, and Tate earned All-American accolades.

The Illini also had a sophomore defensive back who would set many school pass intercep-

Johnny Karras, the "Argo Express"

The 1950 Fighting Illini

tion records. Al Brosky picked off 11 in 1950, still an Illinois single-season record. In three seasons, he collected 29 interceptions, ten more than any other Illinois player, and had a string of 15 consecutive games with at least one interception.

The 1950 Illini went into the final game of the regular season needing only a tie at Northwestern to earn its second trip to the Rose Bowl in four years. Sam Rebecca was the Illini kicker.

"We were down 14-7 and we started marching downfield late in the game. I'm watching them go downfield and realizing that if they score, that extra point could be the difference in the Big 10 and Rose Bowl championship," Rebecca said. "It was probably the most frustrating five or six minutes of my life.

"Anyway we kept pounding it out. Johnny Karras was running well, so was Don Stevens. It was just a couple of yards at a time all the way downfield, but we ended up on their 7-yard line when the clock ran out on us. We lost the championship, we didn't go to the Rose Bowl. We spent a terrible winter thinking all about that."

The Illini that winter had no way of knowing just how much talent was with the junior varsity. Talent that was ready to blossom in 1951.

No one was better than a 195-pound linebacker named Chuck Boerio, who went from junior varsity to Illini MVP and All-American in one season. "In the middle, Boerio challenged everyone," Ray Eliot said 25 years after that season. "Every time he hit somebody, he got up laughing."

The Illini also had outstanding linemen in All-American Charles Ulrich and Chuck Studley, a superb pass-catching end in Rex Smith, and a more-than-capable quarterback in Tommy O'Connell, a transfer from Notre Dame. They had a defensive backfield second to none with Brosky, Herb Neathery, and sophomore Stan Wallace. And, of course, they still had backfield punch in Karras, Stevens, and fullback Bill Tate.

The Illini weren't big. Wallace, a sophomore defensive back, weighed in at 212 pounds. Guard Studley, who would be an All-Big 10 performer, didn't go much over 200. And overall they probably weren't as talented as the previous year's team.

Chuck Boerio

More Roses

Al Brosky, 1951

"Half of us were walk-ons," Boerio once said. "We were not very big, but we loved to play."

A Tenth Anniversary Present

Ray Eliot's tenth season started with Karras scoring three touchdowns, twice plunging over from the one and once dancing from the 11-yard line. The Illini beat UCLA 27-13 in Champaign, and Stevens punctuated the victory with a 58-yard touchdown run.

The next week, a crowd of 56,207 and a television audience watched quarterback Don Engels, subbing for the injured O'Connell, direct a fourth-quarter touchdown drive that overtook Wisconsin, 14-10. During the winning drive, Engels threw a desperation pass that bounced out of the arms of intended receiver Steve Nosek and into Smith's to give the Illini a first down at the Badger 8-yard line. Fullback Pete Bachouros drove for five yards before Karras scored his second touchdown of the game and fifth in two weeks.

The following week, the Illini went east, piled up 416 yards in offense, and manhandled Syracuse 41-20. Stevens ran for 100 yards and a touchdown. Karras added 76 yards and two scores. Engels, still subbing for the injured O'Connell, passed for 180 yards, leading the Illini to victory.

One week later, Illinois was ranked No. 8. O'Connell was back in the lineup and the Illini played before a crowd of 54,000 at Washington. O'Connell directed an 81-yard fourth-quarter scoring drive to give the Illini a 27-20 victory.

Illinois went back to Big 10 business the next week at Indiana. Karras scored three times and ran his touchdown total for the season to eight. His first went for 88 yards. The Illini piled up 374 yards on the ground in an easy 21-0 victory.

Illinois hadn't played in Memorial Stadium in a month, so the Illini were happy to come home to play Michigan. However, the crowd of 71,119 that welcomed them home could barely see the players through a howling blizzard spurred by 35 mile an hour winds. The weather was so awful even the Block I student cheering section gave up trying to put on a show, opting instead to avoid freezing to death.

Reporter Helen Farlow described it like this: "A few panty-waists—a couple of thousand or so—trickled out of the stadium and started homeward at halftime. They were not missed. Their seats were speedily taken by refugees from the temporary bleachers that had been

Tom O'Connell, later an assistant coach

erected at the north of the field, right in the path of a 30-to-45 mile an hour wind. . . .

"Sartorially speaking, it was one of the strangest looking game crowds in Illini history. Ear muffs, sealskin caps, clumsily folded long underwear, motheaten raccoon skin coats and blankets of every kind and description were too commonplace to excite attention. . ."

Illinois marched 84 yards in the final five minutes to post a 7-0 victory and move into sole possession of first place. The frozen fans, who had watched each team punt ten times through the muck, went home cold, but happy.

The following week, Iowa came to Champaign and was easily dispatched 40-13, moving the Illini to 7-0, 4-0 in the Big 10. The Illini sewed this one up early as O'Connell and Joe Vernasco connected for touchdown passes of 38, 17, and 37 yards. Karras scored his 12th touchdown of the season.

A win at Ohio State in the season's next-to-last game would clinch the Rose Bowl berth. It had been a fairly mediocre season in Columbus, but on this day the Buckeyes and the Illini staged one of the most hard-hitting defensive struggles ever seen in the Big 10.

Rebecca had nothing to do but sit on his helmet. Neither team came close to scoring. "In all my years I don't think I've ever seen a more splendid defensive football game," Rebecca said 38 years later. "Neither team got close enough to the goal line to even attempt a field goal, that's how strong the two defenses were. Whenever either team would finally make a few yards or complete a pass or two and get down into scoring area, either an interception or a fumble caused by a tremendous tackle would stop it." The game ended in a 0-0 tie.

The Illini entered the final game of the season needing a victory over Northwestern to earn a trip to Pasadena. With Engels holding, Rebecca kicked a 16-yard second-quarter field goal—his only three-pointer of the season—to give the Illini a 3-0 victory.

"I have to tell the truth, sometimes I tell this story and make them think it was a last-minute kick or it gets longer through the years," Rebecca said. "At the time, I didn't think much of it because I thought the field goal would help, but we'd score more. But when it got to the fourth quarter and it was still 3-0, I really didn't want us to score any more."

1952 Rose Bowl send-off

This victory marked the Illini's first win over the Wildcats since the 1946 Rose Bowl season. The Illini would meet Pac-8 champion Stanford on New Year's Day, 1952, for the first college football game televised live from coast to coast.

Another Trip to Pasadena

By the end of 1951, air travel was more common than it had been five years earlier, but if there was any hint of bad weather, planes stayed on the ground. Eliot, fearing lost time waiting for a plane to take off, put his team on the train.

In Pasadena, Illinois drove 76 yards for a touchdown on the opening possession, with

afterwards. Stan Wallace picked off a Kerkorian pass at the Illini 34-yard line and raced to the Stanford 12. Three plays later, near the end of the third quarter, Tate scored from the 5.

"I was lucky, and I do mean lucky, by intercepting that pass because I had come up on the receiver and we were deep in their territory. I got one arm hung up with the receiver and the other hand caught the ball. I was just fortunate it happened," Wallace said.

Boerio, Brosky and their mates gave up nothing defensively. Shortly the Illini were on the march again from their own 32. Karras, Tate, Bachouros, and O'Connell took turns carrying the ball to the Stanford 7 before Karras went around end to score. That made it 20-7, a

1952 Rose Bowl action

Bachouros driving the final six yards for the score. Rebecca's extra point was blocked, the first time that had happened in his three years of play. Stanford, riding the passing of Gary Kerkorian, marched 84 yards to take a 7-6 lead that held up through halftime. It wouldn't hold up

lead that quickly grew to 27-7 after Wallace picked off his second pass of the day. Tate ended the 44-yard drive with his second touchdown.

"I had no idea I'd gained 150 yards," Tate said years later. "I remember breaking off a 40-

yard run early in the game and when I realized I was in the open, I got so excited I thought my heart was going to pound through my chest."

They would score twice more. Freshman halfback Clarence "Bud" DeMoss raced 53 yards to the Stanford 7, where Don Stevens took it in. In the final minute, Illinois blocked a Stanford punt and Engels tossed a 6-yard touchdown pass to John "Rocky" Ryan to put the wraps on Illinois' second Rose Bowl victory, 40-7, and the sixth straight triumph for the Big 10.

Tate, who later coached a quarterback named John Mackovic at Wake Forest, was the Rose Bowl MVP. Karras, Brosky, Ulrich, and Boerio were All-Americans.

And a group of Illinois seniors heard one last motivational speech from Ray Eliot. "It was the last time he talked to us as players and I'm telling you it was so stirring we were practically in tears," Rebecca said. "The guy could just get you so wound up and make you feel so intense that he could bring tears to your eyes sometimes."

Illinois finished 9-0-1 that year, its first unbeaten season since 1927. There hasn't been one since. It was the centerpiece of one of the most successful years ever in Illinois athletics. Illinois would later add Big 10 titles in basketball, gymnastics, wrestling, fencing, baseball, and both indoor and outdoor track.

It was a giddy time that Illinois fans will never forget. Rebecca has served the University of Illinois in a variety of capacities since his graduation. "When I'm on a speaking engagement, it never fails that two or three people remember when they saw me kick," he said. "It sticks with you forever. It really does."

Loyalty at the Top

By 1952, Ray Eliot was at the top of his profession and it seemed like everybody wanted him. Texas made a pitch and, after the 1950 season, Southern California laid out the red carpet in a bid to lure him West. Eliot's players, friends, and fans begged him to stay in Champaign, and Ray Eliot was loyal to his university.

As the 1952 season approached, hopes in Champaign were again high. But a barrage of injuries left the Illini vulnerable.

The season started on a positive note. O'Connell and Ryan hooked up for 119 yards in passing, and Cliff Waldbeser ran 72 yards for a touchdown with a fumble recovery—still an Illinois record—to lead the Illini to a 33-7 win over Iowa State. The Illini, however, never really got up a head of steam. They lost 20-6 at Wisconsin the following week, then beat Washington 48-14 when O'Connell threw for five touchdowns. Then they lost 13-7 to Minnesota and 40-12 to Purdue, but the next week Illinois upset Michigan 22-13.

The Illini's last victory in 1952 was 33-13 at Iowa, a game where Bachouros ran for 137 yards and O'Connell passed for 306, including 190 to Smith, who had 11 catches that day. The

1952 Illinois vs. Michigan game

next week Illinois lost to Ohio State 27-7, despite O'Connell's 22 completions in 35 attempts, good for 252 yards. The season ended with a 28-26 loss to Northwestern.

When it was over, O'Connell had passed for 1,761 yards and 12 touchdowns on his way to All-American recognition. Ryan and Smith each caught 45 passes, Ryan's good for 714 yards and five touchdowns, Smith's for 642 yards and four scores. By the time that season was over, Illinois had rewritten 14 conference passing marks. Brosky added eight more interceptions to finish his career with 29 pass thefts. Brosky's record is still an all-time NCAA record.

1953: Eliot's Finest Accomplishment

The 1953 season dawned with uncertainty. The uncertainty grew when Nebraska took a two-touchdown lead in the season opener, largely because a quiet sophomore Illinois running back grounded a Cornhusker punt on the Illinois 31-yard line that led to a Nebraska score. He made a handful of other mistakes that helped keep the Cornhuskers in command throughout the first three quarters. But J.C. Caroline came back that day to race 73 yards for

J.C. Caroline, All-Big 10 halfback, 1953

a fourth-quarter score that lifted the Illini to a 21-21 tie.

For the next eight weeks, South Carolinian Caroline and his backfield running mate, sophomore Mickey Bates, ran roughshod behind a line anchored by tackle Don Ernst, who would be the Illinois MVP.

First the Illini dispatched Stanford 33-21 in a non-conference tuneup. Then they ran over Ohio State (41-20), Minnesota (27-7), Purdue (21-0), and Michigan (19-3) in the Big 10, as well as posting a 20-13 non-conference win over Syracuse. By this time, Illinois was rated No. 3 in the nation, and Rose Bowl scents perfumed Champaign again—at least until the Illini went to Wisconsin, the Big 10's 1953 Rose Bowl representative, in the season's next-to-last week. The Badger defense pinched Caroline into ineffectiveness, and Wisconsin posted a 34-7 upset.

Despite the disappointment, Illinois came back the next week to hammer Northwestern 39-14 and to gain a share of the Big 10 title with Michigan State, which got the Rose Bowl bid.

Many called this season Eliot's finest accomplishment. The 7-1-1 season, 5-1 in the Big 10, was Eliot's third—and last—league championship. When it was over, Caroline not only led the Illini with 1,256 yards, dwarfing the 829 yards that Buddy Young gained in 1944, but also his 1,620 all-purpose yards eclipsed anything that Red Grange had accomplished in an Illinois uniform. Six times Caroline, who would be named to everybody's All-American team, ran for more than 100 yards, including 205 yards against Minnesota, 192 against Ohio State, and 184 in the upset victory over Michigan.

While Caroline did the bulk of the running, it was left to Bates, the Kewanee sophomore, to put the ball in the end zone. Bates scored 11 times that season for a team that averaged 25.3 points a game. He complemented Caroline in the romp past Ohio State with 152 yards.

Injury and Ineligibility

The two sophomores had already seen the best of their collegiate playing days. Before 1954, Caroline's biggest battle was with his

Jan Smid

academic eligibility. That problem solved, Caroline ran for 115 yards in a 14-12 season-opening loss to Penn State, but much of the rest of that year he was hampered by a shoulder injury. The Illini, Big 10 co-champions just a year before, came unglued. Only a non-conference 34-6 win over Syracuse separated Illinois from its first winless season ever.

Ohio State beat them 40-7, Minnesota 19-6, Purdue 28-14, Michigan 14-7, Wisconsin 27-14, and Northwestern 20-7. Despite missing much of that season, Caroline was Illinois' leading ground gainer with 440 yards. The Illini didn't light it up through the air either. Quarterback Em Lindbeck completed 38 passes in nine games for 476 yards. Only guard Jan Smid made the all-conference teams.

Caroline wouldn't play in an Illinois uniform again. He was academically ineligible for the 1955 season. Caroline, who later coached high school football in Urbana, played professional football in Canada for a year before settling into a long and successful career as a defensive back for the Bears.

Rising Stars

In 1955 the Illini had talent. Junior Abe Woodson would later distinguish himself in the NFL. Halfback Harry Jefferson was nothing flashy, but he was steady, twice running for more than 100 yards during the early season. And they had a couple of sophomores who, as freshmen, had dreamed that their passing and catching would delight Memorial Stadium crowds.

Of course, Ray Nitschke never played quarterback for Illinois—nor during a long and illustrious NFL career with the Green Bay Packers, for that matter—as he had done at Proviso Township High School in Maywood. But he turned into a pretty good fullback and linebacker for Eliot.

Bobby Mitchell, later a pro football Hall of Famer after a distinguished career with the Browns and Redskins, first brought his 9.7 speed to Champaign.

Nitschke recalled in his autobiography *Mean on Sundays* how Eliot called him into his office. "Ray," Eliot said, "which would you rather be: the second-string quarterback or my first-string fullback?"

Ray Nitschke

Bobby Mitchell (22) makes a run

"Coach," Nitschke replied, "I'd rather be the first-team quarterback."

Lindbeck was the quarterback that fall, and his passing to Bob DesEnfants and Jefferson's 127 rushing yards led to a 20-13 season-opening win at California. A week later, Nitschke scored three of the Illini's six touchdowns and Woodson ran for 76 yards in only three carries, still a school-record 25.3 yards per carry average, in a 40-0 blitz of Iowa State. The next week, defending Big 10 champion Ohio State came to town and quickly put a crimp in Illinois' title hopes, 27-12. Illinois beat Minnesota 21-13 the next week, then suffered losses of 21-7 and 13-0 to Michigan State and Purdue, respectively, before vaunted Michigan, ranked No. 3 and winner of six straight games, came to Champaign.

Enter Bobby Mitchell, then just another unknown halfback, who probably wouldn't have played at all had not Jefferson, who had 60 yards on 14 carries, left the game with sore ribs in the third quarter. Ten times Mitchell carried the ball that day: once for 64 yards for a touchdown, another time for 54 yards to set up another Illinois score. When it was over, Mitchell had 173 yards. Defensively, linebackers Nitschke and Jim Minor shut down the Michigan running game. Illinois had a 25-6 victory, its most lopsided win over the Wolverines since 1924.

The next week Mitchell ran for 118 yards and a touchdown in the Illini's 17-14 win over Wisconsin. A 7-7 tie at Northwestern closed that season. When it was done, Mitchell had 504 yards in just 61 carries, an 8.6 yards per carry average in Big 10 play, which was then a conference record. Despite the late start, Mitchell made the all-conference first team. Jefferson was named to the second team.

The 1956 season was one, as Nitschke said, "the alumni don't do much bragging about." Mitchell was out much of the year with a bad knee. That 2-5-2 record is not much to claim, but a 20-13 victory over Michigan State—then ranked No. 1 in the nation and coming off a 47-14 smearing of Notre Dame—alters those bragging rights.

Illinois, after opening the season with a 32-20 win over California, was in the throes of a three-game losing streak when the Spartans came calling on October 27. The Illini were 21-point underdogs and, once again, calls could be heard from campus for Eliot's coaching scalp.

Michigan State took a 13-0 halftime lead. In the third quarter, Nitschke, who had had four teeth knocked out in the game against Ohio State, got the call and gained 34 yards. Moments later, Woodson finished the drive for the touchdown, the first and least dramatic of his three. Bill Offenbecher would call the screen pass to perfection, Woodson would score on 70- and 82-yard plays, and the Homecoming crowd would go home delighted one more time.

HAIL TO THE ORANGE AND BLUE!

Eliot later called this victory second in satisfaction only to the 1947 Rose Bowl triumph over UCLA. That was to be Illinois' last win in 1956. Ties with Purdue (7-7) and Wisconsin (13-13) were sandwiched around losses to Michigan (17-7) and Northwestern (14-13), but by then Illinois fans didn't care about wins and losses. The Illini had their upset. And, after that win over Michigan State, a sign appeared in front of Eliot's house: "Brother Ray is here to stay."

The 1957 season was another of those nondescript 4-5 seasons. Among the highlights was a 20-19 win over Michigan when L.T. Bonner ran for two touchdowns, one for 58 yards. Gene Cherney blocked a Wolverine extra point that would have tied the game.

That year, Mitchell and Nitschke were among those closing their careers. Nitschke averaged 6.2 yards a carry and had his best day offensively with a 170-yard performance in the season-ending 27-0 victory over Northwestern.

Mitchell and Nitschke were named to All-Big 10 teams as were end Rich Kreitling and guard-linebacker Bill Burrell; both would go on to earn some All-America recognition in the next two seasons.

Rich Kreitling

Mr. Illini

The next year, Illinois would also finish 4-5, but with a different cast. The 1958 Illini lost its first three games, but quarterback John Easterbrook and Kreitling connected on 23 passes for 688 yards to lead Illinois to a respectable year. They paired up twice, once for 83 yards and another time for 60, in the Illini's 21-8 victory over Michigan. Kreitling capped his day catch-

1958 Fighting Illini

More Roses

ing a touchdown pass from reserve quarterback Russ Martin.

In March, 1959, Ray Eliot announced that his 18th season would be his last, setting off a round of tributes to the dean of Big 10 coaches. The announcement had a disastrous effect on recruiting that year, as Eliot's successor would not be named for months. Before that season began, Eliot told his sports information director, Charlie Bellatti, that he doubted this Illinois team could win a game. But it could.

Illinois, led by All-American Burrell and full-back Bill Brown, came into the final two games of Eliot's last season with a 3-3-1 record. The Illini had Big 10 wins over Ohio State (9-0) and Minnesota (14-6) and a 7-7 tie with Purdue.

The Illini went to Wisconsin in the next-to-last week of the season. On the first play from scrimmage, Easterbrook threw a bomb to end Ed O'Bradovich, another player who would later make a name for himself in the NFL. O'Bradovich was so wide open that he streaked for the end zone untouched. The only problem was that somewhere along the way he'd lost the football. Bill Brown plunged over from inside the 1-yard line on the last play of the game to lift Illinois to a 9-6 victory over the Big 10 co-leader.

For 18 years, Eliot had dreamed of winning a game on the final play. When it finally happened, Eliot almost botched it. Eliot thought he

John Easterbrook and Ernie McMillan

Ed O'Bradovich

had an extra timeout as the clock was winding down, a timeout he planned to use in order to send in a substitute with a couple of plays. He didn't have that timeout, and had Burrell, the Illini captain, signalled it, Illinois would have faced its last play of the game from outside the 5-yard line instead of inside the 1. The next week, Northwestern, and coach Ara Parseghian, in the hunt for the Big 10 championship, came to Champaign to close the Eliot era. It was no time to play the Illini.

"If there's ever one we've had to win," Ken Gehler, then a junior linebacker from Mendota, said, "this is it." Eliot, his hat askew, paced the sideline stride for stride with assistant coach Jim Valek. He smiled when Easterbrook scored the first touchdown from short range. Illinois led by two touchdowns at halftime, when the Marching Illini would salute their coach.

In the third quarter, Eliot grimaced as Northwestern drove to the Illinois 18. But the Illini held and soon John Counts scored on a 17-yard run. Later, Bill Brown ran 69 yards for the last of

Illinois' four touchdowns. A 28-0 victory and pandemonium. The 1959 Illini grabbed their coach and carried him off on their shoulders. In the locker room, Eliot led the team in a prayer. Finally he said, "God bless you boys. God bless you all."

The party at Margaret and Ray Eliot's house that night didn't end until darkness had fallen

the next evening. Soon, Eliot settled into his new assignment in athletic administration. He would serve the Athletic Association in good times and in the very bad times that were to come, with dignity, until his death early in 1980.

Eliot is buried not far from Zuppke's grave in Mount Hope Cemetery. The inscription on his tombstone says all that needs be said about Ray Eliot. It reads, "Mr. Illini."

"Mr. Illini"

The Ray Eliot Honor Roll

- 18-year record of 83-73-11 at Illinois

- Served as president of the American Football Coaches Association in 1955-56

- The Amos Alonzo Stagg winner in 1961

- Chicago Midwest Writers Coach of the Year award in 1959

- Honorary life membership in the American Football Coaches Association, 1965

- Coached several All-Star teams:
  —The *Chicago Tribune* All-Star Game
  —East-West Shrine Game four times
  —Blue-Gray game four times
  —North-South Shrine Game two times

- Associate director of athletics, Illinois 1960-73

- Honorary associate director of athletics, Illinois 1973-80

- Served as interim athletic director, Illinois 1979

- Recipient of the Trustees' Distinguished Service Medallion by the University of Illinois Board of Trustees for outstanding service to the university, 1976.

Part IV: From Eliot to Elliott

ILLINOIS

1890   1990

FOOTBALL
100 YEARS OF TRADITION

"Once you have won, the pressure may be greater, but you also try harder. You really bear down because you know what it is to win . . . and it's better than losing."

Pete Elliott

"He [Elliott] is building a solid foundation for the future of Illinois football teams and anyone familiar with the situation knows that this has represented a task which could not be accomplished overnight."

—Duane A. Cullinan
Athletic Board President

In 1959, searching for head football coaches was virtually foreign to the University of Illinois. Ray Eliot's successor would be the third Illini coach in 47 years.

Candidates, attracted by one of the most prestigious and secure jobs in the nation, were aplenty. Oklahoma's Bud Wilkinson, Louisiana State's Paul Dietzel, Bowden Wyatt of Tennessee, and Dave Nelson of Delaware were among those considered. Illinois assistants Mel Brewer, Chuck Studley, and Jim Valek also applied. One newspaper account said just about everybody's name except Fidel Castro's had been linked with the opening.

Three days before Christmas, president David D. Henry announced that 33-year-old University of California coach Pete Elliott would become the youngest coach in the Big 10. Elliott's name might already have been linked with the greats in Illinois athletic history if not for the intervention of World War II.

Elliott grew up in Bloomington where his father, Dr. J. Norman Elliott, a practicing physician, coached at Illinois Wesleyan. Pete and his brother, Chalmers "Bump" Elliott, who was already head coach at Michigan at the time of Pete Elliott's Illinois appointment, were all-state football players in high school.

"Bump and I had both felt all along we would go to Illinois after we graduated from high school. We just took it for granted," Pete Elliott once said.

"Then the war came and when Bump graduated he went into the Marines and when I graduated I went into the Navy. The Navy sent me to Michigan for my training and sent Bump to Purdue."

Pete Elliott stayed at Michigan where he was the only Wolverine with 12 varsity letters. Elliott quarterbacked the Wolverines to a 49-0 triumph over Southern California in the 1948 Rose Bowl. After graduation in 1949, Elliott served two years as an assistant at Oregon State before joining Wilkinson's staff at Oklahoma. There he proved himself a top-notch recruiter and earned Wilkinson's respect and admiration. Elliott got his first head coaching

Pete Elliott, Illini head football coach 1960-66

job in 1956, coaching Nebraska to what was then a respectable 4-6 record.

The Coach from California

The congenial Elliott brought many of his California assistants with him to the Midwest, but his freshman coach, a young guy with some coaching promise named Mike White, opted to stay home. It would be thirteen more years before White would be lured away from his native Bay Area.

Ray Eliot had left some talent on the field, but most of Elliott's first squad were seniors. The dearth of underclassmen would be painfully felt down the road, but as the 1960 season approached, quarterback John Easterbrook, fullback-linebackers Bill and Jim Brown, end Ed O'Bradovich, and tackle Joe Rutgens, who would earn All-American recognition, led an experienced team.

Bill Brown had led Illinois' late-season 1959 charge with 280 yards in the Illini's last two games. Jim Brown may have played a lot for somebody else, but often he played behind his brother at Illinois.

High Hopes, No Depth

Hopes ran high as Elliott's Illini opened the 1960 season with wins of 17-6 over Indiana and 33-0 over West Virginia. A capacity crowd of 71,119—the first full house in Memorial Sta-

Bill and Jim Brown

dium in four years—came out to watch Illinois' Homecoming date with Ohio State. Reality set in with the Buckeyes' victory, 34-7.

The Illini lost 21-10 at Minnesota the next week before posting wins of 10-8 over Penn State and 14-12 over Purdue. Then they went to Michigan. Pete's mother went too, but couldn't quite figure out when to cheer. For the first time in the Big 10, brothers lined up opposite one another as head coaches. The Wolverines got a two-point conversion to post an 8-7 victory, the first of six straight wins Bump Elliott would have over his brother's teams.

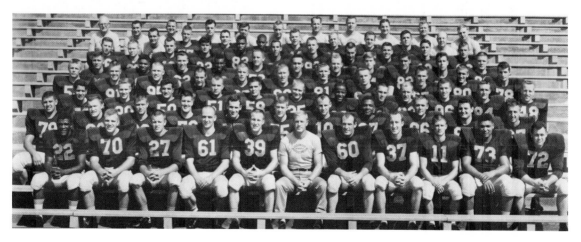

The 1960 football team

The next week Illinois scored a 35-14 win over Wisconsin, lifting its record to 5-3 and delighting the crowd of 43,165. They'd better have enjoyed it; the Illini next lost 14-7 at Northwestern to close out Elliott's first season. The Illini would play another 15 games before tasting victory. Even the school's 1961 media guide cast a pessimistic outlook. "Only change in the University of Illinois gridiron outlook since last spring is for the worse," it read. Elliott had only 14 lettermen to start with and, for various reasons, three of them were gone before the start of fall drills.

"The least experienced Big 10 football squad since the war, and probably the least experienced Illinois team in history," Elliott said. "I don't know how soon we can expect our sophomores to step in and do a job. This isn't a sophomore league, but we've got to have help from those newcomers."

A Long Losing Streak

There wasn't much help that fall of 1961. Week after week the losses mounted. Washington beat Illinois 20-7; Northwestern 28-7; Ohio State 44-0; Minnesota 33-0; Southern California 14-10; Purdue 23-9; Michigan 38-6; Wisconsin 55-7; Michigan State 34-7. Nine games, nine losses. Illinois scored 53 points and gave up 289. No Illini team had ever before lost every game in a season.

The only game Illinois had a chance to win that fall was at Southern Cal. Elliott blamed himself for that loss, as a potential winning drive ended at the USC 2-yard line as time expired. The Illini, out of time outs, drove from their own 11-yard line. They'd never practiced conducting a series of plays without a huddle, and the final gun went off without an Illinois victory.

There were five more losses in 1962 before Illinois finally upset Purdue 14-10 to lay to rest the school-record 15-game losing streak.

"It wasn't much fun," Elliott said later of that streak. "I got hung in effigy a couple of times and there was some pretty sharp criticism here and there. But on the whole people stuck with us—on the campus, among the alumni and in the press."

Nevertheless, in good times and bad, Pete Elliott was always a popular figure in Champaign. Not only did he conduct his normal post-game press conferences with aplomb, but also, after home games, writers were among those invited to the Elliott household for more conversation.

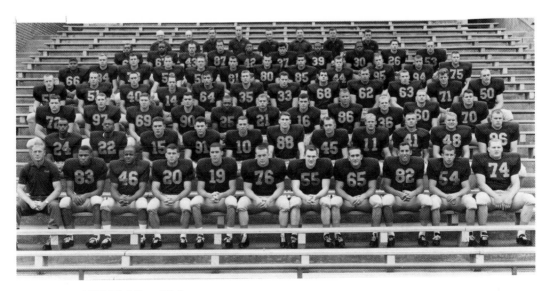

1962 Fighting Illini

A Solid Foundation

Reaffirmed Commitment

Two days before the Illini finally snapped the streak, the athletic board reaffirmed its commitment to Elliott, voting unanimously to extend his one-year contract through the 1963 season.

"The athletic board is 100 percent behind Coach Pete Elliott," board president Duane A. Cullinan said. "He is building a solid foundation for the future of Illinois football teams and anyone familiar with the situation knows that this has represented a task which could not be accomplished overnight."

The Boilermakers were title-hungry that season, and the Illini were downcast, but tackle Gregg Schumacher blocked a Boilermaker punt and end Rich Callaghan ran with it to the Purdue 48-yard line. Mike Taliaferro and Ken Zimmerman hooked up for a 25-yard gain, and three plays later Taliaferro found Thurman Walker in the end zone. Jim Plankenhorn's conversion put Illinois up 14-3.

Late in the third quarter, Bill Pasko's interception gave Illinois the ball at the Purdue 30. On the next play, Zimmerman shook off a pair of tacklers en route to what proved to be the winning touchdown.

Ken Zimmerman

Purdue scored late to make it 14-10 and were driving again when the Illini's Schumacher, Archie Sutton, and Frank Lollino brought the Boilermakers up short on a fourth-down play at the Illini 7-yard line.

After the Purdue upset, Illinois lost twice more, 14-10 to Michigan and 35-6 to Wisconsin, but the Illini upset Michigan State 7-6 in the season finale and the victory provided the springboard for much better things to come.

"If we had lost to Michigan State," one player said later, "the Purdue game wouldn't have meant a thing. That final game sent the Illini on their way."

Despite the gloom and doom on the field, Elliott was proving his worth as a recruiter. He had already brought in a sophomore center-linebacker who racked up 97 tackles, tackles loud enough to echo off every rafter in Memorial Stadium.

The sophomore's name was Dick Butkus.

Mike Taliaferro

HAIL TO THE ORANGE AND BLUE!

"During that 15-game losing streak we had, he never once got down or let team morale fall," long-time assistant coach Burt Ingwersen said of Elliott. "Pete had the team high for every one of those games. But we just didn't have the material and were running into exceptionally good opposition week after week. Sometimes it'd look like we were going to snap out of the streak only to run into bad breaks. But, even that didn't dampen his enthusiasm or his optimism."

"As they were presenting it [the MVP Silver Cup], my dad...walked into the locker room. My dad hugged me and I put my arms around him. I think of the look in his eyes and how proud he was. At that moment, the hard work involved in playing was worth it."

—Jim Grabowski
Illinois fullback

Two victories in 19 games hardly seemed like a foundation from which to build lofty expectations, but lofty they were when Elliott called 77 candidates to the opening of fall drills in 1963. Among that group the Illini welcomed were 26 lettermen, including Dick Butkus. His reputation for twisting opposing ballcarriers into funny shapes was already growing so legendary that he was being touted for the Heisman Trophy.

Butkus of Illinois

Sports Illustrated's Dan Jenkins wrote, "If every college football team had a linebacker like Dick Butkus of Illinois, all fullbacks would soon be three feet tall and sing soprano."

The 6-foot-2-inch, 243-pound Butkus, the nation's No. 1 prospect in 1960, was Illinois' first big recruiting catch.

"Before he's through," Elliott gushed prophetically in 1963, "He'll be the greatest linebacker anybody ever saw."

Butkus and sophomore Don Hansen made a fearsome linebacking duo and they were not a solo act. Tackle Archie Sutton anchored the line, and the secondary of Mike Dundy, Jim Warren, George Donnelly, and Ron Fearn was as sticky as flypaper.

Elliott also had a few sophomores he liked, including fleet halfback Sam Price, quarterback Fred Custardo, and Jim Grabowski, a 205-pound runner who a year earlier had started out as the No. 4 fullback on the freshman team.

Grabowski would carve quite a niche for himself during his next three seasons at Illinois, but he was out with an injury when the Illini opened the season in Memorial Stadium against Elliott's old team, Cal. Elliott had molded an offense that was talented but conservative. If Illinois were to rise from the ashes, it would do so on the strength of its defense.

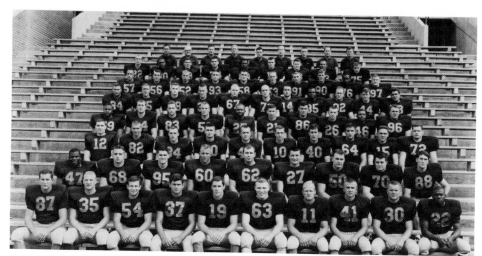

The 1963 Illini football squad

From the Ashes

The Butkus-led defense intercepted Cal quarterback Craig Morton three times and plugged up the middle, leaving the Bears nowhere to go.

Champaign News-Gazette sports editor Ed O'Neil wrote that Morton made a flock of new friends on his brief visit to the Midwest, most of them Illinois pass defenders.

"The big Cal star must have thought he had been trapped in the revolving door of the Violent Ward," O'Neil wrote. Dundy separated Bear back Tom Blankenfield from the football and the Illini's Donnelly recovered on the Cal 13. Two plays later, Price scored the only touchdown in Illinois' 10-0 victory—Illinois' first shutout in 26 games. The next week, fifth-ranked Northwestern, the Big 10 title favorite, and its long-ball quarterback, Tom Myers, presented the obstacle. Elliott had posted a huge sign in the locker room, lest the Illini forget the 45-0 humiliation the Wildcats had handed them the year before. But the Illinois defense asserted itself again. Butkus sacked Myers four times, causing one fumble, and was credited

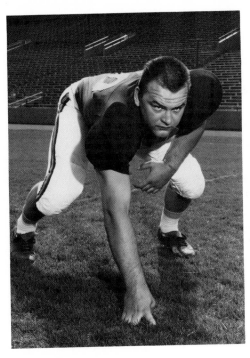

Illinois' MVP 1963, 1964

with seven solo tackles and 12 assists as the Illini won 10-9.

Wrote Bert Bertine in the *Champaign-Urbana Courier*, " In one of the great hitting

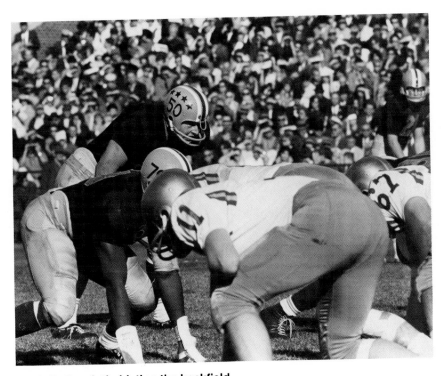

Dick Butkus intimidating the backfield

contests seen in Memorial Stadium in years, Pete Elliott's valiant Illini won a game only wishful thinkers felt they could. A tremendous defensive effort combined with opportunist offense produced the season's first Big 10 upset."

Another week, another major task: Ohio State in front of a record crowd of 84,712 in Columbus. Butkus was even better than before, getting in on 23 tackles and making a diving interception at the Buckeye 24 to set up Illinois' first touchdown. The Illini scored twice in the fourth quarter to take a 20-17 lead. But the Buckeyes' Dick Van Raaphorst kicked a 49-yard field goal late in the game to tie 20-20, and narrowly missed another try from 57 yards that would have put an early end to Illinois' Rose Bowl bid.

What If?

The next week, Minnesota came to Memorial Stadium and, for the first time in a long time, Illinois fans dared to dream. At halftime, the Block I members flipped their panel into position, revealing a beautiful red rose. Beneath it were the words, "What if?"

Don Hansen

What if, indeed. Illinois' 16-6 victory that day made the prospect seem less preposterous. That jarring defense recovered four of five Gopher fumbles, and Grabowski picked up 72 yards in 17 carries to push the Illini to 3-0-1 for the season.

The Illini took a break from the Big 10 the following week, travelling to Los Angeles to spot the Bruins a 12-10 lead after three quarters before fashioning a 16-play 62-yard drive capped by Grabowski's 1-yard touchdown plunge. The Illini came out on top 18-12.

The Illini were winning and were moving up in the national polls, but their close wins were driving fans crazy. Wrote O'Neil, "Some 700 members of the Illini alumni saw why the regular customers back home are clutching their hearts. The Illini turned a romp into a hair-raising finish." So, 61,796 were expecting more of the same the next week when Purdue came to town. They weren't expecting Illinois—ranked No. 2 by this point—to roll up 386 yards in offense and bolt to a 21-0 lead early in the second quarter en route to a 41-21 blowout, their highest point total in ten years. Grabowski ran for 99 yards and three touchdowns, and the Illini averaged seven yards a carry.

F Stands for Flat

Illinois was 5-0-1, one of only six unbeatens left in the nation. Yet, Michigan and humility were coming to Champaign. The roses were wilting.

"F stands for Flat," wrote Bert Bertine. "It also stands for Fumble. It may also stand for Fatal. Put them together and you have the shocking story of what transpired in Illinois' final home game before 55,810 stunned spectators. Illinois lost to Michigan 14-8. The Illini paid the price for forgetting the formula of success which had kept them undefeated in six previous games. They failed for the first time this year to either out-hit an opponent, or at least hold their own in the prime requisite of good football."

The loss dropped Illinois to third place behind Michigan State and Ohio State.

The Illini got a reprieve the next week when Ara Parseghian's Wildcats pushed Ohio

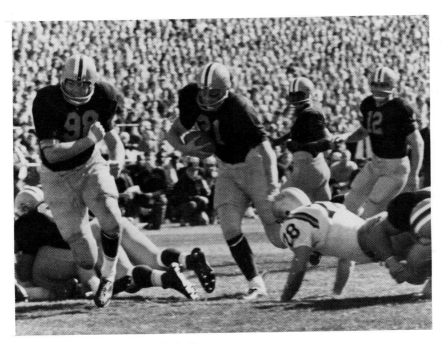

Jim Grabowski runs with the ball

State out of the way, 17-8, at Columbus. Meanwhile, the Illini drove 77 yards for one touchdown and got another on Donnelly's 24-yard interception return to build a 14-0 halftime lead en route to a 17-7 win at Wisconsin.

Showdown in East Lansing

That set up a season-ending showdown. The Illini, 4-1-1 in Big 10 play, got off their plane in East Lansing, Michigan, on Friday, November 22, 1963, needing a victory over the league-leading Spartans (4-0-1).

There was no showdown at Michigan State that Saturday. Four hours before the scheduled kickoff, the game was postponed with respect to the memory of John F. Kennedy. "Football certainly was secondary in the minds of everybody that Saturday," Elliott said. The game was rescheduled for Thanksgiving Day.

Perhaps the abbreviated trip to East Lansing served as a psychological springboard.

"Over there the first time they saw—and heard—about active preparations for Rose Bowl transportation for Michigan State's band and students and others," Chuck Flynn said. "And they had five days to get steamed up about the presumptuous preparations."

The Illini were ready. Elliott shifted his defensive alignment so that Butkus and Hansen would stunt before the Spartans put the ball into play. The move caught Duffy Daugherty's team by surprise, and Michigan State's game-breaking runner, Sherman Lewis, ate a lot of dirt, picking up only 58 yards in 13 carries. "We had

Dick Butkus, 1963 Big 10 MVP

HAIL TO THE ORANGE AND BLUE!

good pursuit and made sure he didn't cut back," Butkus later explained of the defensive maneuver.

Gary Eickman, a defensive end, recalled Butkus' drive that day: "There was one play I really remember. Butkus had been knocked down by a terrific block, but he got up and kept pursuing and got the ballcarrier from behind. And, as I recall, he was playing with a hyperextended elbow."

Inspired defense that picked off four Spartan passes and recovered three fumbles, Grabowski's 14-yard touchdown run, and two Plankenhorn field goals gave the Illini a 13-0 victory, Michigan State's first shutout in 21 games. It was Illinois' 12th conference championship, and for the third time in 17 years, the Illini were California dreaming.

quarterback Bill Douglas drove the Huskies to the Illini 14 before he was knocked out of the game with a knee injury. Later, fullback Mike Kuklenski suffered a broken leg. Halfback Junior Coffey played briefly, ignoring a foot injury suffered in practice. Despite the injuries, the Huskies scored first when, after recovering an Illinois fumble on the Illini 27-yard line, halfback Dave Kopay took a pitchout seven yards for the Pac-8 champ's only score.

The Illini got on the board just two seconds before halftime. After Bruce Capel had recovered a Washington fumble at the Huskie 15, Plankenhorn drilled a 32-yard field goal. Elliott called that play the turning point in the game.

The Illini ground the Huskies down in the second half.

1964 Rose Bowl action

Roses Again

All season long, the Illini had won with rock-em, sock-em football. Their game with Washington in Pasadena would be no different.

Washington took the opening kickoff, and

"We just kept banging away until we got moving," Elliott said.

Wylie Fox recovered three fumbles on the day—including one of Illinois'. A pair of Donnelly interceptions set up both Illinois touchdowns. The first came early in the third quarter and set up Jim Warren's 2-yard run with a Taliaferro pitchout at 8:03 left in the quarter.

"In their films, we saw they liked to fake a short pass, then throw long," Donnelly explained after the game. "I was keying on the quarterback. I knew as soon as he faked it would be a long pass and . . . I just dropped back and intercepted."

The touchdown play was nearly broken up by an official. Taliaferro bumped into the stripes on the rollout and nearly didn't get the pitch away.

"I didn't think those stripes would ever get out of the way," Taliaferro said. Washington drove inside the Illini 10-yard line late in the quarter, but Donnelly got in the way of a Bill Siler swing pass intended for Steve Bramwell. He picked it off at the Illini 4 and returned for ten yards.

From there, Grabowski and his blockers took over. Grabowski picked up 43 yards in the drive and Taliaferro and Fearn combined for an 11-yard completion on third down and eight to keep the drive alive.

Grabowski, who would join Illinois fullbacks Julius Rykovich and Bill Tate as Rose Bowl MVPs, rolled behind Butkus' blocking into the end zone for the clinching score. Grabowski, who would go on to shatter Red Grange's Illinois records and set six Big 10 marks, went 13 yards to the Washington 2 for a first-and-goal situation, but three line plunges left the Illini out of the end zone.

For his work, Grabowski got the MVP

Silver Cup and a very important locker room moment.

"As they were presenting it, my dad (Stanley) walked into the locker room," Grabowski said years later. "My dad hugged me, and I put my arm around him. I think of the look in his eyes and how proud he was. At that moment, the hard work involved in playing was worth it. That, more than anything else, I remember."

The picture of Stanley and Jim Grabowski's locker room embrace went over the wires and appeared in newspapers from coast to coast.

"I got letters and clippings from all over," he said. "People related to the father-son thing more than the game." Also in the locker room that day were University President David D. Henry and Illinois Governor Otto Kerner.

"It's quite an honor to have, first the Chicago Bears, and then these fine Fighting Illini bring important football championships to our state," Kerner told the players.

The Bears had won the 1963 NFL championship days earlier. Three thousand fans greeted the Rose Bowl champions when they returned to Champaign.

Grabowski finished that season with 616 yards. Butkus finished with 144 tackles while anchoring a defense that surrendered only 96 points in 10 games. He, of course, earned All-American accolades and was seriously being touted as the one lineman who could corral the Heisman Trophy.

The 1963 Illinois offensive starters

HAIL TO THE ORANGE AND BLUE!

Dick Butkus' Illinois Career Highlights, 1962-1964

- Two-time consensus All-American selection (1963-64)

- Sixth in 1963 Heisman Trophy voting

- Third in 1964 Heisman Trophy voting

- Named 1964 "Player of the Year" by the American Football Coaches Association

- Big 10 Most Valuable Player in 1963

- Illinois' Most Valuable Player in 1963 and 1964

- Co-captain, 1964

- Second team All-Big 10 in 1962; 97 tackles in 7 games after missing two games due to knee injury

- First team All-Big 10 in 1963; 145 tackles in 10 games

- First team All-Big 10 in 1964; 132 tackles in 9 games

- Finished his career as the career leader in tackles with 373

- His 145 tackles in 1963 stood as a season record until 1976

- Named to Big 10 Diamond Anniversary Team in 1970

- Voted to Sporting News College Coaches All-Time Team

- Elected to College Football Hall of Fame in 1983

- Elected to Pro Football Hall of Fame in 1979

- Second Illinois player to have his number (50) retired. (Red Grange is the only other)

- Namesake of the Butkus Award, given annually to the nation's top collegiate linebacker

- All-pro linebacker for the Chicago Bears 1965-1973

12

RECORDS AND A DARK DAY

"How are Dick Butkus and Archie Sutton going to play any better than they did last year?"

—Coach Pete Elliott

In 1964 Elliott had much different problems than those he faced only a year before. One of the goals of 1963 had been respectability. The goal in 1964 was national prestige. Many around Illinois were dubbing this the Illini's "National Championship Season."

Butkus was back and Elliott was openly touting him for the Heisman Trophy. Grabowski returned also. In fact, only nine players who saw significant duty in the Rose Bowl had graduated. Fred Custardo, who had split time with Taliaferro at quarterback, took over that spot full-time. Only the defensive backfield required extensive rebuilding.

Playing on Top

Roy Damer wrote in the *Chicago Tribune*, "If Illinois football players can fit their heads into their helmets this fall, they should be among the finest teams in the country." Elliott did his best to keep things in perspective.

"A lot of people feel we should improve as much as we did last year and this couldn't happen," Elliott said in pre-season. "We have to play our best to be as good as in 1963. . .How are Dick Butkus and Archie Sutton going to play better than they did last year?"

In addition, Illinois entered 1964 without the incentive of the Rose Bowl. The conference's no-repeat rule was still in effect, so even a league championship wouldn't get Illinois into post-season play.

The Illini found out how tough staying on top could be when Elliott returned to his roots in the season opener at California.

Craig Morton, so harassed by the Illini defense a year earlier, fired an apparent game-tying touchdown to sub Jerry Bradley in the final seconds, only to have Bradley ruled out of bounds on the catch. Even though Morton connected on 22 of 32 passes for 234 yards, that inch let Illinois hold on for a 20-14 victory.

Fred Custardo

Grabowski ran for 110 yards, including an 18-yard touchdown, and Custardo threw for 99 more and ran for a pair of 1-yard scores.

Northwestern was dispatched 17-6, as the Illinois defense wreaked havoc on Myers again, in the Illini's Big 10 opener. A week later,

No. 2-ranked Illinois faced fourth-rated Ohio State. The six-point underdogs humbled the Illini in front of a Homecoming crowd, 26-0. The loss ended a five-game Illinois winning streak and marked the Illini's first shutout loss in 19 games.

The following week, Butkus got the Illini going again with 16 tackles and a fumble recovery to set up a score, leading the Illini to a 14-0 win over Minnesota. Grabowski ran for 98 yards and a touchdown and Custardo threw for 112, including a touchdown pass to Bob Trumpy.

Grabowski Breaks the Records

The next week, Grabowski smashed for 171 yards and three touchdowns in what was considered his finest performance since the Rose Bowl as Illinois routed visiting UCLA 26-7. Illinois had improved to 4-1 for the season.

On the next two Saturdays, Illinois lost 26-14 at Purdue and 21-6 at Michigan—Pete Elliott's fifth straight loss to his brother's team. The Illini needed a boost, and Wisconsin would be the

Jim Grabowski

unwilling foil. Grabowski unfurled the greatest rushing day in 69 years of Big 10 football to surpass both the Illinois and Big 10 single-game rushing marks with a 239-yard performance in 33 carries.

Red Grange's 212-yard performance against Michigan in 1924 was finally eclipsed. J.C. Caroline's 30-carry mark set in 1953 was also history. Gone too was Minnesota's Bill Daley's 1943 Big 10-record 216-yard game.

"I heard an assistant coach or somebody on the sidelines say something like 'he needs 18 yards for an offensive record,' " Grabowski said afterwards. "I thought they meant 18 yards for a team record of some kind."

Typically, Grabowski cloaked his accomplishment in modesty: "Heck, it was never a case of finding a hole today . . . it was just a matter of picking which one to take . . . The line made big holes and those halfbacks (Sam Price and Ron Acks) were springing me on the outside plays."

Meanwhile Illinois' defense, whose pride had been stung in the two previous losses, held the Badgers to 23 yards rushing. The Illini finished with 332.

The next week, Grabowski added 185 yards, including a 58-yard touchdown run, as the Illini closed out the season with a 16-0 win at home over Michigan State. That gave him 1,006 yards for the season, second in the nation and only 40 yards behind Wake Forest's Brian Piccolo. Custardo completed 9 of 16 passes for 92 yards to give him 1,012 for the year.

Butkus Finishes College Career

A crowd of about 32,000, braving 18-degree temperatures, and a regional television audience bid good-bye to Dick Butkus' fabulous college career on that last day of the 1964 season.

Butkus had added 132 tackles to the 244 he had in previous seasons. He would finish third in the Heisman balloting and be named the 1964 Player of the Year by the American Football Coaches Association. The linebacker would join Grange, Agase, and Burrell as a winner of

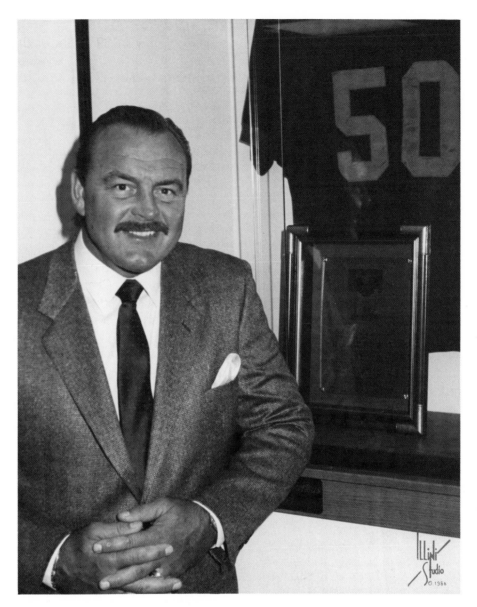

Dick Butkus with his retired jersey

the *Chicago Tribune* MVP Silver Football. Butkus would go on to a Hall of Fame NFL career with the Chicago Bears. College football's award for the nation's best linebacker would ultimately be named for him. Finally, in 1986, No. 50 would join Grange's 77 as the only Illini numbers ever retired.

Just about everybody in the game paid tribute to him, but perhaps none so eloquently as Pete Elliott.

"He is," said Elliott, "the finest football player I have ever coached."

The 1965 Green Team

The 1965 Illini had only 12 lettermen and 29 sophomores and were, as one writer observed, "as green as the grass in old Memorial Stadium." Defensive stalwarts such as Donnelly and Sutton were not part of the line-up.

"Frankly," Elliott said before the season, "we do not expect to set the Big 10 football conference on fire this season."

However, the Illini still had Grabowski, who had more Illinois and Big 10 records to set.

Records and a Dark Day

Dick Butkus receiving plaque commemorating his induction into the National Football Foundation Hall of Fame

They still had Custardo, Price, and linebacker Hansen, finally emerging from Butkus' considerable shadow.

Butkus might have come in handy in the muggy season opener at home against Oregon State. Illinois led 10-5 with three minutes left and the Beavers facing a fourth-and-seven try on the Illinois 9-yard line.

Oregon State quarterback Paul Brothers dropped back to pass and then lobbed a desperation heave into the end zone where Hansen, Ron Acks, and Grabowski, who had come into the game at linebacker, waited for it to come down. All three went after the ball, and Hansen succeeded in tipping it—into the waiting arms of Oregon State's Clayton Calhoun. Oregon State won 12-10.

The next week, Custardo and sophomore John Wright combined for touchdowns of 49 and 64 yards, and Grabowski ran for 127 yards to top the mile mark in his collegiate career in a 42-0 rout of Southern Methodist University.

The following week, Hansen was forced out of the game with a head injury and Michigan State scored twice in the final period to post a 22-12 victory. Ohio State held Grabowski to 44 yards in handing the Illini a 28-14 loss.

The following week a Homecoming crowd of 61,257 watched Grabowski bang out 186 yards and two touchdowns in 30 carries to give him 2,071 career yards and pass Red Grange's 40-year-old total in the all-time record book.

The next week, sophomore Cyril Pinder ran 80 yards for a score. Hansen, back in the lineup, had 19 tackles as the Illini drilled Duke 28-14. Bo Batchelder intercepted Purdue quarterback Bob Griese twice. Custardo threw for two touchdowns and Grabowski had 163 yards in a 21-0 rout of Purdue.

That set the tone for Elliott's annual battle with his brother and Michigan. Pete was 0-for-6 after the Wolverines ground out 306 rushing yards and another 117 through the air en route to a 23-3 victory.

Illinois took out its frustrations on a weak Wisconsin team, handing the Badgers a 51-0 loss, their worst beating since 1916. In that game Grabowski added more records to his name, running for 167 yards to go over the 1,000-yard mark for the second straight year.

It Was an Honor

All that remained was for Grabowski to close his collegiate career. When the contest with Northwestern was over, Illinois had finished a 6-4 season with a 20-6 victory and Grabowski had tacked 187 more yards to his career totals. He left Illinois with an Illini-record 1,258 yards for the season and 2,878 for his career. He also left with both the Big 10 season (996) and career (2,106) rushing records.

Grabowski, who went on to play with a Super Bowl champion team in Green Bay, was to win the Silver Football in a close vote over quarterbacks Steve Juday of Michigan State and Griese of Purdue.

At the end, Grabowski and Elliott stood together in the locker room beneath Dyche Stadium. Said Grabowski to his coach, "It was an honor to play for you."

Custardo got in the Illinois record books as well. His 204 career completions eclipsed Tommy O'Connell's record of 195. Wright finished the season with 47 catches, good for 755 yards.

In 1966 Illinois would lose its first three games en route to a 4-6 season. Highlights of that season included a 74-yard drive in the final six and a half minutes of an Illini 10-9 win over Ohio State, Illinois' first win over a Woody Hayes-coached Buckeye team. Illinois' defense intercepted Griese five times, including Bruce Sullivan's 93-yard interception return for a touchdown, but Purdue beat the Illini 25-21. Quarterback Bob Naponic completed eight of 14 passes for 142 yards including six to Wright good for 136, as Illinois dedicated newly named Zuppke Field with a 49-14 hammering of Wisconsin. And, Pete Elliott's Illini finally got a win over Michigan, 28-21 in Ann Arbor.

Pete Elliott with his most famous player

The Darkest Day

Most of the news in the waning months of 1966 did not center on the field itself. Elliott, 40 years old and extremely popular throughout the conference, was being heavily wooed by Northwestern to succeed Stu Holcomb as athletic director. The job he really wanted belonged to Illinois athletic director Doug Mills, who abruptly resigned in November after 25 years.

In mid-December, Elliott had a photo session scheduled with a Champaign newspaper to coincide with the announcement of Elliott's selection as athletic director at the University of Illinois. At the same time, he planned to announce that assistant coach Bill Taylor would succeed him as football coach.

Mid-morning on December 12, Elliott abruptly cancelled the photo session. There would be no announcement; there would be no athletic director post.

What the public didn't know then was that hours earlier, assistant athletic director Mel Brewer, spurned in his own bid to assume the number one job, had walked into Illinois president David Henry's office with a bag full of documents detailing unauthorized payments to athletes by Illinois alumni.

The darkest day Illinois' athletic program had ever known had dawned.

Jim Grabowski's records

1964

- Big 10 and Illinois records for most rushing yardage in one game, 239, against Wisconsin. Old Illinois record was 237 by Red Grange against Pennsylvania in 1925. Old Big 10 conference record was 216 by Bill Daley, Michigan, against Northwestern in 1943.

1965

- Illinois career rushing record, 2,753 yards. Old record was 2,071 by Grange 1923-25.

- Illinois career total offense record, 3,022 yards. Old record was 2,424 by Tom O'Connell, 1951-52.

- Illinois record for most rushing attempts in one game, broken first with 36 carries against Purdue, and later with 38 against Wisconsin. Grabowski held the old record of 33 against Wisconsin, 1964.

- Illinois record for most rushing attempts in career, 579. Old record 403, John Karras, 1949-51.

- Tied Big 10 record for most rushing attempts in one game, 38, against Wisconsin. Record shared with Ernie Parks, Ohio State, against Illinois, 1943.

- Illinois record for most rushing yardage in one season, 1,258. Old record 1,256, J.C. Caroline, 1953.

- Big 10 record for most rushing attempts in one season, 201, in seven Big 10 games. Old record 178 by Bob White, Ohio State in seven games in 1958.

- Big 10 record for highest average rushes per game, 28.71 in seven games. Old record 26.25 by Bob Westfall, Michigan in four games in 1940.

- Big 10 record for yards gained in career (three years or less) Big 10 games only, 2,106. Old record 2,019, Alan Ameche, Wisconsin, 1951-53.

- First Big 10 player to gain over 1,000 yards in two seasons, 1,004 in 1964, 1,258 in 1965.

Souvenir program from 1899

UNIVERSITY OF ILLINOIS BANDS.

An early postcard for the University of Illinois bands

Score for the Illinois Loyalty Song

The Marching Illini in action

The Block I at work

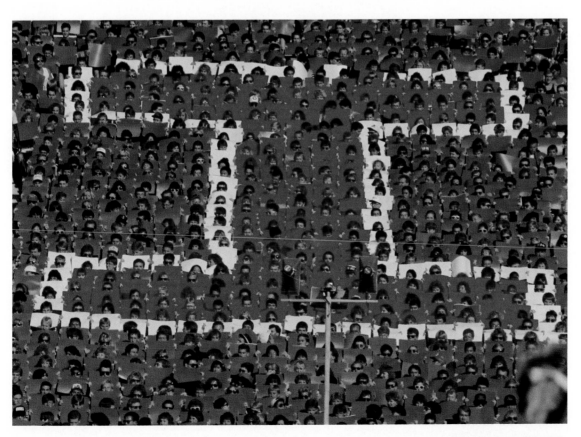

The famous Block I

ILLINOIS
1890   1990
FOOTBALL
®

Memorial Stadium

1947 Rose Bowl Program

1952 Rose Bowl Program

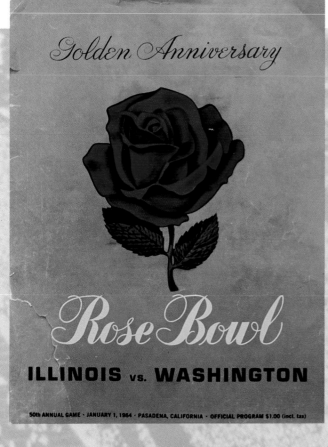

Golden Anniversary

Rose Bowl

ILLINOIS vs. WASHINGTON

50th ANNUAL GAME · JANUARY 1, 1964 · PASADENA, CALIFORNIA · OFFICIAL PROGRAM $1.00 (incl. tax)

THE 1984
ROSE BOWL

UCLA vs. ILLINOIS
January Two, Nineteen Eighty Four/Three Dollars

ILLINOIS
1890   1990
FOOTBALL

Chief Illiniwek

13

THE SLUSH FUND SCANDAL

"Dr. David D. Henry, president of the University of Illinois has reported to me this afternoon that there have been brought to his attention certain irregularities with respect to grant-in-aid assistance to athletes at the university.

"He believes he is in possession of all the facts and has invited my inquiry into the matter with an offer of full cooperation on the part of the university in any investigation that we undertake.

"We will begin an investigation in accordance with regular conference procedures. I will have no further comment until that investigation is completed."

—Bill Reed, Big 10 Commissioner
December 16, 1966

The slush fund scandal, as it quickly came to be known, was an episode that shattered one of the nation's proudest and most respected athletic programs.

Nobody liked losing and there were so many losses during the late 1950s and early '60s that a group of alumni established a fund in 1962 that would be used for providing bonus financial aid for a number of Illinois football and basketball players. That fund, originally directed from a particular contributor toward a particular player, was altered two years later so that all fund monies were distributed from the same pot.

Throughout its existence, the total fund—about $21,000—wasn't large. Most of the money was earmarked for athletes in need. However, the fund was a major violation of NCAA rules, and carefully documented evidence was hard to ignore.

When Melvin Brewer, once the captain of Illinois' 1939 team, later an assistant coach to Ray Eliot, and then an assistant athletic director, walked into Henry's office with documented evidence of violations, the University of Illinois athletic department was turned on its ear.

Henry immediately turned over the evidence to Big 10 Commissioner Bill Reed. Two days before Christmas, Illinois and the Big 10 suspended a dozen football and basketball players indefinitely and put Elliott (who by now had announced that he wanted to remain as football coach) and basketball coach Harry Combes on probation for a year. They were barred from recruiting and told that another violation would cost them their jobs.

Elliott never denied his awareness of the fund. Mills, who resigned before the scandal broke, was also informed. Naturally, Illinois officials hoped that the Big 10 would look favorably on their internal policing actions.

It did not. The league's athletic directors voted, and its faculty representatives later reinforced that vote, to invoke a conference rule that would require Illinois to fire Elliott, Combes, and assistant basketball coach Howie Braun "or show cause why its membership in the conference should not be suspended or terminated."

The league decision was denounced throughout Illinois. Henry went to bat for his coaches. Governor Otto Kerner called it "excessive." The football team issued a petition signed by players urging Elliott's retention. Newspapers throughout the state called for Illinois to stand up and fight or to get out of the Big 10, and the state high school coaches association threw its voice in support of the Illini coaches.

A Violation is a Violation

Only the *Daily Illini* disagreed. It said in an editorial,

"The university is at a crucial point of its

athletic history. To keep the coaches and risk being dropped from the conference is simply too great a gamble, for if the coaches are retained, years of probation for the entire athletic program could ensue.

"Some may say that to ruin the lives of these three men who have served the university so long is much too harsh. But at times like this, personal feelings and close friends must be secondary. It is more a matter of principle. The future of the university athletic program is more important at this point.

"A violation is a violation regardless of what anyone else is doing and regardless of what we think of those who have broken the rules. It often is harder to acknowledge that a good friend has done something wrong, but when the evidence is there, there is little room for discussion.

"We agree with the Big 10."

Three months after the scandal broke, Henry made an impassioned, three-hour plea to the faculty reps, but to no avail. The University of Illinois was ordered again to fire its three coaches or face indefinite suspension from the conference.

The next day, March 18, 1967, Elliott, Combes, and Braun resigned, effectively putting an end to the showdown.

"It is apparent to everyone that the commissioner, athletic directors and faculty representatives of the Western conference (Big 10) have 'fired us,'" the coaches said in a statement issued that day.

"We are therefore reluctantly stepping down from our respective coaching responsibilities at this time rather than to allow the conference to unjustly force the University of Illinois to act on an impossible situation. We emphatically believe that the final decision in this matter must be made by the conference rather than the university and consider the announcement of March 18, 1967 as that final decision.

"We have contemplated the future of athletics at Illinois in the light of the various possibilities available. We believe that the NCAA would necessarily support any conference action that would mean at some future date, if the NCAA suspended or expelled Illinois from membership, there would be no athletic program at Illinois. We do not believe we should jeopardize Illinois or intercollegiate athletics to this extent so that Illinois should be forced to make a choice that would lead to such a result."

NCAA Sanctions

Even though the Big 10 then considered the matter closed, the NCAA did not. It imposed sanctions, barring Illinois from television appearances and post-season play in football and basketball for two years. Elliott, Combes, and Braun were barred from again coaching in the Big 10. Three football players were among five athletes who permanently lost their eligibility at Illinois.

Coaches' Honors

A month after their resignations, the three coaches were feted before a capacity crowd in Urbana.

"I am truly sorry there were violations of the rules and I think this is wrong," Elliott told the gathering. "But the Big 10 had two choices: make examples of the university, the coaches and the athletes—which it did. The other was to have some human feeling toward people. And I think it is horrible when people are not considered. I'd rather be wrong helping people, than right hurting them."

Months later, Elliott, still hugely popular at Illinois, entered private business. Later he coached at the University of Miami and, briefly, worked for his mentor, Bud Wilkinson, with the St. Louis Cardinals before accepting the position of executive director of the Pro Football Hall of Fame.

To this day, Elliott will say little about those trying times:

"I truly and honestly can say that what we did at Illinois was never in the vein of an advantage for Illinois. I don't think anyone ever gave anything special to anyone to go to Illinois. We didn't have any deep sense of guilt in any form.

"There was no use trying to justify it. I knew I'd have to be doing something else, so I did. You don't always feel bad about the things you can't change, you just can't let that get the better of you."

"I loved Illinois," he said. "I truly enjoyed being there."

Elliott left Illinois with a 31-34-1 record over seven seasons. After his departure, Illinois would enjoy only one winning season for the next 15 years.

The school that had once been the nation's most stable, with three athletic directors in 71 years and three football coaches in 54 years, would go through three athletic directors, three football coaches, and three basketball coaches in the next 13 years. Some say the millions of pieces that Illinois' athletic program was broken into were never fully repaired.

Statement of the Faculty Representatives:

The faculty representatives of the Intercollegiate Conference, after full consideration of the University of Illinois' appeal from decisions recorded by the directors of athletics of the conference on February 22, have voted to concur in those decisions as follows:

1. That Coaches Elliott, Combes and Braun have been in violation of certain of the conference rules and regulations;
2. That in consequence there be invoked the penalties stated in rule 7 section 12a and regulation VIII, section 11a of the conference handbook, to wit: "Any member university which employs or retains on its athletic staff anyone who has violated or who has been a party to a violation of the provisions of this rule or who upon inquiry by the commissioner withholds knowledge of the violation of this rule by others, shall be required to show cause why its membership in the conference should not be suspended or terminated."

In accordance with the latter action, the University of Illinois is invited to respond to the commissioner on or before March 17, 1967 concerning the following:

A. Will the university retain on its athletic staff Coaches Elliott, Combes, and Braun—If the answer is "no" the case is closed.
B. If the answer to the above question is "yes" as to any of these coaches, will you discuss with the commissioner dates convenient for a hearing at which the university is invited to show cause why its membership in the conference should not be suspended or terminated. We are grateful for your cooperation.

Sincerely Yours,
Verne C. Freeman,
Chairman

PART V: THE MODERN ERA

ILLINOIS
1890   1990
FOOTBALL
100 YEARS OF TRADITION

"Just as much an objective, [as winning the Big 10] is to continue in a steadfast manner to see that everyone does graduate, does have the diploma and will look back at their years at the University of Illinois with pride and accomplishment both on and off the field. There is something I find good about that."

John Mackovic

"I've had winners in every geographic location in this country. I don't intend to settle for less in Illinois."

—Coach Bob Blackman

The stability that marked Illinois' football program for more than 50 years was shattered by the slush fund scandal. It would be a long time before calm again settled over Memorial Stadium. Jim Valek couldn't have known that when he accepted the task of restoring Illinois' fortunes and prestige little more than a month after Elliott had been banished from the Big 10 forever.

A native of Joliet, Illinois, Valek was a friendly, outgoing athlete who had won four varsity letters as an end for Ray Eliot's teams in 1945-48. After being named the Illini's MVP in 1948, Valek began his coaching career as an assistant at Wichita.

Valek's Impossible Task

After six years in the high school ranks, Valek returned to Illinois and served as an assistant in Ray Eliot's final season and during Pete Elliott's first year. He then served four years as an assistant at Army before joining South Carolina's staff in 1966.

The ashes of the scandal left a grim, if not impossible, task. Even those players not directly affected by the slush fund were demoral-

Jim Valek and Athletic Director Gene Vance

1967 Illini varsity football team

ized. Yet Valek was a personable coach with a penchant for recruiting. Jim Brown, the former Illini fullback, was an assistant to both Elliott and Valek.

"As far as recruiting, he was fine. His biggest downfall was I don't know if he was quite the knowledgeable and the organizational man he should be," Brown said. "I don't think he was quite the person to guide us at that time."

A Season of Promise

Nevertheless, Valek's first season held some promise. Valek adapted himself to the Elliott system in the transition, reasoning that "I can learn the Illinois way of doing things faster and easier than the returning players and coaches can learn mine."

After Illinois lost its 1967 season opener 14-0 at Florida in 94-degree heat, the Illini began their home season on a positive note by routing Pittsburgh 34-6. The next week, injuries took their toll as Bob Naponic, who had missed much of the previous season with a knee injury, suffered another knee injury. Halfback Bob Bess also came up lame in that 20-7 loss at Indiana.

The next week, John Wright, one of Illinois' best receivers of all time, caught his second of four touchdown passes that season, from Dean Volkman, but a fourth-quarter Minnesota field goal gave the Gophers a 10-7 victory.

The following week, a capacity crowd came to Memorial Stadium—the only full house during Valek's tenure—to watch Notre Dame hand the Illini the fifth worst defeat in Illinois history, 47-7.

Of that massacre, Loren Tate wrote in the *Champaign News-Gazette,* "If there was any doubt the University of Illinois football operation has regained its amateur status, this was established beyond question Saturday at Memorial Stadium."

Courier writer Bob Leavitt was blunt: "Chief Illiniwek and cornerback Ron Bess were the only men to get near Notre Dame's tightly guarded end zone."

About the only highlights the home crowd could enjoy were Bess' two interceptions, good for an Illinois-record 152 yards. One of them went 75 yards for the Illini's only score.

Bess also set a record that season for interception yards returned. His 198 yards topped Bruce Sullivan's mark of 193 yards set one year earlier. Following the Notre Dame game, Davis Jackson's 1-yard plunge with 34 seconds left in the game pushed the Illini past Ohio State 17-13 in Columbus. It was the Illini's last triumph in Ohio Stadium until 1988.

In a 42-9 loss to Purdue, Dan McKissic's 51-yard field goal hit the crossbar and then bounced up and over. Illinois jumped out to a 9-0 lead fueled by Johnson's 15-yard touchdown run, but the Wolverines rallied in the second half to win 21-9. Illinois closed that 4-6 season by beating Northwestern 27-21 in Evanston and Iowa 21-19 in Iowa City.

Lopsided Losses

Among those missing in 1968 were the graduated Wright, then the Illini's career pass receiving leader with 159 catches for 2,284 yards. This was the year the bottom would fall out on the field. For recruiting purposes, Illinois might as well have been New Mexico as far as the talent-rich Chicago area was concerned. In just that year alone, Illinoisians Dave Butz, Darryl Stingley, and Otis Armstrong, who all went on to successful NFL careers, went somewhere other than their state university.

Only a 14-0 win over Northwestern in the next-to-last game, on touchdown runs by Naponic and Johnson, separated Illinois from a winless season. The lopsidedness of some of the losses—47-7 to Kansas, 44-0 to Missouri, 58-8 to Notre Dame—was disturbing.

The next year was worse. Illinois seemed to have started the 1969 season an 18-16 winner over Washington State when it blocked a field goal attempt with only 33 seconds to play. But the Illini were penalized for holding on the play and the Cougars took advantage, winning 19-18.

"One moment we were elated . . . jubilant; the next second we were a loser, our chins dragging on the floor," Valek said afterwards. "It really took a lot out of us. Who knows how the season would have gone if we'd won that first game."

What did happen was that Illinois lost nine more times, usually by such lopsided scores as 37-6 to Missouri, 48-20 to Iowa State, 41-0 to Ohio State, 49-22 to Purdue, 57-0 to Michigan, 55-14 to Wisconsin, and 40-0 to Iowa. The Illini were outscored that season 397-106. The Illini were a national joke, topping the syndicated "Bottom 10" rankings.

"They did it on the strength of their defense," cracked *Los Angeles Times* reporter Steve Harvey, the column's creator.

An All-time Low

Average attendance dropped below 40,000, and season ticket sales for 1970 were down another 19 percent from 1969 levels.

Revenues were sinking like a rock. Jim Valek would win in 1970 or he would be gone. He won only three of ten games. He was gone.

Loren Tate watched that season from his perch as sports editor of the *Champaign News-Gazette*:

"The most traumatic day of that time for me was the day we played at Northwestern and I remember watching (Jim's wife) Lois Valek being taken out of the stands with tears rolling down her eyes. The final score was 48-0 and it was awful at the half.

"We knew at the end of that game that it was over. It was only the fourth game of the season, but crowds were down, there was no talent coming in. Things had reached an all-time low."

The athletic board voted to remove Valek after the October 24 game with Ohio State, citing critical player dissatisfaction. No sooner had Illinois finished with a 22-16 loss at Iowa, a game that ended with typical Valek luck (the Illini were stopped inside the 1 as time ran out), then Valek was gone for good. His teams had won only eight of 40 games and only two of their last 21 Big 10 games.

Ron Bess

1970 University of Illinois football team

Blackman's Challenge

The search committee was back in business. It was looking for a big name. It came up with the biggest the Ivy League had to offer in one of the nation's winningest coaches, 52-year-old Bob Blackman.

In 16 years at Dartmouth, Blackman posted a 104-37-3 record. He'd had three undefeated seasons, the final one being the just-completed 1970 campaign. At Dartmouth, the DeSoto, Iowa, native turned down numerous offers. He had three chances to coach in the Big 10, including one in his home state. He might have succeeded Bud Wilkinson at Oklahoma. Only the challenge Illinois presented coaxed him out of his lifetime job at Dartmouth.

"I was only five years old when I decided to be a championship football coach," Blackman said after accepting the Illinois job. "We were living in Chicago and Bob Zuppke and Red Grange were legends to me. I always was thinking of Illinois."

By the time he arrived at Illinois, Blackman had 150 wins, fifth on the all-time active coaching list at the time. Still, skeptics wondered how anybody could successfully make the leap from the Ivy League to a moribund Big 10 program. However, Blackman had a reputation as a superb organizer and possessed a penchant for multiple offensive formations, a concept that had become foreign to the Illini.

Disappointment and Victory

He also had a reputation as a hard-nosed defensive coach. That made guys like Tab Bennett, the defensive tackle who would cap his Illinois career in 1972 with 231 career tackles, smile.

Bob Blackman, Illinois football coach, 1971-76

There weren't many smiles, however, as Blackman's 1971 Illini proceeded to lose their first six games. It was obvious that Blackman's complex offensive schemes would take getting used to. Quarterback Mike Wells and company managed only six first downs in the season-opening 10-0 loss to Michigan State.

Illinois didn't score its first touchdown of the Blackman era until the 52-14 loss to Wash-

Tab Bennett

ington in the season's fourth week. Times were so bleak that Terry Masar's 85 punts that season is still an Illinois record.

Then Illinois started winning. After a 35-6 loss to Michigan dropped the Illini to 0-6, 0-2 in the Big 10, the Illini, with Wells passing and

Wells, George Uremovich, and John Wilson running, won all five remaining games.

Twenty-five years had passed since Illinois had won five straight games in the Big 10. Blackman could be forgiven the bright orange outfit, including orange shoes, that he wore to stalk the sidelines. The 1972 Fighting Illini were set to turn the corner. Unfortunately, academic ineligibilities decimated the team. Illinois opened the season with seven straight losses before rebounding to win three of their last four games. Despite the disappointing season, Blackman turned down overtures from the NFL.

Almost a Winning Season

Blackman was finding Big 10 recruiting much different from Ivy League recruiting.

"At Dartmouth, he could do a lot of his recruiting by mail," Tate said. "He had his coaches go out and the Ivy League had attraction. He came here and he couldn't crack Chicago. And, of course, you can't win without Chicago because it's the big city and if you don't get those guys, somebody else is going to get them and beat you."

Nevertheless, the '73 team appeared close to achieving Illinois' first winning season since 1965. The 5-3 Illini led Minnesota 16-6 late in the fourth quarter of the season's next-to-last game. But the Gophers scored with 4:24 left, recovered a fumble on the ensuing kickoff, and scored again to win 19-16.

The Illini lost 9-6 at Northwestern the following weekend and would have to wait yet another year to find that elusive winning sea-

1973 Illinois football team

son. One of its wins however, was 27-7 over Mike White's California team. In addition, back-to-back wins over Purdue (15-13) and Michigan State (6-3) came without a touchdown; Dan Beaver kicked seven field goals in those games.

Conflicts and a Reprimand

Meanwhile, Blackman's off-the-field problems were becoming apparent. He hadn't developed the rapport with his players that Eliot and Elliott had with their teams. The problem grew worse as he tried in vain to relate to young players.

"There was really nothing wrong with him," Tate said. "The mistake he made was he got old." He was at constant odds with incoming athletic director Cecil Coleman, a feud that would ultimately require that somebody leave.

Illinois got off to a fast start in 1974, winning four of its first five games, including a 41-7 rout of Stanford. "Stanford was leading the nation in passing and nobody believed our 3-deep defense could stop them," Blackman said years later. "But Mike Gow returned an interception for a touchdown, Chubby Phillips scored three times, and we won."

Losses of 49-7 to Ohio State and 14-6 to Michigan and a 21-21 tie with Michigan State in Memorial Stadium's golden anniversary game left the Illini going into the final two weeks of that season with a 4-4-1 mark.

Victories over Minnesota (17-14) and Northwestern (28-14) in the final two games put Illinois over the .500 mark for the first time in nine seasons. Linebacker Tom Hicks and offensive lineman Revie Sorey, who each spent many seasons with the Chicago Bears, made the All-Big 10 teams that year. So did Gow, who closed his Illinois days with 19 career interceptions.

Blackman had a quotation from Vince Lombardi hanging in his office. "Winning is not a sometimes thing. It's an all-time thing." When it involved twin Big 10 terrors Michigan and Ohio State, it was a no-time thing, a fact that grew to a painful point when in 1975, after a 40-3 trouncing by the Buckeyes, Michigan turned back Illinois 21-15, its third successive close win over Blackman's teams.

The Decisive Season

That 1975 loss separated Illinois from its second straight six-win season. Blackman went into 1976 with the ax over his head. Decisive victories over Iowa (24-6) and at No. 6-ranked Missouri (31-6) in the season's first two games and a 3-1 start had the Illini ranked as high as 18th in one wire-service poll. The

Coach Bob Blackman talks with a player

Scott Studwell

campus was in a frenzy. But linebacker John Sullivan—who would go on to become Illinois' all-time leading tackler with 501 tackles—damaged a knee against Missouri and was lost for the season. Even early success couldn't quiet the rumblings.

Blackman told the *Chicago Tribune*'s David Condon, "I've had winners in every geographic location of this country. I've had championship teams in high school, junior college, service, and major college competition. I don't intend to settle for less at Illinois . . . When fans ask when Illinois is going to turn the corner, they're really asking when we'll start beating Michigan and Ohio State."

They wouldn't. Ohio State would win again that year 42-10, and Michigan 38-7. Despite All-American performances from Beaver, who erased Red Grange's career scoring record, and linebacker Scott Studwell, whose 177 tackles that season eclipsed Butkus' single-season record, Illinois finished 5-6. Blackman's career record against the rest of the Big 10 was 24-21-1. Against the twin powers it was 0-12.

Coleman and Blackman made little effort to keep their feud private. Coleman ordered Illini coaches off the recruiting trail. One day before Illinois closed its 1976 season with a 48-6 win over Northwestern, Blackman pleaded his case with the athletic board.

"It's gotten so bad that the kids [recruits] are asking us what in the world is going on," an assistant coach said. Recruiting was in shambles and many of the players already on campus were publicly mocking their coach and his attempts to communicate with them. Blackman got his audience with the board. Then, in November, 1976, he got fired.

Moeller's Turn

Coleman wanted his own man, and when he hired Michigan assistant Gary Moeller, he got him. Moeller was 35 years old when he signed a five-year contract to become the third Illinois football coach in a decade. For ten years, he had been at the side of Bo Schembechler, two seasons at Miami of Ohio and eight at Michigan, including four as defensive coordinator. He was known as an outstanding recruiter and had never been associated with a losing program. These images would take a severe beating over the course of the next three years.

Gary Moeller at press conference accepting head coaching position

The Lean Years

The 1976 Fighting Illini

"I'm not looking for a great rebuilding year," Moeller told a packed news conference on the day of his appointment. "I want to go out and play right now."

He was enthusiastic and he wanted to cultivate both Chicago and downstate Illinois, areas Blackman had virtually abandoned, to the point where the Illini stood an even chance of recruiting that talent.

Moeller had a promising start when two months after he took the job, the Illini got commitments from three of the state's top players. New Trier East quarterback Rich Weiss, whom Michigan coveted; West Chicago 250-pound lineman Tim Norman; and Geneseo all-state fullback Wayne Strader signed with the Illini.

What no one knew then was that, for one reason or another, none of those players would match his high school credentials in an Illinois uniform. But Moeller's most immediate problem was preparing for the 1977 season opener in Champaign against Michigan. "The Mo and Bo Show" it was billed to the record opening-day crowd of nearly 63,000. They would see teams that mirrored each other both offensively and defensively. They would even see Illinois' Dave Finzer kick an early field goal to put the Illini on top 3-0. Unfortunately, they'd see more talent on the Michigan side of the ball. As usual, the show was Bo's, 37-9.

That game set the tone of a 3-8 season. Even though Illinois scored only seven points in its final three games, this would be the most success Moeller would realize in Champaign.

Moeller said after that season, "Coming in with a new program, maybe we didn't blend in

Gary Moeller in an intense moment

the way we should have . . . Our No. 1 goal is to get better every day and every week. We need to be winners every day, in individual practice, group workouts, statistically, in all ways."

The Futility Bowl

The Illini's 0-0 tie with Northwestern in the 1978 season opener—dubbed the "Futility Bowl" by those who were forced to sit through it—screamed volumes about the Moeller era at Illinois.

Loss after loss after loss piled up. More and more every week, Memorial Stadium was not the place to be. Crowds dwindled to an average of less than 45,000 in 1979. Ohio State, as usual one of the nation's best teams, drew fewer than 42,000 on a beautiful fall day. If there were 30,874 spectators as was announced for Moeller's final home game, a 45-14 loss to Indiana, many were well hidden.

After three seasons, Moeller was 6-24-3. His teams had suffered through 19 consecutive Big 10 games without a victory, a futile streak finally snapped in Illinois' 29-13 win over Northwestern in Moeller's finale.

Worse, his schemes showed little imagination, and athletic director Cecil Coleman had already been fired earlier that year. Coleman's successor, Neale Stoner, started on the job three weeks before the end of that season. Stoner was a much different character than Cecil Coleman.

"Unfortunately, Moeller was not prepared to leap into a lion's den for his collegiate coaching debut," wrote Bob Shiplett for the *Galesburg Register-Mail*. Shiplett was a walk-on at Illinois during Moeller's tenure. "Illini support declined with each defeat and attendance figures plunged. It was very disheartening to a dedicated Fighting Illini football player to see 'fair-weather fans' leaving early in the second half,

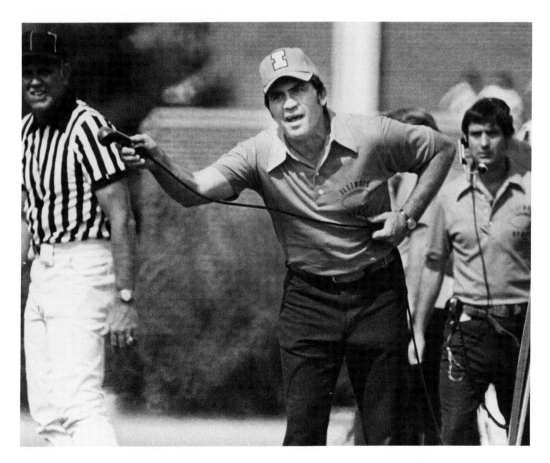

Gary Moeller in action

The Lean Years

as their resounding footsteps seemed amplified throughout Memorial Stadium. Equally depressing was viewing a half-filled stadium late in the season. What disturbed the players must have bothered the coaching staff, too. During my sophomore year, we could not believe our eyes as the pressure of a losing program began taking its toll.

"One example that will always remain implanted in my mind occurred during contact drills preceding the Minnesota clash. Perturbed by the offensive backs' unacceptable intensity, the backfield coach grabbed each one in full view of the crowd, and smashed his own face into their protective headgear—the same equipment used to punish the opposition. Point made, the coach stormed off the field screaming obscenities, and bleeding profusely from several gashes on his face. Such antics destroyed morale, and did little to generate respect for our leaders."

A half-dozen players, led by Weiss, Norman, and Strader, threatened to quit if Moeller was axed. Others, however, were less enthusiastic about Moeller's performance. Moeller charged Illinois with breach of contract and loudly went public, pleading his case. "I demanded a five-year contract when I came to Illinois because if you're honest and don't cut corners, it takes that long to establish your program," he said.

"I inherited a football house that couldn't be remodeled. It had to be torn down and rebuilt. I felt good when Ray Eliot (who was serving as interim athletic director) assured our staff that we were on the right track." But the track that Gary Moeller was on led back to Ann Arbor where he would spend the 1980s as Schembechler's top aide.

Illinois, meanwhile, once the cradle of coaches, set out to find its fifth head coach in 20 years. Like Coleman before him, Stoner was in search of his own man. He liked Wake Forest's John Mackovic very much, but not as much as he liked one of Pete Elliott's former players and assistant coaches, Mike White.

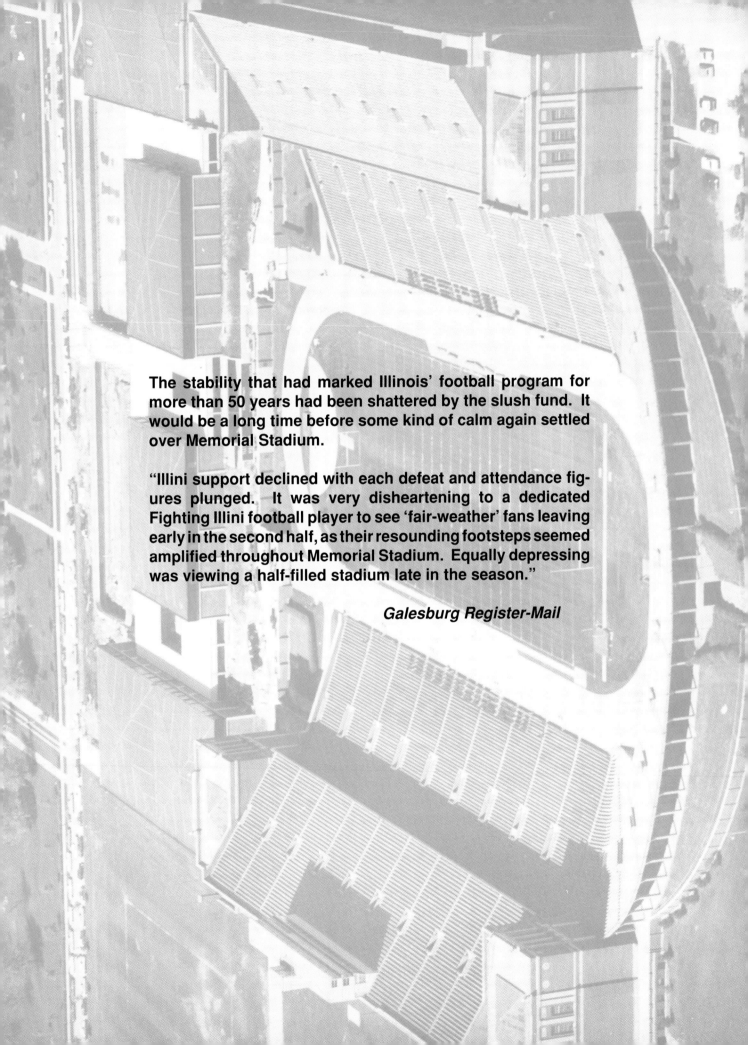

The stability that had marked Illinois' football program for more than 50 years had been shattered by the slush fund. It would be a long time before some kind of calm again settled over Memorial Stadium.

"Illini support declined with each defeat and attendance figures plunged. It was very disheartening to a dedicated Fighting Illini football player to see 'fair-weather' fans leaving early in the second half, as their resounding footsteps seemed amplified throughout Memorial Stadium. Equally depressing was viewing a half-filled stadium late in the season."

Galesburg Register-Mail

THE QUARTERBACK COACH

"There are a couple of junior college quarterbacks we'll look at in California."

—Coach Mike White

Neale Stoner had not yet officially begun his duties as Illinois athletic director when he first contacted Mike White—then an assistant to Bill Walsh with the San Francisco 49ers—about the job that Moeller would soon lose.

White had credentials. From the day Pete Elliott steered him toward a coaching career at Cal, White had learned football from some of the game's biggest names—Walsh, John Ralston, Dick Vermeil, and Marv Levy.

He served eight years as Ralston's offensive coordinator at Stanford before taking over a downtrodden Cal program in 1972. Three years later, the Bears were Pac-8 co-champions and led the nation offensively, averaging 458.6 yards a game. White was a winner at Cal, but he was also at odds with athletic director Dave Maggard. White got fired after an 8-3 season in 1977.

Promise and Proclamation

His resume included development of a long list of stellar quarterbacks—Craig Morton, Jim Plunkett, Steve Bartkowski, and the late Joe Roth, among others. All of that had come to him in the San Francisco Bay Area. Ever since he had declined Elliott's overtures to join him at Illinois in 1960, White had turned his back on several opportunities outside his native California.

Then Stoner came along. Stoner introduced White as Illinois' 20th head coach ten days before Christmas, 1979, at a packed news

Neale Stoner proclaiming "the 80s belong to the Illini"

conference in the Ray Eliot Varsity Room. White got the job over a list of candidates that included Wake Forest's Mackovic, Syracuse's Frank Maloney, Dick Jamieson of Indiana State, and Larry Smith of Tulane.

The '80s, Stoner proclaimed, belonged to the Illini.

"I believe in the 'key man' theory, and this is the right man for the job at this time," Stoner said.

For his part, White said all the right things. He said Moeller left a decent nucleus and that the University of Illinois would be only as good as the players it got from within the state, even though he knew there would be no quick fix without a huge transfusion of junior college talent. He hired people who were to concentrate on nothing but recruiting. He left an impression.

"If Mike White can't get the job done where Jim Valek, Bob Blackman, and Gary Moeller did not," wrote Larry Harnly in the *Springfield State-Journal Register*, "maybe it simply can't be done at Illinois."

California Quarterbacks

White said one other thing that day: "There are a couple of junior college quarterbacks we'll look at in California."

They were Tony Eason, whose impact on Illinois football would not be felt immediately, and Dave Wilson, whose influence would be nearly instantaneous.

Six weeks after White took the job, Wilson, recovering from a broken leg suffered while playing for Fullerton Junior College, was the first player signed for Illinois. He was the first of many junior college transfers who would find their way to Champaign over the next eight years. Wilson's arrival set off a complex series of maneuvers that would have Illinois staring eyeball to eyeball with the Big 10.

As a junior college freshman in 1977, Wilson had broken his hand on his first play from scrimmage. He dropped out of school without going to a class, then reapplied to the junior college governing body for two seasons' eligibility. It was granted.

When he transferred, the Big 10 ruled Wilson had but one year of eligibility remaining and should be classified a senior. He did not have enough credit hours for senior status. Therefore, the Big 10 ordered that he was not eligible until 1981.

Wilson went to court to get his eligibility established for 1980. That he did, but only after the case took such bizarre twists and turns that nobody knew from one week to the next if Wilson would get the green light to suit up Saturdays.

Even though it filled a lot of space in the sports pages for months to come (ten years later Illinois partisans still marvel at the complexity of it), all that was off the field. Illinois fans learned quickly that Dave Wilson could make news on game day as well.

The 1980 U of I football team

HAIL TO THE ORANGE AND BLUE!

Mike White, head football coach, 1980-87

Dave Wilson Astounds

Somewhere amidst the red tape, Illinois opened the Mike White era against Northwestern on September 6, 1980, in front of a modest Memorial Stadium crowd of 44,222. White sent the message that no matter what happened, football at Illinois was not going to be the same. *Chicago Tribune* columnist David Condon checked his watch. It was 1:08 p.m. when Illinois got off its first offensive play under Mike White. Immediately he called for Wilson to throw long.

Wilson, effortlessly it seemed, hung the ball out as far as he could throw it, and it fell incomplete. No matter. The Memorial Stadium crowd had seen nothing that even remotely resembled that kind of pass for a long, long time. The crowd roared its approval. Neither Wilson nor Illinois, a 14-point favorite, were effective as Northwestern took a 9-0 halftime lead.

After halftime, the Illini drove 70 yards, buoyed by John Lopez catches of Wilson passes good for 21 and 15 yards, to set up Mike Murphy's 4-yard touchdown plunge. Meanwhile, Illinois defenders John Gillen, Tony Scarcelli, Dave Dwyer, and freshmen Terry Cole and Mark Butkus, nephew of Dick Butkus, showed flashes of brilliance. Later, Mike Holmes ran 53 yards around right end to put Illinois on top for good. After that, Wilson didn't throw another pass, but the Illini took advantage of Northwestern mistakes to open the White era a 35-9 winner.

Dave Wilson

"I guess you could say I was nervous, kind of uneasy, from the mental standpoint. . . , " Wilson said. "I can't say the court case wasn't on my mind a great deal." White got a game ball.

A week later, Wilson threw for 170 yards and his first Illini touchdown and Mike Bass kicked a 38-yard field goal with no time remaining as Illinois knocked off Michigan State 20-17.

The next week, Wilson, despite having his eligibility rescinded—and restored—in the days and hours before game time, threw 43 passes, completing 20, for 158 yards, but Missouri humbled Illinois 52-7. The following week Calvin Thomas ran for 105 yards and Wilson threw for 198, but the Illini could only forge a 20-20 tie with Air Force.

Illinois was 2-1-1 at that point and had won as many games as Moeller's last team. The 1980 Illini would win only once more, 20-14 at Iowa. It would lose 28-21 to Mississippi State, 45-20 to Purdue, 45-14 to Michigan, 21-18 to Minnesota, 49-42 to Ohio State, and 26-24 to Indiana to finish 3-7-1. Even in a losing season,

White and Wilson showed the type of aerial assaults that Illinois fans would come to expect.

Take the October 18 date with Purdue and its quarterback, Mark Herrmann, in Memorial Stadium. Herrmann hit 24 of 35 passes, including four touchdowns, and he passed for 371 yards, eclipsing the Big 10 record of 369 thrown by Michigan State's Ed Smith in 1978. Hardly anybody noticed that.

Trailing 24-0, Wilson unleashed his right arm. He threw 58 passes that day and completed 35, both Big 10 records at the time. These were good for 425 yards, his longest pass a 77-yard strike to Mike Martin.

"It certainly wasn't three yards and a cloud of dust," quipped Purdue coach Jim Young.

White wasn't amused. "We got beat," he said afterwards. "A lot of times records are broken in defeat because of the circumstances. I don't want to glamorize it. The bottom line is that our program has a long way to go."

Wilson would not throw for less than 310 yards in each of the Illini's final four games that season. And all the records he set that sunny day in Champaign were obliterated just three weeks later, November 8, 1980, during Homecoming at the cloud of dust capital of the world, Columbus, Ohio.

"Ohio State was rated about seventh in the nation and, deep down, we really didn't figure to win," Wilson later recalled. "Coach White told us to just go out there and have some fun, not to worry about it.

"We studied Ohio State film and put together a game plan. And I'll never forget as I came up to the line that day, it was like watching that film over again. When they tried the strong safety blitz, we had a play for it. When they brought the free safety, I threw to Greg Boeke for a touchdown. The coaches had me prepared and I recognized each defense as it came up."

Illinois ran 76 offensive plays that afternoon, 69 of them Wilson passes and 43 of those completions. Six turned into touchdowns. Six hundred twenty-one yards. All, except the six touchdown passes, bettered or equalled NCAA records. This was against perhaps the best secondary in the league.

Illinois, after trailing 35-7 at one point, had the partisan Buckeye fans cheering wildly for the Illini before the curtain finally fell on a 49-42 loss. Ten Big 10 and NCAA records fell.

"It's a good thing Wilson didn't have a good first half or he would've had a thousand yards," said stunned Ohio State coach Earle Bruce.

After the season, Wilson would be in court for many more months, but he would never play again for the University of Illinois. His memory would linger, though, as the Big 10 would hand out stiff sanctions to the Illini football program. Originally those sanctions called for three years' probation, a two-year ban from post-season play in all men's sports, and exclusion from sharing conference TV revenue for two years. That was softened, however, and the Big 10 ultimately slapped only the football program for only one year.

Wilson would lose his battle for another year of eligibility and would go on to sign a $1.6 million contract with the New Orleans Saints.

With or without Wilson, the Illini's 3-7-1 record did not represent significant improvement, but everybody knew that with Mike White running the show, something was cooking.

Mike Bass, Illinois kicker

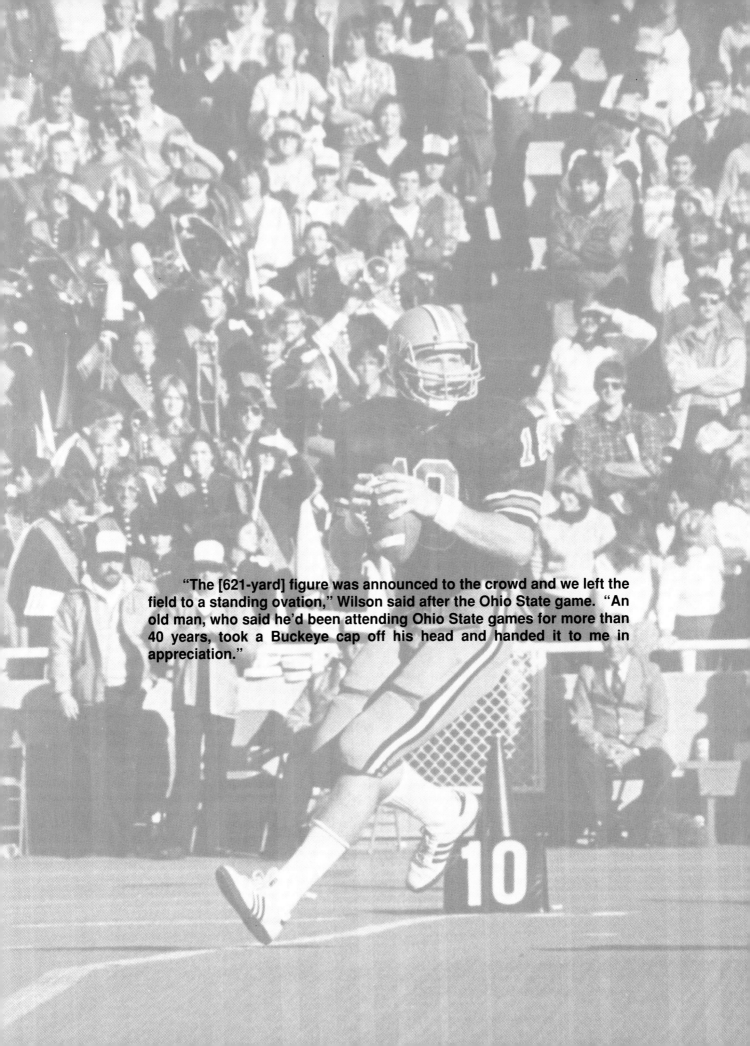

"The [621-yard] figure was announced to the crowd and we left the field to a standing ovation," Wilson said after the Ohio State game. "An old man, who said he'd been attending Ohio State games for more than 40 years, took a Buckeye cap off his head and handed it to me in appreciation."

"Three years ago Coach White sat in our living room and said he was going to take us to a bowl game. That's what I went to Illinois for . . . I believed him. I wouldn't have gone to Illinois if I hadn't."

—Terry Cole
Illini defensive end

In the midst of the Wilson controversy, White and Iowa coach Hayden Fry visited at midfield before the two teams played in 1980. Fry, naturally enough, said he hoped everything worked out well and that Wilson would be in an Illinois uniform in 1981.

White thanked the Iowa coach for his concern and said he hoped so too, but if not, he had a quarterback in the wings who he believed would be just as good, if not better, than Wilson. Fry thought he was nuts.

The Emerging Tony Eason

Tony Eason, the man about whom White spoke, wasn't so sure either. After all, he had spent much of his high school career in Walnut Grove, California, handing the ball off, and although he had thrown for 14 touchdowns as a sophomore at American River Junior College in Sacramento, his major college scholarship offers equalled exactly zero.

On the recommendation of Fred Besana, a former backup quarterback for White at Cal, White offered Eason the last available scholarship in 1980. While Wilson spent that season throwing bombs and filing affidavits, Eason was red-shirted.

"I came to Illinois for two reasons," Eason said before anybody outside the football office had any idea who he was. "First, there was the history of Mike White as a coach of quarterbacks. Second, I didn't have any other offers."

Of course when September came around, Wilson had signed a large NFL contract and Eason was one of 19 junior college transfers in the Illinois spotlight.

"I haven't turned my back on the Illinois high school coaches," White said, responding to criticism that he had done just that. "They don't play my style of football here, so it's hard for me to find my style of athletes . . . We want

Tony Eason

to base our recruiting in the state, but we couldn't start that way or we would have been out of business fast."

White's vaunted offensive system was squarely in Eason's hands. White had brought in players who could catch the ball, such as Oliver Williams, the first of three brothers who would distinguish themselves at Illinois, Mike Martin, John Lopez, and Kirby Wilson.

But could the defense stop anybody? Did it really matter that Big 10 sanctions would keep bowl hunters away from Champaign? After all, they'd had no reason to show up before now. Even White was cautious.

In preparation for the first 1981 game, at Pittsburgh, White told Eason to forget about trying to read the Panthers' defensive alignments once he had called a play. White thought it would be too much pressure for the quarterback's first major-college game. Perhaps partly as a result of this concern, Eason spent much of the afternoon on the seat of his pants as the Illini lost 26-6. Nevertheless, Eason doled out 23 completions to eight different receivers, good for 204 yards and a hint of things to come.

The next week the Illini opened the Big 10 season at Michigan State. Eason, by now given the green light to call an audible, unleashed virtually his entire repertoire. He threw for 320 yards, including touchdown passes of 26 yards to Martin and eight yards to Williams. Illinois won 27-17.

Mike Bass preparing to kick barefoot

The Illini's new air show flew home for the first time in the season's third game against Syracuse, and 57,579 fans boarded the flight, but the Orangemen sat on the football offensively for almost 37 minutes. Nevertheless, the Illini rallied from a 14-7 deficit in the second half to post a 17-14 victory.

Kirby Wilson spearheaded the game-tying 77-yard drive, catching an Eason pass and squirming 19 yards to set up Mike Murphy's 1-yard touchdown plunge. Bass won it with a 23-yard field goal against a stiff wind. Eason threw for only 132 yards that afternoon in what would be his lowest output as an Illini.

An Assembly Line Spiral Pass

The next week, Eason was grumpy. "I made more mistakes than in the first three games put together," he said. Nobody else, including a crowd of more than 63,000, complained about his 21 completions and three touchdown passes as the Illini dumped previously unbeaten Minnesota 38-29. So impressive was Eason already that Gary Childs wrote in the *Peoria Journal Star* that Eason threw perfect spiral passes "until they looked as if they were being produced on the perfect spiral pass assembly line."

Equally important, Calvin Thomas ran for 56 yards and a touchdown and the Illinois defense held the Gophers to only 144 rushing yards in the first win over Minnesota since 1975.

The Illini were 3-1 for only the third time since the 1963 Rose Bowl season. By now Eason had hit 63 percent of his passes for just under 1,000 yards. He was ranked ninth nationally in total offense and 16th in passing efficiency.

Could the Illinois fans, giddy enough to pop out of the woodwork in droves, dare dream?

Building Enthusiasm

Road games awaited at Purdue and Ohio State. Eason would pass for 728 yards and four touchdowns in those games, but he would also throw five interceptions. The losses were 44-20 at Purdue and 34-27 at Ohio State.

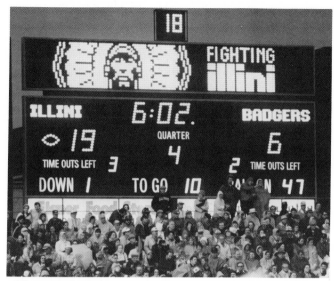

Illini scoreboard

In Columbus, the Illini turned a 24-10 deficit into a 27-24 lead in the third quarter, but were called for six penalties in the last 20 minutes. Art Schlichter passed the Buckeyes back into the lead, and a last-minute Illinois drive was thwarted when Eason threw his third interception of the game. Ohio State came out on top. The losses did not sit well.

"He [White] told us 'the hell with moral victories,' " Lopez said after this loss. ". . . The year before there were people in the locker room actually happy that we'd stayed close. This year, we were down."

Nevertheless, Homecoming fever was rampant as the first sellout crowd in five years awaited Wisconsin's arrival. The Badgers, already upset winners over Purdue, Ohio State, and Michigan, boasted a take-no-prisoners defense. But Eason escaped the Badgers' wrath, completing 26 of 38 passes for 357 yards and three touchdowns in Illinois' 23-21 victory. He equalled the Big 10 record with five straight 300-yard passing games. Eason and Williams combined on an 86-yard scoring strike, and the quarterback found tailback Darrell Smith twice for 5- and 16-yard scores.

Next up, resurgent Iowa invaded Champaign. Eason again: 22 of 34 for 263 yards and two touchdowns. The Illini defense stepped to the fore, falling on four Hawkeye fumbles. One was recovered by Pete Burgard for a touch-

down. Illinois was a 24-7 winner, but Iowa would go on to its first Rose Bowl in over 20 years.

"When the defense plays like that," Oliver Williams said afterwards, "you just want to kiss each one of them individually." Williams deserved a peck on the cheek too, catching two touchdown passes, including a 56-yarder that put the Illini on top 17-0. Defensive bows went to back Dennis Bishop, who had a 46-yard interception return and was named Player of the Week by both wire services; his backfield mates Charles Armstead, who had a 46-yard interception return, and Rick George; and linebacker Ron Ferrari, who forced the Iowa fumble that Burgard recovered .

By now, the recharged Illini were worshipped in Champaign-Urbana. Two businesses contributed $150,000 apiece to help build a new scoreboard. One grocery store decorated its shopping bags with Illinois' schedule and pic-

Oliver Williams

tures of Illini players, while another piped the game broadcasts into its store. Tailgate parties were turning into celebrations complete with Dixieland bands and picnics accentuated with gold candelabras.

A Championship Denied

Next came Michigan in Ann Arbor. Bo Schembechler, it was well noted, never tried to hide his disdain either for Illinois' treatment of Moeller or of White's methods. Any chance Schembechler had to pour it on, he gladly accepted. That chance came this day.

An early 21-7 Illinois lead looked good. And even a 21-21 halftime tie seemed promising. Then, the Wolverines poured four of their 10 touchdowns over the goal in the final period. Final score: 70-21.

"I thought we had them early in the game," linebacker Jack Squirek said afterwards. "Then they got a lot of big plays on us. We had to apply

Mike White gets into the game

pressure like we did against Iowa, but we couldn't do it."

"After the first quarter, everybody just came apart," White said. "Tony [who threw for a then season-high 386 yards] came apart, our field goal kicker came apart. It was a complete disintegration."

Still this whipping didn't bother White nearly as much as the earlier tough loss at Ohio State. It was indeed a whipping and it took Illinois out of the running for the Big 10 championship. Yet it didn't tear the Illini to pieces.

The next week Indiana came to Illinois. The Illini responded with their best rushing performance of the season, as backs Joe Curtis, Darrell Smith, and Calvin Thomas combined to give the Illini 198 rushing yards in a 35-14 victory. It was Illinois' sixth win and assured the Illini of their second winning season since 1965.

"We're proud of the winning season because that in itself is quite an achievement," White said. "Normally, you look to the third or fourth season for that, but we've taken the step from a losing to a winning season in two years."

Culminating a Winning Season

A winning season would not translate into a bowl bid, so the 1981 Illini played their "bowl" game in icy and nearly dark Dyche Stadium. The Illini, after building a 35-12 halftime lead,

Champaign Tony

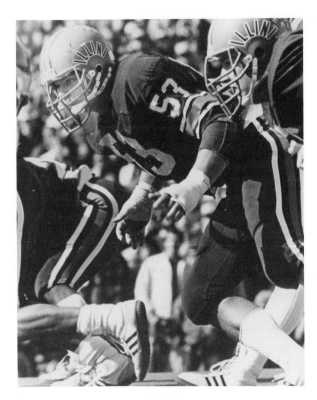

Mark Butkus, nephew of Dick Butkus

pummelled winless Northwestern 49-12 to finish 7-4, 6-3 in the Big 10.

The two teams threw 110 passes over the ice-covered turf, only 14 passes short of the major-college record. The football flew 70 times in a one-hour, 45-minute first half. Had that pace continued throughout the short November afternoon, the game would have ended in the dark of night.

Eason, who threw for 409 yards in the Wildcat contest, rewrote four conference season records in 1981: 20 touchdowns, 211 pass completions, 407 plays, and 3,360 passing yards. Already he held a bundle of Illinois career records. Unlike Wilson, he knew he would return for another season—a season where "Champaign Tony," as he was dubbed, would be hyped for the Heisman Trophy.

More fans—311,826—filled Memorial Stadium that year, more than any other to date, and Illinois' 5-0 home record was its first perfect mark at home since 1951.

White gave credit to the playing of defensive end Willie Young, a 25-year-old Army vet-

eran; fifth-year offensive linemen Greg Boeke and Troy McMillin; junior college tranfers Dennis Bishop and Charles Armstead in the defensive backfield; and sophomores like defensive linemen Mark Butkus and Don Thorp, who would provide the nucleus for even more success down the road.

White called this his most enjoyable season in coaching. "I had hoped for a five-win season and considered six victories a dream, but we had a lot of pieces fall into place, and Tony Eason replaced Dave Wilson without a hitch. In fact, after a year as a redshirt, Eason was more advanced in the beginning than Dave was."

Thomas Rooks

Although the Illini could not go bowling in 1981, White, whose contract was extended to a full five years, coached the Blue-Gray Game in which Boeke, McMillin, Squirek, and Thomas played. Kelvin Atkins, Ron Ferrari, and Rick George also were selected for post-season play.

Rose Bowl Contenders

During that off-season, Illinois was touted as a 1982 championship and Rose Bowl contender. During that same off-season, a pair of junior college players visited the Illinois campus

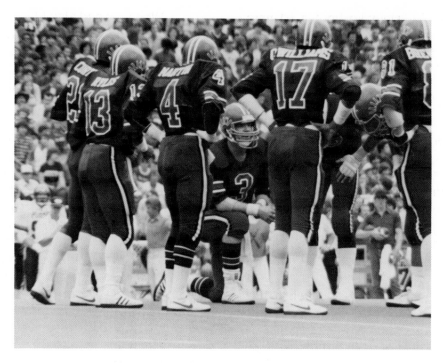

Eason and the Fighting Illini in the huddle

one bitterly cold January weekend. The weekend that became known as the "Elton and Delton Affair" triggered an NCAA investigation into the recruitment of junior college players Elton Veals and Delton Edwards. Both apparently enrolled, but hustled back to California after only four days on campus. The probe, which would drag on for more than two years, would ultimately come back to haunt White and Illinois.

Good times were about to roll first. In 1982 no sanctions were hanging over the Illini's heads. Bowl scouts would scramble to find dusty maps of central Illinois. The Illini would get Top-20 recognition. The hype, Heisman and otherwise, was on. A music professor even wrote a song about Eason, one that got plenty of play on local radio stations. Ticket sales were booming. In fact, 424,711 would pass through the turnstiles for six home dates. The Illini would be unmerciful to those fans—six games would be decided in the final seconds, but they'd be entertaining to the end.

"I don't want to be blunt or too bad," said Williams, who had caught 38 of Eason's passes for 760 yards and six touchdowns the year before. "We're going to the Rose Bowl. It's like we're a bunch of tigers waiting to be let out of a cage. Last year we were on probation, this year it's like taking the lock off the cage and letting us loose. We're going to be running wild."

The season opener against Northwestern was pushed back to a 6 p.m. starting time, all the better to show off the stadium's new lighting system and to allow more partying time for Stoner's new Tailgreat promotion, a marketing move that launched tailgating to even loftier standards.

White expressed fear that the confidence in his team was being oversold. "But we like it," he said. "This community has needed it, the state's needed it."

They liked it when Eason passed for 245 yards and ran for one touchdown, when Mitch Brookins ran for two touchdowns and caught a 15-yard pass from Eason for another, and when three Illinois running backs—Dwight Beverly, Thomas Rooks, and Richard Ryles—combined for over 200 rushing yards in the 49-13 win over the Wildcats.

Steaming to Syracuse

The next week, the Illini watched Michigan State's Ralf Mojsiejenko boot a 61-yard field goal early in the first quarter, but Bass drilled three field goals of his own—of 34, 21, and 23 yards. Illinois went to 2-0 in the Big 10, 23-16.

Eason threw for 301 yards that day. Mike Murphy caught seven passes, Williams six, and tight end Tim Brewster four. It was freshman Craig Swoope's third-quarter interception that really turned the momentum. The Spartans led 16-13 and were driving again when Swoope picked off a John Leister pass and returned it 40 yards to set up Joe Curtis' 2-yard scoring run.

Then, Illinois went to the Carrier Dome at Syracuse to hold the first Illini game indoors since before the turn of the century. They came out 47-10 winners behind Bass' four field goals, Eason's 293 passing yards, and a defensive charge that allowed the Orangemen 120 yards in total offense. A defensive highlight was Mike Heaven's 27-yard interception return for a third-quarter touchdown.

That game got the Illini ranked in both wire service polls for the first time in six years, and it got the hype, particularly the Marino-Eason Heisman hype, boiling. Top-rated Pittsburgh and Marino were coming to Champaign. What kind of an aerial circus would a crowd of 71,547 get to see?

Reality Reestablished

"I can't wait to play Pitt again," Eason said.

For the most part, however, Illinois' air show was grounded. Pitt's defense sacked Eason nine times and forced five interceptions, including one that defensive tackle Dave Puzzuoli scooped up and lumbered 95 yards for a touchdown. The Panthers won 20-3.

"We must have had a hundred attempts [actually, it was 93]," Marino said. "The thing is, you gotta complete 'em."

Marino completed 18 of 35 for 215 yards. Eason completed 30 of 58 for 275, but for most of those he was running for his life. The 82 yards he lost on sacks dropped Illinois' rushing total to minus-27 yards.

"You felt sorry for Tony," White said. "It looked like he was in a revolving door."

White praised Max McCartney's defense, which held the Panthers to 136 rushing yards. The Illini intercepted Marino four times, including twice by Swoope.

With reality reestablished, the Illini went indoors again the next week, meeting Minnesota at the Metrodome in Minneapolis. Bass found the indoors to his liking, booting field goals of 28, 45, 47, and 50 yards. The Illini scored 22 unanswered fourth-quarter points to post a 42-24 victory. Eason threw touchdown passes of 80 and 42 yards to Martin and Williams, respectively. Week five approached and Illinois was 4-1, 3-0 in the Big 10.

The air show was outdoors the next week at Memorial Stadium, but it was in full flower with Purdue in town. Eason threw for 358 yards and four touchdowns, including a 50-yard strike to Brookins with less than seven minutes to play. The Illini won, 38-34. Brookins caught five passes, good for 116 yards. Martin had nine

Mike White concentrates on the game

Winning Again

catches for 132 yards, including an 8-yard touchdown, and Armstead intercepted a Scott Campbell pass and returned it 36 yards for another score.

Smelling Roses

Illinois had passed the season halfway point undefeated in the Big 10. The Illini were smelling roses. Next up was a home date with Ohio State, uncharacteristic loser of three straight. The matchup was not only so attractive that it drew a crowd of 73,488—the biggest throng in Memorial Stadium in 36 years, but it was also so appealing that bowl scouts and even *Sports Illustrated* showed up.

Unfortunately, Illinois' defense got a late wake-up call, allowing a 74-yard first-quarter scoring pass from Mike Tomczak to Cedric Anderson and then a 44-yard touchdown run by Tim Spencer halfway through the second period. But Eason was on target. After a 37-yard touchdown pass to Martin, a 5-yard scoring strike to Kirby Wilson, and Rooks' 21-yard touchdown run, the two teams went deep into the final quarter tied at 21.

The Illini might have gone up by three had not Bass' 56-yard field goal attempt bounced off the right upright with three minutes to play. Then Tomczak engineered a 14-play, 69-yard drive in the final four minutes that ended with a 27-yard Rich Spangler field goal with three seconds in the game. Eason was tackled in the end zone on the game's final play. The Buckeyes left town with a 26-21 victory.

That put a damper on the Illini's spirits, but not for long. Another challenge loomed against Wisconsin. With only 52 seconds remaining, the Badgers turned a surprise bounce lateral play into a 40-yard touchdown pass from Al Toon to Jeff Nault to go up 28-26. All the Illini were devastated . . . except for Bass, the kicker.

"I'll try anything up to 60 yards," Bass, who had already kicked field goals of 19, 21, 30, and 44 yards, told White on the sideline.

Eason, who would finish the day with a career-best 479 yards, took most of those precious remaining seconds passing the Illini 51 yards to the Wisconsin 29. Bass made good on his promise. Tim Damron took the snap and set it down, and Bass kicked it through from 46 yards, snatching victory from the jaws of defeat, with the Illini winning 29-28.

"I thought it was down the middle all the way," Bass said after emerging from the huge pile of orange and blue that descended on him, a pile that included the head coach.

The Rose Bowl dream was alive again, but it dimmed the next week in Iowa City in a 14-13 loss to Iowa. Eason, playing even though his parents had been involved in a serious automobile accident on their way to the game, completed 31 of 46 passes, including an early 47-yard touchdown to Williams. Bass kicked field goals of 52 and 45 yards.

A Bruising Liberty Bowl

The next week Michigan was at Champaign, and although the Rose Bowl seemed out of the question, a victory might have sent Illinois to the Gator Bowl. Anthony Carter ran 90 yards with a pass from Steve Smith, and Ali Haji-Sheikh kicked field goals of 30, 45, and 47 yards as the Wolverines held on 16-10. Illinois had not beaten Michigan or Ohio State in its last 31 tries.

Despite that disappointment, the Liberty Bowl folks were still keenly interested in asking the Illini to spend the Christmas holidays in Memphis. All the Illini had to do was win at Indiana in their season finale.

Eason threw three first-quarter touchdown passes, and Illinois had a 31-0 lead by halftime before settling for a 48-7 victory. Brookins scored three times this day, giving him ten touchdowns for the season even though he touched the football only 47 times all year. The Illini were 7-4 for the second year in a row and had their first back-to-back winning seasons since the Pete Elliott days.

For the first time in 19 years, they were going "bowling." They would meet Alabama—appearing in its 24th consecutive post-season game—at the Liberty Bowl in Memphis. This was to be retiring Alabama coach Bear Bryant's final game.

"Three years ago coach White sat in our living room and said he was going to take us to

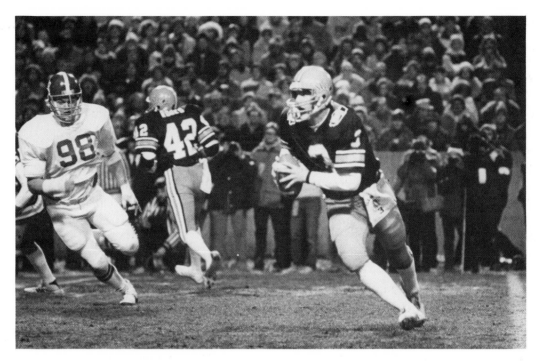

Tony Eason at 1982 Liberty Bowl

a bowl game," said junior defensive end Terry Cole. "That's what I went to Illinois for . . . I believed him. I wouldn't have gone to Illinois if I hadn't."

White relished the idea of sharing the spotlight with the 69-year-old Bryant's swan song.

"All these circumstances surrounding Bryant's retirement have thrust Illinois into the national spotlight and nothing could accelerate our program faster," White said.

Yet, there would be no bowl victory for Illinois that December night, and Eason would end his college career with both a host of Liberty Bowl records and the pain of disappointment.

Pete Wickham wrote in the *Memphis Commercial-Appeal*, "The first hint Tony Eason had as to what kind of night this 24th Liberty Bowl would be came early. His kidneys found out first. Street gangs have been more merciful."

" I had just thrown the ball and they got to me. Oh, they got to me," said Eason, after a cold, lonely evening of trying to preserve his skin and Illinois' upset chances against an angry Alabama defense.

Three times crushing Crimson Tide hits forced Eason from the game, the last after he had moved the Illini from their own 18 to the Alabama 30 in the final minutes. He didn't even know that backup quarterback Kris Jenner—who had previously thrown only three passes in his collegiate career—had thrown his third interception of the night (and Illinois' seventh) to seal Bryant's 323rd collegiate victory, 21-15.

"I wound up with my eyes bobbing up and down. I couldn't find the ground," Eason said.

When he regained his bearings, Eason realized that he owned just about every Liberty Bowl passing record on the books. Among them were records for total offense (413), passing yardage (423), most passes attempted (55) and completed (35), and most interceptions (four). Martin shared in the record books with 115 yards, and his eight catches tied a mark.

In the first half, Eason threw for 247 yards and the Illini had five scoring opportunities, but two interceptions, a fumble, and a blocked field goal left the Illini with only Curtis' 1-yard scoring run. They missed the kick and trailed 7-6 at the half.

The Tide went up 14-6 in the third quarter

Winning Again

on Jesse Bendross' 8-yard score on a reverse, but the Illini came back early in the fourth quarter. Eason threw a touchdown to Williams on fourth and goal from the 2. Now, Illinois' two-point conversion failed. Alabama scored again to go up 21-12 before Bass got the Illini within winning distance with a 23-yard field goal.

They had two more chances. The first came when Cole recovered a fumble at the Alabama 24 with 4:38 remaining. Eason completed passes of five and three yards before crumbling under a sack. That brought out Jenner, whose pass went directly to Alabama's Eddie Lowe.

The last chance came when the Illini got the ball back on their own 18 with 1:43 left. Eason pulled himself back together to complete passes of 24, 13, and ten yards. He got dizzied again, bringing Jenner back in for a try that the Tide's Robbie Jones picked off with just 16 seconds left.

Eason, who would go on to quarterback the New England Patriots into a Super Bowl, finished his Illinois career with 7,031 yards and 38 touchdowns. When he left, he owned nine NCAA passing and total offense records. He had more Big 10 and Illinois records than he could count. Martin would finish his final season with 69 catches for 941 yards. Bass had several NCAA and Big 10 records, and three Illinois records, including a then-record 209 points.

Even though all of them were leaving Illinois, White's system was just getting in gear. A new year, 1983, was about to dawn.

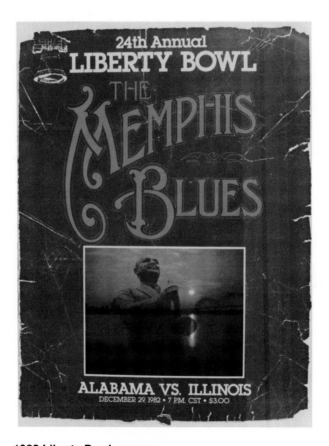

1982 Liberty Bowl program

HAIL TO THE ORANGE AND BLUE!

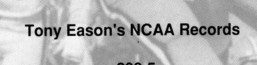

Tony Eason's NCAA Records

Most total yards per game, career: 299.5
Most passing yards per game, career: 300.4
Most completions per game, career: 23.9
Most attempts per game, career: 38.9
Most total yards, first two seasons: 6,589
Most seasons gaining 2,500 yards, 2 (tie)
Most seasons gaining 3,000 yards, 2 (tie)
Most games gaining 200 yards or more, season: 11 (tie)
Most consecutive games gaining 200 yards or more, season: 11 (tie)

RETURN TO ROSES

"You have to assume a position of pride, and dwell upon the factors that put Illinois in the Rose Bowl in the first place."

—Coach Mike White

As 1982 ended, the NCAA continued to probe the Illinois football program. White spent a lot of time denying that he was about to return to professional football—either to the NFL or to the fledgling United States Football League—as a head coach.

On the field, however, there was no question that the moribund program that White had taken over just three years earlier was alive and kicking. Thanks was due to California passing arms, more junior college imports than the Big 10 had ever seen, and a solid Midwestern work ethic.

Season ticket sales were 12,000 in 1979. By 1983, they were cut off at 50,000. Seventeen of the 25 new team members came from the high school ranks. Of the seven returning defensive players, most had been in the program four years, including Don Thorp, Mark Butkus, Terry Cole, and Ed Brady, all Illinois high school players.

Trudeau: A Worthy Quarterback

Offensively, for the first time, Illinois boasted a physical front line. Greatness was seen for sophomore Jim Juriga, and he was flanked by returnees Rick Schulte, Bob Stowe, and Chris Babyar. Tight end Tim Brewster was one of the league's best.

White openly predicted that tailback Dwight Beverly, the Illini's rushing leader in 1982 with 390 yards, could become Illinois' first 1,000-yard back since Jim Grabowski. Sophomore Thomas Rooks could run too. Beverly would finish with 685, Rooks 842.

About the only question marks Illinois had were in the kicking game, where somebody had to replace Bass; in the receiving corps, where only Brewster returned; and at quarterback. The quarterback job was being given to redshirt sophomore Jack Trudeau, another California import, and no one knew how he would respond to stepping into White's quarterback system.

Jack Trudeau, one of White's California quarterbacks

White wasn't saying how good he thought this team would be, but he did think it would turn out to be a little better than the fourth- or fifth-place team that pundits predicted. "Our transition is coming back the other way, toward the running game," White said. "And there is one consistency in the Big 10—the best defensive team wins."

There was also the delicious prospect that the Illini would play the league's strongest teams—Michigan, Ohio State, and Iowa—in Champaign. That taste soured, though, when the Illini, who had looked less than fine-tuned offensively in pre-season scrimmages, opened the season against Missouri in sweltering Columbia. White had no choice but to shelve his new-found running game after the Illini fell behind 21-0 early in the second quarter. The Illini had the ball for only five first-quarter offensive plays.

If nothing else, Trudeau proved he was a worthy successor to Wilson and Eason. He completed 26 of 38 passes for 293 yards, including touchdown passes of 45 and four yards to Mitch Brookins, who had switched to flanker after spending three years in the backfield. Kicker Chris White, son of the head coach, made his collegiate debut with a 50-yard field goal, but the Illini hardly looked like world-beaters in a 28-18 loss. The heavily hyped defense did nothing to live up to its reputation.

"It hurts when all the talk this year has been about how strong our defense is supposed to be," Cole said. "We were supposed to go out and conquer the world this year . . . and then this."

Neither was the team impressive the next week against Stanford in their second non-conference tuneup, before 72,852 Tailgreat fans, but the Illini won 17-7. Beverly ran behind improved line play for 116 yards—the first Illinois runner to gain more than 100 yards since 1980—and Trudeau hooked up with sophomore wide receiver David Williams, Oliver's younger brother, nine times for 111 yards, including a 30-yard touchdown.

Joe Miles blocked a Stanford punt and John Ayres fell on it in the Cardinal end zone for Illinois' other touchdown. Chris White kicked his second field goal of the season. The Illini

Chris White, all-time leading scorer

actually gained more rushing yards (215) than they did passing (198), an unheard-of statistic in the White era. "That might be a Ripley's Believe It Or Not," White quipped.

Taking the Big 10

Thus, Illinois was 1-1 as it headed into its nine-game Big 10 schedule. The schedule would begin at 2-0 Michigan State, which was coming off a 28-23 upset victory over Notre Dame. The two teams would play in front of 75,867 at Spartan Stadium, the largest crowd to watch these schools play each other since the 1963 Rose Bowl showdown.

Michigan State

Seldom before had the Big 10 played a round-robin league schedule. Never before had one team defeated all nine Big 10 foes in a single season. The punishing Illini sent seven Spartans to the sidelines with injuries, including starting quarterback Dave Yarema, his backup, Rich Kolb, and All-American linebacker Carl Banks, who got a helmet in the knee.

"I felt like we intimidated them right from the start," said Butkus, whose eight tackles contributed to the Spartans' 42-yard rushing day. Meanwhile, the Illini strung together second-quarter scoring drives of 11 and 16 plays. Beverly scored from three yards for the season's first rushing touchdown, and Trudeau and Brookins connected on a 5-yard scoring pass. Chris White drilled 29- and 35-yard field goals. Final score: Illinois 20, Michigan State 10.

Iowa

Unbeaten fourth-ranked Iowa was due up in Champaign. The Hawkeyes, fresh from knocking off Ohio State, came to town sporting the league's best offense, averaging 38 points and 507 yards a game. The Illini hadn't forgotten their 14-13 loss in Iowa City a year before. They dubbed this "pay-back day."

A packed house, 80-degree sunshine, and an all-blue Illinois team greeted the Chuck Long-led Hawkeyes that Saturday. Illinois players came out for warm-ups wearing their usual blue jerseys and orange pants, but by game time the orange pants had been discarded in favor of blue.

First, Chris White kicked a 30-yard field goal with 8:59 left in the first quarter. Less than two minutes later, Trudeau and Brookins connected on a 54-yard scoring strike. Trudeau, who would finish with 23 of 32 for 286 yards, hit Cam Benson from 12 yards out. Less than a minute into the second period, it was David Williams whom Trudeau found free in the end zone, this time with a 6-yard pass. It was 24-0 almost before the tailgaters had packed up their picnics. White added a 24-yard second-quarter field goal to put Illinois on top 27-0 at halftime, then had fourth-quarter kicks from 47 and 45 yards out to put the finishing touches on the Hawkeyes' debacle. It was an Illini victory, 33-0.

The Illini's stunting defense so muddled the Hawks that Iowa gained only 15 yards on the ground and Chuck Long was sacked seven times and completed only 12 of 27 passes, the only time he would be at less than 50 percent in his college career. "We're driving the bus," Mike Heaven said, in reference to the Rose Bowl race.

"I don't know if we're this good a football team," said Trudeau. "But I do know I had a blast out there today."

David Williams

Return to Roses

Don Thorp, #96

Four games into the season, Illinois ranked first in the Big 10 against the rush, allowing just 70.5 yards a game. It also ranked first in scoring defense with 11.2 points per game. Now the 19th-ranked Illini were to travel to Wisconsin, which had posted a 21-20 victory over Illinois-conqueror Missouri.

Wisconsin

The defense and running game would come in handy during a bone-jarring afternoon at Camp Randall Stadium that featured 22 penalties and more than a dozen injury timeouts. The Illini completed less than 50 percent of their passes for the first time in 30 games, but Beverly would run for 113 yards and Rooks would add 88. It was a 27-15 Illini victory.

Ohio State

The winning streak was four, Ohio State was coming to town, and the hype was on. Even at Memorial Stadium, Illinois had won over Ohio State only four times since 1934. Could Illinois, who had come so close a year earlier, really

beat the Buckeyes for the first time since 1967?

Sixth-ranked Ohio State led 13-10 with 8:18 left to play when the driving Illini were stopped at the Ohio State 11. Under a heavy defensive rush, Trudeau was intercepted by OSU safety Kevin Richardson.

That interception started Ohio State, moving into a stiff wind, on one of its long-patented three-yards-and-a-cloud-of-dust marches. Butkus, Cole, and linebacker Moe Bias were all nursing injuries on the sidelines. Thorp limped back into the game with braces on each knee. With 230-pound tailback Keith Byars running up the middle on almost every snap, the Buckeyes drove to the Illinois 19 where they faced fourth down and four.

Coach Earle Bruce spurned the field goal attempt, instead allowing reserve quarterback Jim Karsatos—filling in for the injured Tomczak, out with a concussion—to roll out. Vince Osby bumped Karsatos out of bounds at the 17, giving the Illini 1:43 to figure out how to move 83 yards.

Mike White was hoping against hope they'd get close enough for his son to try a game-tying field goal. As it turned out, they only needed 37 seconds to score. The first play: Trudeau fired a sideline pass to little-used walk-on Scott Golden, good for 24 yards. Next snap: same play; same combination; virtually the same result, this time for 22 yards. Now, after Golden dropped a pass, Trudeau had to scramble, which he did 16 yards to the OSU 21. Before the Buckeyes could gather their senses, Trudeau audibled a pitch to Rooks on a sweep. Rooks followed blocks by Juriga and Brewster into the end zone.

During the next Buckeye offensive play, Illinois safety David Edwards, who had scored the first half's only touchdown on a 47-yard interception return, grabbed his second interception to give the Illini the 17-13 victory and push them to 4-0 and a deadlock with Michigan in the Big 10 race. It also started the fans on to the field in waves that would dismantle both goal posts—a first at Illinois.

Purdue

Illinois travelled to Purdue's Ross-Ade Stadium. The Boilermakers were pass-happy—Scott Campbell would throw from the shotgun for 388 yards and three touchdowns. But the Illini would intercept Campbell four times—including twice in the end zone in the final quarter. The Illini, meanwhile, stuck to the ground, where Beverly erupted for 179 yards and three touchdowns and Rooks added 70 yards. The Illini held on to win 35-21. They would carry a six-game winning streak, Illinois' longest since 1953, into the next weekend's showdown with co-leader and No. 8-ranked Michigan.

Michigan

Newspapers from throughout the country

Illini fans take down the goalposts in victory

"Ohio State was going to find a way to win—that's how they do it," Mike White said. "The satisfying thing is that we found a way to win, and we've never done that before. We didn't have any doubters and there were times when there could have been doubters."

Five games remained in the regular season. There were few doubters that Illinois could go to the Rose Bowl.

requested space in the Memorial Stadium press box. The game was played in front of a stadium-record crowd of 76,127 and a national television audience.

Trudeau had the foresight to cart several dozen rosebuds to the stadium that morning. "You might say I anticipated the demand," he later said. Thousands of fans had the same idea.

Jim Juriga

Michigan took the opening kickoff and, as Schembechler loved to do, pounded out an 8-minute, 16-play drive. Finally, after the Wolverines had reached Illinois' 17-yard line, Swoope ran down Rick Rogers for a 4-yard loss on a screen pass that forced Michigan to settle for Bob Bergeron's 38-yard field goal. Trudeau drove the Illini right back to the Michigan 24, but fumbled a snap on a messed-up audible that Michigan recovered on the 26.

The Illini defense, helped by Chris Sigourney's masterful punting, would give up no more long drives this half, and after Luke Sewall got a finger on a Wolverine punt that travelled only 14 yards to the Michigan 49, Trudeau went back to work. The sophomore, who deftly avoided the Wolverine rush to complete a 17-yard gain to Williams, found Rooks from 9 yards out, and the big fullback lunged the final three yards into the end zone.

Michigan closed to within 7-6 on Bergeron's 28-yard third-quarter field goal. The Illini might

Jack Trudeau

HAIL TO THE ORANGE AND BLUE!

have folded again when they botched a third-quarter scoring chance. Facing third and one at the Michigan 4, Trudeau was to hand off to Beverly, who was supposed to leap over the Wolverines into the end zone. But Beverly caught the ball with his elbow, and it skipped out of Trudeau's hands and into the arms of Michigan's Carlton Rose.

Yet for the Illini on this day, adversity was no problem. The Thorp-led defense forced a Michigan punt, and the offense quickly drove 59 yards for the winning touchdown.

Later, Joe Miles would spin Michigan punt returner Evan Cooper down in the end zone for a safety and the final points. Illinois' 16-6 win was its first over Michigan at home since 1957. Suddenly Illinois was 6-0 in the Big 10, its best conference start since 1914. It had its longest winning streak in 32 years, and the media started figuring out Illinois' long-shot scenario for the national championship. Down came the goalposts again. And up went the sign in at least one Champaign travel agency offering Rose Bowl vacation trips.

For the second time in 72 games, Michigan did not score a touchdown. Swoope was credited with 11 tackles, Butkus nine, and Thorp eight. "This was the year of the Illinois defense and you saw it at its finest," said Mike White. "Max McCartney and the other defensive coaches kept the pressure on all day long."

Minnesota

All that separated Illinois from the Rose Bowl now was Minnesota, Indiana, and Northwestern, three conference doormats. The Illini were admittedly lackluster in the Metrodome. They rushed for only 34 yards against a defense that had allowed an average of nearly 250 yards a game. Trudeau threw for 342 yards and three touchdowns, including a 77-yarder to Williams. Edwards scored on a 35-yard interception return as the Illini cruised to their eighth straight win, 50-23. Thorp, who by now had become Illinois' career leader in tackles for a loss, (he finished with 37), had nine tackles and was named Midwest Defensive Player of the Week by the Associated Press.

Indiana

Now only Indiana stood between Illinois and the Rose Bowl. Nobody expected the Hoosiers to stand long. The *Chicago Tribune* had full-color headlines prepared, complete with bright red roses strewn across its front page. Other newspapers had special sections waiting in the wings.

The 73,612 who came to Memorial Stadium that day to watch 27 Illinois seniors play their final home game knew the Hoosiers would offer little obstacle. Beverly ran for three touchdowns. Rooks collected two, and backup quarterback Ken Cruz got a touchdown pass and scored on a run as the Illini rolled up 565 yards in offense. Score: 49-21. Illinois' first nine-game winning streak since 1927-28. "Rose Bowl," said Mike White afterwards. "Those two words say it all."

Don Thorp in Rose Bowl-clinching Indiana game

Chris White

Northwestern

Only the finale at Northwestern now could prevent Illinois from becoming the first school to beat all nine Big 10 opponents in the same season. About 30,000 Illinois faithful streamed into Dyche Stadium that Saturday—fueling Northwestern's first sellout in ten years. Sure, the 662-yard offensive effort was nice. So were the 56 points, the most for an Illinois team since 1947. But what was really great about Illinois' 56-24 victory was that Brewster, who had caught 100 passes in his long Illinois career without crossing the goal line, finally got a chance to snare not one but two 3-yard passes from Trudeau in the end zone.

Home to Roses

"I'm real happy about it and the guys were excited for me," Brewster said. "But now we can look forward to the Rose Bowl." They were to meet Pac-10 champ UCLA in a rematch of 1947's first meeting between the two conferences.

First there were the accolades for a team that had given Illinois ten victories for the first time since 1902 and averaged a school-record 30.7 points a game. Six Illini made AP's first-team All-Big 10: Dwight Beverly, Jim Juriga, and Chris Babyar on offense and Don Thorp, voted the team MVP, Mark Butkus, and Swoope on defense. Juriga, Swoope, and Thorp gleaned All-American recognition and Thorp, who had built himself up from a 210-pound freshman to a 260-pound senior, joined past Illini greats Red Grange, Alex Agase, Bill Burrell, Dick Butkus, and Jim Grabowski as winner of the *Chicago Tribune* Big 10 MVP Silver Football.

For White and 19 Illinois players, including Tim Brewster, Vince Osby, Moe Bias, Archie Carter, and Curtis Clarke, whose home field was the Rose Bowl when they played for Pasadena City College, it was time to go home to California.

"From a psychological standpoint, we're getting killed out here this week," Stoner said days before the January 2 kickoff. "Veteran members of the Los Angeles media are rehashing that 1947 game, quoting former Illinois players how they left the Bruins bloodied and beaten. And Terry Donahue is being quoted on how great this Illinois team appears on film. It's brutal."

It should have been brutal. After all, Illinois was 10-1, ranked No. 4, considered the best Big 10 representative in years, and the bearer of a 10-game winning steak. Unranked UCLA, on the other hand, had limped into the Rose Bowl 6-4-1 after an 0-3-1 start.

Thirty-seven years earlier it had been Illinois that had to defend its right to play in this game. Now it was the Bruins. "We played a tough schedule, had early injuries and finished as the undisputed Pac-10 champion," coach Terry Donahue said. "Finishing 6-4-1 after an 0-3-1 start is a testament to our character and resiliency."

Wilting Roses

Thirty-seven years earlier Illinois had roared onto the field with something to prove. Now it was the Bruins. Game day, January 2, 1984, was, for lack of a better term, ugly. Not the weather—that was 84 degrees, a temperature similar to the September Saturday at Missouri. Perhaps that was an omen.

Illinois' dream season started popping at the seams ten plays into the game when, oddly enough, Luke Sewall leaped in front of a 43-yard UCLA field goal attempt. He got it swatted down, and the ball landed near the Illinois 5-yard line where Swoope picked it up and started to run. When he reached the 14, the Bruins separated Swoope from the football and recovered. Four plays later, quarterback Rick Neuheisel feathered a 3-yard pass to tight end Paul Bergmann in the corner of the end zone.

Chicago Sun-Times writer Bob Pille wrote, "At 7-0, the 70th Rose Bowl game was over." That may have been a bit harsh, but not much. Illinois' dream season crashed into a nightmare that Monday afternoon and early evening.

There were six turnovers. Illinois ran the ball on its first two offensive plays, good for 12 yards. Then, inexplicably, the Illini hardly ran again. On its seventh possession, Illinois charted its fourth running play and Beverly fumbled. By halftime, Illinois had run the football only six times and trailed 28-3.

The defense crumbled as well. The Illini had given up an average of only 94 yards a game on the ground. This day it surrendered 213.

Through the air, 298 UCLA yards were even worse. Four times Neuheisel threw touchdown passes. Three times freshman defensive back Keith Taylor was the victim, including one where Neuheisel found Michael Young for a 53-yard strike.

The 45-9 score was the most lopsided Rose Bowl score since 1960. "It's humiliating, it's a fiasco," Mark Butkus said.

"We're living with what happened on January 2," Trudeau said months after the debacle. "Because it was the last game, it's what we have in our minds. But the other reality was the regular season. That helps."

Mike White accepted accolades from the Walter Camp Foundation, Washington Touchdown Club, *Sporting News*, UPI, Kodak, and the Washington Pigskin Club as Coach of the Year, but the honors seemed hollow. "You can't feel guilty and you can't feel sorry for yourself," White said. "You have to assume a position of pride, and dwell upon the factors that put Illinois in the Rose Bowl in the first place. Do I think about it? Sure, I wake up in the middle of the night thinking about it . . . it's like a death in the family. We blew it before we ever teed up the football."

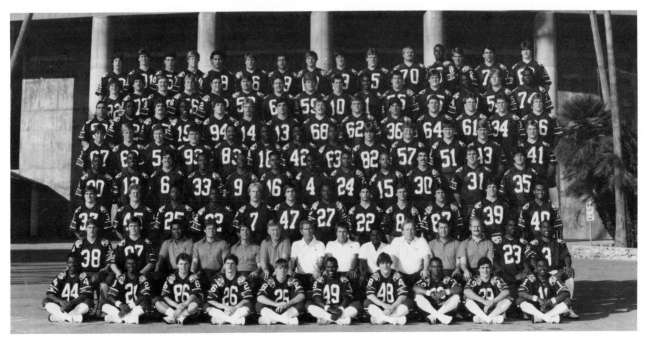

1984 Rose Bowl team picture

Mike White in a triumphant moment

Illinois has come up with a lot of innovations over the course of a century of football. Homecoming, Dad's Day, the Block I, and the first marching band formations. But none have been as widely enjoyed as Stoner's innovative Tailgreat promotion, turning tailgating into an all-day or all-weekend party. Tailgating—the art of eating and drinking out of the trunk—was long established before 1982. But Stoner turned it into an art form, establishing a themed tailgate party, complete with prizes for the most innovative displays, ranging from dinner at a local restaurant to Rose Bowl tickets to Carribean cruises.

"I think at one time, there was a Mike White edge. That sure as heck isn't prevalent now . . . that has to resurface. If there was something we did right, we have to find it again."

—Mike White

As spring drills progressed in 1984, Mike White left a message flashing on the stadium scoreboard: U-C-L-A.

"It's a four-letter word as far as I'm concerned," Rooks said. "Every time you look up it's there. It may have been January 2, but for me it's always in the back of my mind."

At the same time another four-letter word was flashing in everyone's mind: NCAA.

NCAA Sanctions

In later July, the NCAA finally wrapped up its two-and-a-half year investigation. It found the Illini guilty of 47 violations ranging from the purchase of airline tickets to the purchase of orange socks for prospective recruits. Most of the charges, however, involved automobile transportation to or around Champaign, meals, and hotel lodging. All violations were charged to assistant coaches.

There would be two years of probation, no post-season play in 1984, and no TV appearances for a year (that penalty served during the 1985 season). Scholarships were trimmed from 30 to 20 for a year.

In addition, after Illinois' own investigation into the matter, White and McCartney were barred from recruiting off-campus and their salaries were frozen. The university took steps to beef up its internal investigating capacity.

"I was not aware of the violations. I think that's one of the areas I was vulnerable in my administration of the program," White told an interviewer. "When they came to my attention, I was put in a position of accepting the responsibility, but I was aware of very, very few of them."

So, with the NCAA having spoken, the Illini would get all dressed up in 1984 with no place to go.

"We're still defending Big 10 champs, there's still plenty of incentive out there," Trudeau said.

Incentive, perhaps. But the defense that had allowed only one touchdown in the final 13:42 of any game in 1983 was decimated. Thorp and Butkus were gone up front. The line-backing corps was missing. Eight new junior college transfers were in place.

Only the defensive backfield had experience with Heaven, strong safety David Edwards, Taylor, and Swoope, but there was trouble there too. Taylor had been injured in an auto accident. Swoope, meanwhile, faced trial on a drug charge; he was later cleared.

If Illinois was going to succeed in 1984, the offense would have to carry a green defensive unit. This season Illinois would have to face Iowa, Ohio State, and Michigan on the road.

Neale Stoner and New Construction

The September 1 home opener against Northwestern was the earliest starting date in Illinois history. Despite the off-season bad news, there was plenty of good news as well. More than 60,000 season-ticket applications had been received by Memorial Day, so many that Stoner cut off filling applications. The grants-in-aid program, which had brought in less than $500,000 in 1979, received nearly that much in a single month in 1984.

Stoner's economic campaigns were wildly successful, and new construction—ranging from a football office complex to a baseball stadium to replace ancient Illinois Field—was either in progress or deep in the planning stages. Before the year was out, Illinois would have $6 million in reserves.

The Williams Connection

In the season opener with Northwestern, Trudeau passed for 315 yards, including a 33-yard touchdown to Williams, to move into third place behind Eason and Wilson on the all-time passing list. Williams caught 11 passes that day, starting the junior on his way to a phenomenal 101-catch season. The Illini rallied for a 24-16 victory. That stretched their Big 10 winning streak to 11 games.

The next week Missouri came to Champaign. A record crowd of 78,297 came to greet the Tigers. They watched Illinois pile up 466 yards of offense, Rooks score twice, and the defense hold off a fourth-quarter rally as the Illini held on to win, 30-24.

By the season's third week, Swoope had been acquitted and reinstated to the team. The Illini hoped to ease their Rose Bowl nightmare when they took a 12-game regular-season winning streak on a return trip to California. This time they met Stanford, a 1-10 finisher in 1983. Stanford spotted Illinois an early 3-0 lead on Chris White's 28-yard field goal, but went ahead 24-13 by halftime en route to humbling Illinois, 34-19.

Twice the Illini recovered Cardinal fumbles inside the Stanford 30. They wound up with only 3 points to show for it. David Williams got thrown out of the game for scuffling with Stanford players. It was another California disaster.

"We laid a big fat egg in California," Mike White said.

With Michigan State next on the schedule, Illinois had just 353 rushing yards on the season. The Illini did do something about the running game this day, handing the ball to Rooks 26 times for 132 yards. The Illini cruised to their 11th straight Big 10 victory, 40-7.

At Iowa the next week, Fry wanted no part of keeping the ball in either Trudeau or Williams' hands. So Ronnie Harmon ran for 191 yards and three touchdowns, and Owen Gill added 115 yards in the Hawkeyes' 21-16 victory.

Architect's model of Stoner's proposed athletic center

The next week, the Illini would vent their frustrations on Wisconsin. Trudeau threw for 301 yards, Rooks ran for 139, Chris White kicked five field goals, and Swoope registered 11 tackles and an interception in a 22-6 romp.

That took Illinois to Columbus, a place where White's teams always seemed to be entertaining, but never victorious. Four times the Illini struck in the game's first 16 minutes to take a 24-0 lead. The crowd of 89,937 was stunned, but not for long. Ohio State—behind Keith Byars' 274 rushing yards and Tomczak's 236 passing yards—roared back with 28 unanswered points to take a 28-24 lead early in the fourth quarter.

A Bit of Disappointment

The two teams traded points until—after kicker Chris White drew the Illini even at 38 with a 16-yard field goal with 3:18 left—Byars capped a drive with a 3-yard run with 36 seconds left to give the Buckeyes a victory, 45-38. The Illini were 2-2 in the Big 10 and effectively out of the championship race.

Illinois came home the next week to meet Purdue. Williams had eight catches for 85 yards in the Illini's 34-20 win. That pushed him to 951 yards for the season, best in the nation and an Illinois record.

The Illini went to Ann Arbor where the Wolverines were still smarting from their loss to Illinois a year earlier. Williams caught 12 passes for 132 yards and Rooks ran for 110 yards, but

Oliver Williams

Michigan rallied from a 13-10 halftime deficit with ten unanswered third quarter points and posted a 26-18 victory, Illinois' fourth straight road loss.

Williams' 12 catches equalled the Illini single-game mark established by Mike Martin against Ohio State in 1982. Now he had 80 catches and was well within range of becoming only the third player in NCAA history to finish a season with more than 100 receptions. "It goes into the stats category, but it goes into the loss category too," Williams said. "We still gotta win the next two games to make it look like we got a decent ball team." Minnesota posed no problems in Memorial Stadium the next week.

The Illini racked up 541 yards in offense, and the defense allowed only a 26-yard Chip Lohmiller field goal in a 48-3 rout. Williams' count went to 91 after 11 catches good for 142 yards.

Illinois closed its season the next week against Indiana at the Hoosier Dome in Indianapolis. The Illini started slowly with only a 27-yard White field goal and Swoope's 73-yard interception return for a touchdown on the scoreboard as Illinois led 10-7 at the half. The Illini erupted for 24 unanswered second-half

David Williams

points to post a 34-7 victory. Illinois, with nowhere to go for the holidays, was 7-4, 6-3 in the Big 10. Williams caught ten passes, good for 53 yards and a touchdown. His 101 catches put him No. 2 on the all-time single-season NCAA list.

Accolades

All the Illini could do that December was add up their accolades. Williams, whose final count was 101 receptions and 1,278 yards, became Illinois' first consensus All-American since Grabowski in 1965. Rooks ran for 1,056 yards, also a first for an Illini runner since Grabowski. That combination made the Illini the first team in Big 10 history to have a 1,000-yard rusher and receiver in the same season.

Trudeau completed 65.3 percent of his passes and 66.2 percent in Big 10 play, second best in conference history. Tight end Cap Boso caught 44 passes. The offense averaged 441.8 yards a game, and its 4,860-yard total broke the previous year's school record of 4,661.

Chris White hit 24 of 28 field goals, breaking Mike Bass' Big 10 single-season record. Heaven moved into third place on the all-time interception list with 13. Sophomore Sam Ellsworth recorded 71 tackles.

The Illini's winning season was their fourth straight. It was the first time since 1929 that Illinois had enjoyed four straight winning years and the first time since 1904 that it had won at least seven games four straight times.

"This team was 7-4, yet we're disappointed," White said. "But we're pleased in the fact we now have three key factors working for us: stability, continuity and support. The future is very promising."

A Promising 1985

With Trudeau, Rooks, Williams, Juriga, Boso, and Swoope leading a long list of returnees for 1985, the future indeed looked promising. It seemed so promising, in fact, that terms like national championship contender were mentioned in the same breath with Illinois. Although nobody would see them play on tele-

Thomas Rooks

vision, the 1985 Illini could go back to the Rose Bowl. All they'd have to do was qualify.

Coach White, normally a sandbagger when it came to his teams' abilities, gushed over this one. He compared it to his 1975 California team, which featured quarterback Joe Roth and running back Chuck Muncie, that racked up over 5,000 yards in offense.

"Some of our statistical guys on offense may have to take an unselfish role," said the coach. "David Williams may have to settle for only 50 passes this year instead of the 101 last year in order to help the team."

Fumbles, Interceptions, Disillusionment

Those championship thoughts were chilled in the season opener when the Illini, ranked No. 11 and three-point favorites, fumbled seven times (two were lost). Trudeau threw four interceptions and sixth-ranked Southern Cal scored 17 unanswered points in the first 16 minutes en route to an easy 20-10 victory. Trudeau and company heard plenty of boos from the Memorial Stadium crowd of 76,369.

"I hope it's the worst I've ever played," said Trudeau, who did complete 21 of 37 passes for 310 yards and an 83-yard touchdown to Boso. "I still feel we have a good offensive team, but today wasn't our day. It was frustrating."

Much of the work Mike White did the next week involved explaining why Illinois would have Southern Illinois on its schedule. The Salukis were moved in to provide a third non-conference game after the Big 10 had abandoned its round-robin format. The Illini narrowly avoided a huge embarrassment when, after getting only Chris White's 25- and 46-yard field goals in the first half, they had to rally from a 14-6 halftime deficit with three third-quarter touchdowns to post a 28-25 victory.

The next week powerful Nebraska racked up 456 yards on the ground and scored at will in a 52-25 romp in Lincoln. Disillusionment was mushrooming. Trudeau had already thrown ten interceptions, and 11 Illinois turnovers had turned into opponents' points. The Illini had two weeks to think about this humiliation before the Big 10 opener. Illinois' 18th straight sellout crowd turned out for the opener against unbeaten and third-ranked Ohio State in Memorial Stadium.

Ohio State

Illinois drove for touchdowns on its first two possessions, with Keith Jones and Ray Wilson taking turns scoring from a yard out to take a 14-0 first-quarter lead.

Ohio State came back with a drive of its own to make it 14-7. The Illini were five yards away from a two-touchdown lead when Mike White called for Jones to throw a halfback pass, which he did— directly to Buckeye safety Terry White in the end zone. The Buckeyes drove 80 yards to tie.

Then Ohio State took a 14-point third-quarter lead on a pair of Karsatos-to-Carter touchdown passes, but the Illini came back with two more touchdowns to make it 28-28 as time dwindled. Four seconds remained when Chris White got the call: 38 yards.

"Don't miss," Ohio State linebacker Eric Kumerow hollered across the line of scrimmage. He didn't.

Chris White, who had been strictly a basketball player in high school, kicked the Illini to a 31-28 victory. This time it was he at the bottom of a jubilant pile of Illini after his first last-second game-winning field goal.

"When I got off the bottom of the pile, my dad was on the bottom and I was kind of worried about him," Chris White said afterwards.

"I can't remember a sweeter victory in my coaching career," added Mike White, after he'd untangled himself from the pile. "I felt we had not lived up to our expectations, that we let a lot of people down."

Purdue, Michigan State, Wisconsin

The season, however, sputtered to a stop the next weekend in Ross-Ade Stadium at Purdue. Trudeau threw 66 passes for 413 yards and three touchdowns. Williams caught a league-record 16 of those passes.

Boilermaker quarterback Jim Everett, on the other hand, threw for 464 yards and four touchdowns, and that was the difference in Purdue's 30-24 victory. Trudeau threw 66 times without an interception this game, a big chunk of the NCAA-record 215 straight pass attempts he would record without a theft. Five games down. Only two three-point victories to show for them. It looked like more of the same the next weekend when Michigan State took a 17-7 lead early in the second quarter. The Spartans still led 17-14 at halftime.

"Max [McCartney] came in and told us we were the saddest defense in the Big 10," cornerback Todd Avery said. "That got our defense going."

Going so they would hold tailback Lorenzo White, who chewed them up with 103 first-half yards, to just 19 in the second half. That, eight quarterback sacks, and an inspired offensive performance turned the tables in a 30-17 Illinois victory—the Illini's first win away from Memorial Stadium in nine tries. Chris White, who kicked three field goals, became the Big 10 career field goal leader with his second, a 27-yard shot, early in the fourth quarter.

The next week the Illini had a 21-point first-quarter burst in an easy 38-25 win over Wisconsin.

Michigan

That brought Michigan, reeling from a

last-second 12-10 loss at Iowa the week before in a battle for the nation's No. 1 ranking, to Champaign. The Illini came within a fingernail of sticking in the Big 10 race.

For more than three quarters, the two teams pushed each other all over the field with only a field goal apiece to show for it. Then, in a typical Schembechler drive in the final minutes, Michigan pushed the ball on the ground from their 20 to the Illinois 12. The Wolverines' Gerald White fumbled.

The Illini's Bob Sebring recovered, and Trudeau went to work against Michigan's vaunted defense. He hit Stephen Pierce twice and scrambled to put Illinois in position for a game-winning field goal. The clock approached zero. Chris White lined up from 37 yards. Robert Markus described what happened next in the *Chicago Tribune*:

"The finger of fate is attached to the left hand of an obscure Michigan linebacker named Dieter Heren. It rose from a desperate mass of sweating, shoving, gasping humanity here Saturday to deflect a Chris White field-goal attempt and alter the course of destiny.

"With Illinois on the brink of seizing control of the Big 10 race, Heren got just a tiny piece of White's game-ending 37-yard field-goal try. It was enough. With 76,397 wrung-out fans and members of both teams staring in silent agony, the ball continued on its course for what seemed an eternity.

"Then it hit the crossbar and fell back on the field, and a large share of Illinois' hopes and dreams came crashing down with it."

In this 3-3 tie, Trudeau eclipsed Jerry Rhome's NCAA record for consecutive passes thrown without an interception. Under the circumstances, however, he was not impressed. The Illini that day felt like losers.

"This is awful," Mike White said. "I don't ever remember feeling worse after a football game. I feel sick. I'm devastated."

"It feels like a loss," Chris White said.

But it wasn't. The Illini went to Iowa the next week. That was a loss.

Iowa, Indiana, Northwestern

Chuck Long threw a 49-yard touchdown pass to Robert Smith on the sixth play of the game. That was just the beginning. There was still a minute left in the first quarter when Iowa led 35-0. It was 49-0 at the half and 59-0 when it ended. The third worst defeat in Illinois history was finally, mercifully over. There were nine turnovers, including four interceptions, a mark that ended Trudeau's NCAA record at 215.

Florida Citrus Bowl representatives watched that game in Iowa City. They quickly lost interest in Illinois. The question was no longer whether the Illini would go to the Rose Bowl, but would 4-4-1 Illinois be good enough to go to any bowl?

Chris White and the Fighting Illini after the 1985 Ohio State victory

HAIL TO THE ORANGE AND BLUE!

Coach White lobbied that they were, and the Illini kept their hopes alive with a 41-24 win over Indiana, stretching their home winning streak to 13. Rooks ran for 163 yards and three touchdowns to move him past Grabowski as Illinois' all-time leading rusher. He would finish with 2,828.

The next week the Illini stated their final argument for a bowl bid with Trudeau throwing three touchdown passes, including a pair to Williams, in a 45-20 win at Northwestern. The game ended 15 minutes after sunset. Williams caught seven passes for 109 yards to finish his regular-season career with 250 catches, 11 shy of Howard Twilley's all-time NCAA record.

ended with Illinois fans groping for rose-colored glasses.

"The glasses needed windshield wipers. Indeed, the Illini's long-awaited day in the sun turned out to be just another day in the rain.

"A dismal season ended on an equally dismal day in Atlanta Fulton-County Stadium. It ended with the Illini coming up short time and time again in a 31-29 Peach Bowl loss to Army.

"It ended with four turnovers leading to 24 Army points. It ended with a pair of failed two-point conversions. It ended with a field-goal attempt hitting the crossbar. It ended with Army, a wishbone team that supposedly couldn't pass, burning the Illini for two touchdowns on

The Illini at the 1985 Peach Bowl

The Peach Bowl

The Peach Bowl went for Illinois' lobby. The Illini would play Army on December 31 in Atlanta. They were back on television . . . a mixed blessing. Joel Bierig described that cold, rainy New Year's Eve day in Fulton County Stadium for the *Chicago Sun-Times*:

"A season that began with visions of roses

halfback options.

"It ended with the Illini (6-5-1) counting statistics and second-guesses and Army (9-3) counting heroes."

Trudeau completed 38 of 55 passes for 401 yards (Peach Bowl records) and three touchdowns. Williams caught seven passes for 109 yards and two scores. Chris White, who finished his career as Illinois' all-time leading scorer with 254 points, hit the crossbar from 40 yards out with less than three minutes to play. Army's Peel Chronister intercepted two Trudeau passes and broke up Illinois' last-ditch two-point conversion try that would have forged a tie.

On the bright side, Illinois finished with its fifth straight winning year, a first since 1929; its 37 wins over that span hadn't been seen since 1905, and its fifth straight finish of fourth place or better in the Big 10 hadn't been accomplished since 1911.

Trudeau owned three NCAA passing records, including a record 734 pass completions in three seasons. He finished the season with 2,938 yards and 15 touchdowns and his Illinois career with 8,146 yards and 51 touchdowns.

Williams, who caught 85 passes for 1,047 yards and eight touchdowns, wound up as a two-time consensus All-American, the first Illinois player to earn that distinction since Butkus. His 3,195 career receiving yards placed No. 4 on the all-time NCAA list. Williams, Rooks, Juriga, Swoope, Chris White, Guy Teafatiller, and Mark Tagart all earned All-Big 10 accolades.

All the veterans would be gone in 1986. Gone too would be Illinois' winning ways. First, sophomore quarterback Jim Bennett, an Illinois high school player from West Aurora, the centerpiece of Illinois' heralded—but disappointing—1984 recruiting class and heir apparent to Mike White's quarterback crown, recognized that big-time football wasn't for him and left school.

Players Missing, Suspended

When fall drills opened, nearly a quarter of the players who had been expected to report were nowhere to be found. White wasn't telling anybody why. At least two of the players were suspended because of drug use, and a handful of others were in academic trouble. Many of the missing were fringe players that White simply didn't want getting in the way.

Eighteen players would end up suspended for the season. The whole mess turned into a public relations fiasco.

Bennett's departure left the quarterback's job to fifth-year senior Shane Lamb, another California junior college transfer. His backup would be a red-shirt freshman from near St. Louis, Brian Menkhausen. Offensively, White tried to switch the Illini to an option, but that was shelved when Lamb was hurt in the season's third game.

Lack of Confidence

The season opener looked all right when Lamb passed for 223 yards and a touchdown in a 23-0 win over a weak Louisville team. However, in the next three weeks, Illinois had to face Southern California, Nebraska, and Ohio State. The Illini lost all three, 31-16 to USC, 59-14 to Nebraska in front of a home crowd of 75,865, and 14-0 at Ohio State.

"I was secretly hoping that this would be a bowl team, but we lacked the confidence," White said late that season. "There hasn't been the right circumstances. So many things would have to happen early. We would have to beat USC or Nebraska and then probably Ohio State. That's what didn't happen."

With those debacles finally past, the next week Ray Wilson scored from three yards out with little more than a minute left to push Illinois past Purdue, 34-27. In that game, Lamb returned to pass for 252 yards, and Menkhausen added 127 yards and a touchdown.

However, it was Purdue's quarterback who ultimately would spark the most interest for Illinois fans. Boilermaker freshman Jeff George, running for his life behind an inexperienced offensive line, completed 21 of 46 passes for 217 yards.

Then came a 29-21 loss to Michigan State, a 15-9 loss at Wisconsin, and a 69-21 humiliation at the hands of Michigan, as the Wolverines scored 42 unanswered second-half points.

A Two-game Winning Streak

Illinois looked bad in the newspapers. It looked bad on the field too. The Illini made another appearance in the "Bottom 10" rankings. A 20-16 win at Iowa the next week, a game

Coach White gives instructions to Jack Trudeau

in which the Illini entered as 17-point under-dogs, helped some. Menkhausen threw a 54-yard touchdown pass to Stephen Pierce, Keith Jones ran for 97 yards, and the Illini defense gave up just 34 yards on the ground.

The next week Illinois enjoyed its only two-game winning streak of the season as Jones rushed for 100 yards and Jerrold Reese caught 8 passes for 120 yards in a 21-16 win at Indiana.

The 1986 season would close with North-western at Memorial Stadium. The Wildcats' come-from-behind 23-18 victory caused months of frustration to spill over the edge. "We've been playing patty-cake football," White said of that 4-7 season, 3-5 and tied for sixth in the Big 10.

The recruiting woes of probation-scarred seasons had taken their toll. In part because of off-the-field problems, White was not able to focus his attention on high school recruits. A winter of both soul-searching and changes were in order.

First, White brought in six new coaches, including for the first time an offensive coordina-tor. Dwain Painter would run the offense, How-ard Tippett the defense, and White would free himself to oversee a program many felt was becoming out of control. He would also, for the first time, make himself freely available to the media.

"We hope to get the kids feeling good about themselves," White said.

New Approaches

White and the Illini tried the feel-good approach for 1987. They got some good news when George, the much-heralded quarterback who fled Purdue when pass-happy coach Leon Burtnett was fired in favor of Fred Akers, announced he wanted to play for Mike White and Illinois. He would not, of course, be eligible until 1988.

So the Illini had new coaches, new attitudes, and a new approach, but the same quarterback troubles. Menkhausen, who had thrown for 991 yards and four touchdowns as a freshman, was No. 1 at the position, while junior college transfer Scott Mohr and holdover Peter Freund would challenge.

Despite a broken foot suffered by 1986 MVP Keith Jones on the opening day of practice, there was still a feel-good feeling around pre-season drills.

White also felt good because there was no Nebraska-caliber team on the non-conference schedule to run up lopsided scores and shatter any fragile confidence the Illini might have.

A Rough Beginning

The happy feelings dissolved, though, in the rain and humidity in the opener at North Carolina. Illinois led 7-3 late in the first half and might have stretched the lead when the Tar Heels were forced to punt deep in their own territory. The snap was low. Illinois' Howard Griffith and John Wachter closed in to block the kick, but missed it. Tar Heel punter Kenny Miller, who ran like he had a load of pianos on his back, somehow eluded Illini tacklers until Darryl Usher ran him down at Illinois' 14-yard line. The Tar Heels went on to score a late second-quarter touchdown, and then they watched the Illini unravel both offensively and defensively in the third quarter en route to a 34-14 blowout.

The next week, running back Ken Thomas delighted a crowd of 70,060—the last of 28 consecutive sellouts in Memorial Stadium—with a third-quarter 57-yard touchdown dash, but Arizona State rallied for a 21-7 victory.

"Brian's taking too much blame and he's trying to overcompensate," White said of his first-string tosser. "Consequently we're not getting the performance out of the quarterback position we'd like."

Mohr in Charge

The following week Mohr was at the controls. He completed ten of 19 for 187 yards with two interceptions, and the Illini won 20-10 over East Carolina.

Two weeks later, Ohio State came to town. The Buckeyes scored early after Jones, making his first appearance of the season, fumbled inside the Illinois 20. Despite an in-

The 1987 Fighting Illini

spired Illini defensive performance, Ohio State led 10-0 deep into the fourth quarter when Mohr—who would complete 24 of 42 passes for 243 yards—threw an 11-yard touchdown pass to Anthony Williams. Doug Higgins' kick failed, so when Illinois drove inside the Ohio State 20 late in the fourth quarter, the Illini had to have a touchdown. They ran out of downs, and the Buckeyes held on to win 10-6.

The next week the Illini took a 1-3 record to Purdue. The rain was there too. So was one of the worst Illinois offensive performances ever seen. The Illini lost eight of ten fumbles, including one inside the Purdue 1-yard line, and many came when Mohr couldn't pick up the center snap in the face of a Purdue blitz. Meanwhile, Jonathan Briggs kicked 44-, 23-, and 37-yard field goals to give the Boilermakers a 9-3 victory, the first for Akers. Illinois' ten fumbles matched their own 39-year-old Big 10 record.

"This is rock bottom," said White. "Basically, I've lost faith in them. It's a total loss. Obviously, we have to give them leadership, hopefully a plan that will allow them to finish off the season with some enthusiasm and give them a chance to win some games.

"Until today I had a lot of faith in this team in terms of improvement, the will to win, the opportunity to get the job done. Obviously, that's gone."

Things looked up a little bit the next week when Higgins' 34-yard field goal in the final minute pushed Illinois to a 16-14 win over Wisconsin. Mohr and Usher combined on 32- and 38-yard touchdown passes.

Quarterback Rotation

The next week the Illini had a chance to salvage everything when they outplayed Michigan State in East Lansing. Even that almost went up in smoke until 6-foot-7 defensive end Scott Davis blocked a Spartan field goal attempt in the final seconds to preserve a 14-14 tie with the team that would win the Big 10 and Rose Bowl championships.

Illinois' offense was abysmal. The Illini were rotating quarterbacks sometimes as often as every series. The offensive line was in a state of confusion, having abandoned the run-blocking concepts it had been taught earlier in order to return to pass-blocking.

The offense looked a little better the next week when it scored two touchdowns in four minutes and got 45- and 52-yard field goals from Higgins in a 27-17 victory over Minnesota.

The following week, Illinois grabbed a 16-3 lead against bowl-bound Indiana, but backup quarterback Dave Kramme and the Hoosiers adjusted to the Illini's furious pass rush with four second-half touchdowns en route to a 34-22 victory.

Downhill Slide

Michigan was coming to Champaign and, despite a 3-5-1 record, maybe the Illini could salvage something. The Illini led 14-7 going into the final quarter, and they still had a four-point lead after Mike Gillette's field goal with less than seven minutes to play. With the Wolverines down to their last breath, a fourth-and-eight situation, Michigan quarterback Demetrius Brown passed the Wolverines to a first down and the Wolverines marched 60 yards in the final seconds to win 17-14. It was the first time a White-coached Illinois team had lost a lead it held going into the final quarter.

The Illini seemed not the least bit interested in their season finale, a 28-10 loss to inspired Northwestern.

Illinois finished 3-7-1, the same as White's first Illini squad seven years earlier. Worse, Illinois ranked last in the league in both scoring and total offense. White, whose contract ran through the 1990 season, was given a vote of confidence by Stoner, but with attendance dwindling, another losing season could easily cost White his job.

Jeff George would be eligible in 1988 and, fair or not, he was being hailed as a program savior.

White's Resignation

"I think at one time, there was a Mike White edge," White said in a season post-mortem. "That sure as heck isn't prevalent now, but if in fact there ever was such an edge, that has to resurface. We have to find out the circumstances that happened eight years ago. If there was something we did right, we have to find it again."

Only days after that statement, what Mike White and Illinois found was yet another letter from the NCAA alleging more recruiting violations.

Most were not crucial, but one, arranging to pay a hotel bill for a prospective recruit by an assistant coach, was quite serious. This, the third run-in with Big 10 and NCAA officials in eight years, was more than the administration could tolerate. In January, 1988, Mike White resigned under pressure.

He left a team that would face another year of NCAA probation—although this time, in part because Illinois moved quickly to remove White, there would be no sanctions. He left a team that would, for the first time in three years, have a first-rate quarterback. He left a team with talent on both sides of the line of scrimmage.

Mike and Chris White celebrate with the Fighting Illini

By the end of 1979, the Illinois football program had fallen to its lowest point in decades.

The last three coaches had compiled a combined record of 43-83-2, and Illinois failed to win in its last 13 home games. Attendance was at an all-time low, and both fans and prospective high school athletes were losing interest in the program.

Neale Stoner looked to California for a coach who could turn the program around under such adverse conditions. Mike White had been an integral part of two similar reversals, first as offensive coordinator at Stanford and then as head coach at his alma mater, Cal-Berkeley.

White was a master of the passing game and a whirlwind recruiter. While he stirred up controversy by bringing a number of California junior college transfers to the UI campus, the flamboyant Californian had the personality and drive to put fans back in the Memorial Stadium seats and provide them with victories.

Illinois became the dominant passing school in the Big Ten during the 1980s as three California quarterbacks—Wilson, Eason, and Trudeau—put their names high in the conference record book. Much of Illinois' success in the 1980s can be traced to White and the California Connection.

Loren Tate

19

NEW COACH, NEW CENTURY

"Illinois football is today in a position where we enjoy a great deal of prestige and recognition nationally as well as in the Big 10. There is still a lot of work for us to do to establish ourselves as a perennial favorite for the Big 10 crown, but that's one of our objectives."

—Coach John Mackovic

While White still sat in the coach's office, his staff was rounding up what appeared to be an outstanding high school recruiting class. When he was pushed out, less than three weeks remained before those recruits could sign binding national letters of intent. Nobody knew what would happen to them. Stoner knew, however, that Illinois had to find a coach quickly. Presi-

dent Stanley Ikenberry and Chancellor Morton Weir were among those insisting that the new coach bring with him a reputation beyond reproach.

They talked seriously with Boston College coach Jack Bicknell, but Bicknell did not want to leave his school in the lurch so close to signing day. Former Northwestern coach Dennis Green was interviewed, as was Ohio State offensive coordinator Jim Colletto and Illinois defensive coordinator Howard Tippett.

John Mackovic was also interviewed. Mackovic had been out of coaching for more than a year since he was fired as head coach of the NFL's Kansas City Chiefs just weeks after that franchise had made its first post-season appearance in 15 years. Little more than two weeks after White quit, Mackovic, who had been seriously considered for the Illinois job eight years earlier, was the man Stoner recommended. Six days before signing day, he was

John Mackovic with Morton Weir and Neale Stoner, accepting head coaching position

formally introduced to the Illinois media as the school's 21st head football coach.

"My responsibility as the head coach is to ensure that everyone who works in that [recruiting] process—everyone—understands and appreciates that we will operate accordingly with the rules and that the responsibility for that is mine ultimately, but it's each individual's responsibility," Mackovic said that day.

John Mackovic grew up in Barberton, Ohio. After quarterbacking Wake Forest for three seasons, Mackovic signed on as a graduate assistant to Bo Schembechler at Miami of Ohio in 1965. For the next 13 years, he served with a number of teams as an assistant coach. He served one season at his high school alma mater and the rest in the college ranks.

Mackovic took over as head coach at Wake Forest in 1978, directing a school that had won just 13 games in six seasons to a Tangerine Bowl invitation in 1979. After three years at Wake Forest, he moved into the NFL, working with quarterbacks for Tom Landry. Under Landry he was given considerable credit for the development of Dallas Cowboy quarterback Danny White. Before the 1983 season, Mackovic, at 39 became head coach of the Kansas City Chiefs. Four years later, the Chiefs were in the playoffs, but Mackovic was out of a job.

"It hurt. I would be less than honest if I didn't say it hurt," Mackovic said of his dismissal. "It didn't hurt just me and my family, but it hurt a lot of people. But we also learned that we can't dwell on the past. We try to learn from it, try to go on our way. It doesn't erase it and perhaps the best way to feel good about yourself is to go on and continue to achieve things perhaps someplace in another vein."

There was plenty in need of achievement at Illinois.

Building Cautious Optimism

The Illini would land only nine players, none of whom White had recruited. Of White's staff, only Bob Gambold and Tim Harkness stayed on. However, the NCAA was kind in its evaluation, giving Illinois a single year of probation without sanctions attached. Mackovic managed to assemble a staff by the time spring practice opened in mid-March. White had left a talented but very young team.

From the beginning, Mackovic spelled out his goals for Illinois.

"At our first meeting with the players, I laid out for them what I felt were two basic responsibilities of the student-athlete in our program," he said. "The first would be to make sure that each member did in fact graduate. Secondly, each member of our team would put in the necessary work and effort to help us have a winning program."

Mackovic inherited, of course, the much-heralded Jeff George. He had running back Keith Jones, back at full strength after recovering from a broken foot, and wide receiver Steven Williams, the last of the three brothers. He had defensive back Glenn Cobb, one of the league's best. He had defensive lineman Moe Gardner, who had distinguished himself as one of the league's top young players as a freshman in 1987.

Even though 13 sophomores and freshmen were listed among the Illini's top 22 players, there was some cause for cautious optimism as the 1988 pre-season drills and non-conference games approached. Mackovic's positive attitude and his strategy of dividing the

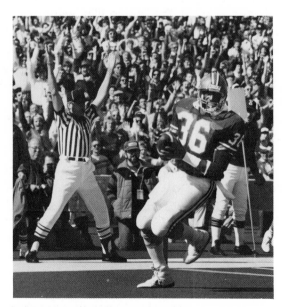

Keith Jones scoring an Illini TD

season into a series of stages sparked some of the hopeful attitude among Illini fans.

That optimism was shaken to its core in front of a home crowd of 54,458 in the season opener when Washington State ran up 601 yards in total offense, including 382 rushing yards, and scored virtually at will against a confused Illinois defense. It was a rout, 44-7. About the only bright spot for Illinois was that sophomore fullback Howard Griffith ran for 85 yards, including a 53-yard second-quarter touchdown run. Reality had set in.

"Many times you can't compare what you have until you play other teams so our first spring was an exciting spring of learning. Everyone had high expectations, but when we stepped on the field, we were thoroughly defeated," Mackovic said about the debut. "I believe then our players realized the stark reality of how much work and effort was needed.

"We looked after that game—of course it was our first game together—at least as a point of reference for everyone. It was a point for our coaches, for me as head coach and certainly a point of reference for our players as to where we were lacking, what needed to be done to be more competitive. We set out to do those the very next week."

Mackovic, defensive coordinator Lou Tepper, and the staff spent much of the next week bolstering both the defense and the team's confidence before the young Illini went on the road to nationally ranked Arizona State. That game, which didn't begin until nearly 10 p.m., central daylight time, opened in 102-degree heat. On the field, it looked like another rout as Sun Devil quarterback Danny Ford drove Arizona State 69 yards for a touchdown on its first possession.

However, the Illini came back, driving 82 yards for the tying score. George and Williams hooked up for completions of 21, 18, and seven yards before George hit tight end Jeff Finke with a 4-yard touchdown, George's first scoring pass in an Illinois uniform. The Illini defense, led by Gardner and linebackers Steve Glasson and Darrick Brownlow, showed signs of huge improvement.

Arizona State did get second- and third-

Jeff George attempts a pass

quarter touchdowns to go ahead 21-7, but the Illini came back with a 78-yard third quarter drive, capped when Jones hit Williams for a score on a halfback option pass. Then twice in the fourth quarter, including a drive when Peter Freund relieved an injured George at quarterback, Illinois drove deep into Sun Devil territory. Yet the game was a 21-16 loss, dropping the Illini to 0-2.

"Although we did not win, we definitely made strides forward. We established confidence that we were going to play a tougher brand of football," Mackovic said.

Firing a Winning Streak

Freshly charged, Illinois got its first Mackovic victory a week later when Jones scored on runs of 54 and 53 yards and Griffith galloped 78 yards—the longest Illinois run since 1965—in 88-degree temperatures to bring the Illini a 35-24 win at home over Utah.

Jones ran for a career-high 186 yards; Griffith gained 148; George passed for 165. The Illini totalled 513 yards in offense. Defensively, sophomore Brownlow continued to impress with 14 tackles.

Illinois had two weeks to think about the next stage of Mackovic's plan and the Big 10 opener at Ohio State, where the Illini hadn't won since 1967. What a way for Mackovic to celebrate his 45th birthday.

George dissected the Buckeye defense for 224 yards and a 24-yard touchdown to Steven Williams. Pat Donnelly recovered a fumbled punt snap for a touchdown. Safety Mark Kelly intercepted a fumble and sacked Ohio State quarterback Greg Frey twice. The Illinois defense allowed only 38 rushing yards as the Illini dominated 31-12.

Now, the Illini were starting to believe. The next week Jones and Griffith each ran for more than 100 yards, the Illini defense giving up just six first downs and 54 total yards. George passed for 152 yards and a touchdown in his first appearance against his old school as the Illini recorded a 20-0 shutout of Purdue.

"I had a lot of dreams about this game," George said of the win that gave Illinois its first three-game winning streak since 1983. "I'm just glad it's over with, glad we came out on top."

The streak ran to four the next week as George passed for 306 yards and the Illini

Wide Receiver Steven Williams sprints downfield after a completion

"I always have remembered my 10th birthday because my mother bought me a football suit, and since that time I've either been playing or coaching this game," Mackovic said afterward. "I don't think I have had a more memorable birthday since that time until today."

scored 27 points in a nine-minute, second-half span en route to a 34-6 rout at Wisconsin.

Amazingly, it seemed, 4-2, 3-0 Illinois shared the Big 10 lead with Indiana. The Illini defense had given up just one touchdown in ten quarters.

Mike Bellamy with game-winning catch against Indiana

Reality and Rose Bowl Dreams

Reality set in the next week when defending Big 10 and Rose Bowl champion Michigan State spotted Illinois an early 14-0 lead, then capitalized on a fumbled punt and an Illinois defense that suddenly sprang leaks for a 28-21 victory in front of an Illinois Homecoming crowd of 65,771.

Reality nearly turned into disaster a week later in the Metrodome at Minnesota when the Illini watched a 24-7 third-quarter lead dissolve into a 27-24 deficit before Doug Higgins kicked a game-tying 44-yard field goal as time ran out.

What would happen now to the upstart Illini? A crowd of 66,201 braved a cold biting wind when Indiana came to town the next week to find out. Most fans thought they'd seen enough when Hoosier cornerback Erick Coleman stole the ball from Jones and returned it 43 yards for a touchdown that put Indiana up 20-9 with less than four minutes to play. The stands were just about empty when George drove the Illini 80 yards in 1:27, capped by a fourth-down 21-yard touchdown pass to Shawn Wax, to make the score 20-15.

Moments later, fewer still saw cornerback Chris Green meet Indiana quarterback Dave Schnell head-on at the Illinois 30-yard line. Had the Illini fans stayed, they would have seen the football pop out of Schnell's grasp and into the arms of Illinois linebacker Julyon Brown with 1:58 to play. With 26 seconds left, George flipped a 5-yard touchdown pass to Mike Bellamy that gave the Illini an amazing 21-20 victory. Even more amazing, Illinois would go to Michigan the next week with the Rose Bowl at stake.

"It's one of the greatest comebacks I've ever been around, I guarantee you that," Mackovic said.

Much was made of Barberton, Ohio, that week, hometown to both Mackovic and Schembechler. Much was made of the considerably more friendly relationship between the two schools with Mackovic instead of White running the Illinois show. However, in front of a Michigan Stadium crowd of 105,714, the young Illini were not ready to match Michigan's strength. Leroy Hoard ran for 137 yards and two touchdowns, and the Wolverines clinched their fourth Rose Bowl berth of the 1980s, 38-9.

"I don't believe we were prepared for that game in the sense that I'm not sure everybody understood what it was going to take to become the champions," Mackovic said. "We weren't ready and that only means that our young players had not been in that position before."

Mackovic and Schembechler share a moment before the Illinois-Michigan game

John Mackovic receives 1988 Big Ten Coach of the Year award

Birmingham Bound

Even though the Illini wouldn't go to the Rose Bowl, Illinois officials were negotiating a bowl bid. The Illini signed to go against Southern California in the first-ever Glasnost Bowl, scheduled for Labor Day weekend, 1989, in Moscow.

The 5-5-1 Illini were hardly out of the post-season bowl picture. All they needed for an official invitation from the All American Bowl in Birmingham, Alabama, was a home-field win over Northwestern in the season finale.

That prospect looked like a piece of cake when Illinois drove 84 yards, capped by a slick 11-yard halfback option touchdown pass from Jones to George to put Illinois up 7-0 early in the first quarter. It was Jones' fourth career touchdown pass. Before the first period was out, the Illini had a 14-0 lead, but Northwestern's Ira

Adler kicked two 35-yard second-period field goals and added a 37-yarder in the third quarter. Suddenly, Illinois could do nothing offensively against the Wildcat defense.

Illinois clung to a 14-9 lead in the final minute when Wildcat quarterback Greg Bradshaw, working from the Illinois 24, hit tight end Bob Griswold with a fourth-down pass near the goal line. Safety Marlon Primous, who had broken up a Wildcat pass in the end zone on the previous play, grabbed Griswold and hung on for dear life, both keeping Griswold out of the end zone and forcing the ball loose. Brownlow recovered on the Illinois 2-yard line.

Somehow the Illini had escaped to finish 6-4-1 and earn the bowl bid. Jones passed the 1,000-yard mark, becoming only the fourth Illini back to pass that barrier in a single season. His career total of 2,194 yards put him No. 3 on the all-time list. Mackovic's six victories were the most for a first-year Illinois coach since Ray Eliot went 6-4 in 1942. Mackovic was named Big 10 Coach of the Year.

Birmingham couldn't be mistaken for Pasadena, but it sure was a lot nicer than spending the holidays in the sleet and snow in Champaign-Urbana. The Illini defense, however, looked as if it had slipped on the ice when Florida's All-American runningback Emmitt Smith ran around end for a 55-yard touchdown on the game's opening play from scrimmage. Fortunately, the Illini shook that off, and after Jones broke free for a 30-yard score early in the second quarter, the two teams went into the half tied 7-7. They were still tied at 7 when Higgins' 44-yard field goal put Illinois up 10-7 with 8:55 left in the game.

This night would not end Illinois' 25-year post-season victory drought. The Gators got a turnover at the Illinois 26-yard line, and after Smith's dramatic 16-yard gain on a third-down situation, he scored from the 2 with 4:28 left in the game. By this point Jones was on the sidelines with a sprained ankle, but George drove the Illini to the Florida 35 in the final minutes before they ran out of downs. Florida was a 14-10 winner.

The curtain fell on Mackovic's first season, a 6-5-1 finish. Seniors Jones, Cobb, and offensive lineman Mark McGowan would earn some All-Big 10 accolades. So would George, Williams, Gardner, Finke, Brownlow, Primous and defensive lineman Mel Agee. All of the latter group would return in 1989, a season that would see Illinois seriously touted for top 20 and Rose Bowl consideration.

Athletic Director Mackovic and Glasnost

First, though, Mackovic assumed the duties of athletic director after Stoner was forced to resign in the wake of allegations of misuse of Athletic Association personnel, funds, and equipment. The scandal brought an end to the 97-year-old autonomous Athletic Association. By mid-1989 athletics had been moved under the university umbrella and retitled the Division of Intercollegiate Athletics.

One of Mackovic's first duties in 1989 was a trip to Moscow to check out Moscow's 50,000-seat Dynamo Stadium, site of the proposed Glasnost Bowl.

"One of the things I've always dreamed of is to take American-style football around the world," Mackovic said at the time.

The Moscow game, however, which was to have been televised worldwide, fell through in midsummer. Field conditions, accommodations, and logistics couldn't meet the standards of major college football. The game against Southern California, ranked No. 1 in many preseason polls, was rescheduled for Labor Day at the Los Angeles Coliseum.

Opening the Second Mack-Season

To accommodate a date with USC, Illinois had to drop its scheduled home opener with Cincinnati. It also had to cancel Tailgreat for 1989.

Barring something unforeseen, with 18 starters back, Illinois would be better in 1989. There was experience, but there was not much depth.

George, who had passed for 2,451 yards the year before, was seasoned and had six of his top seven receivers back. The offensive line, anchored by center Curt Lovelace and guard Tim Simpson, had considerable experience. Keith Jones was gone, but fullback Howard Griffith returned. Also the Illini had re-

Darrick Brownlow awaits the snap

New Coach, New Century

cruited a pair of highly touted high school running backs in Steve Feagin and Wagner Lester.

Defensively, Gardner and Agee anchored a fearsome line. Brownlow, who'd averaged 14 tackles a game as a sophomore, and Steve Glasson led the linebackers, and the secondary, even with the loss of Cobb, had three returning starters. Higgins, who converted all 27 extra points and ten of 14 field goals, was back too. So was punter Brian Menkhausen.

The early schedule did Illinois no favors with a road game at Colorado following the opener at USC. Colorado would go on to play for the national championship. "We felt in our own minds that if we could split with USC and Colorado, that would be a good start," Mackovic said.

In its opener, Illinois would run into a rock-solid Trojan defense that had three returning All-Americans. George and the Illini found out just how solid that defense was as they couldn't move the ball for more than three quarters. Yet George set the tone for this season when, with Illinois trailing 13-0 midway through the fourth quarter, he connected with Shawn Wax, who grabbed the tipped pass and ran into the end zone, good for a 53-yard score.

Moe Gardner

After a Trojan punt, the Illini got one more try and George pieced together a 10-play, 80-yard drive, capped by a 20-yard scoring pass to Steven Williams with 2:19 left. The Illini were 14-13 winners. They earned their first appearance among the nation's top 10 since the Rose Bowl season.

Their giddiness crashed in the Rocky Mountains the next weekend, however, as the Buffaloes rolled up 475 yards in offense and crushed Illinois 38-7. This one had Mackovic upset, not so much because of the result, but because of the statements floating around Boulder, attributed to George, downgrading the Colorado program. George, of course, denied it all and Mackovic was so worked up that he offered to personally sell tickets for the September 15, 1990, rematch in Champaign.

"The week against Colorado brought everybody back to reality of how hard you have to work," Mackovic said. "That was a shocking week and it was good for us."

Victory, Vandalism, and Injury

The Illini took out their frustrations the next week on Utah State, in front of a crowd of 61,553. The Illini gave up three first downs, 65 rushing yards, and only 17 yards passing in a 41-2 rout. Offensively four Illinois backs, including little-used Errol Shavers, gained at least 64 yards as the Illini racked up 507 yards of offense, including 322 on the ground.

That was the Illini's first home game of the season. For a time it looked like it might be the last. Vandals broke into the stadium later that night, setting fire to the artificial turf and destroying nearly half the playing surface. Amazingly, representatives of AstroTurf Industries got the damaged turf replaced in time for the Ohio State game two weeks later.

The good news that day was that everybody got to play. The bad news was that backup quarterback Jeff Kinney would be diagnosed with a blood clot under his arm and would miss the rest of the season. If anything were to happen to George, only little-used redshirt freshman Jason Verduzco was in reserve.

Something did happen to George in the

Football field damaged by vandals

34-14 victory. George completed 12 of 20 passes for 130 yards, and Griffith ran for 117 yards. The Illini added a little sleight of hand to their offensive repertoire when wide receiver Williams threw a 34-yard touchdown pass to fellow wide receiver Mike Bellamy. Defensively, Gardner racked up nine tackles and a fumble recovery and was named the Associated Press Midwest Defensive Player of the Week.

"Perhaps the most rewarding thing as we headed into the Big 10 season was that this year we knew teams were waiting for us," Mackovic said. "But also people were beginning to talk about Illinois as a real favorite, a serious contender for the title." That set up the next week's date at Purdue, marking George's only appearance at his old school in an Illinois uniform.

Big 10 opener against Ohio State in front of a Memorial Stadium crowd of 69,088, largest to date of the Mackovic era. Five minutes into the game, George didn't get up after a sack by Ohio State's Aaron Spellman. Verduzco,though, rose to the occasion, completing nine of 14 passes for 126 yards, and led the Illini on two scoring drives that gave Illinois a 10-7 halftime lead.

George, limping on a sore knee, came back for the second half and the Illini rolled to a

Serious Rose Bowl Contenders

He came in pumped up, directing the Illini on an 80-yard game-opening scoring drive. The offense looked good then. It would have looked good all day long except that penalties stalled drive after Illinois drive. The Illini piled up 421 yards in offense. The defense held Purdue's run-and-shoot to just 144 yards, but thanks in large measure to their own mistakes, the Illini didn't wrap this 14-2 victory up until they marched

Mackovic on the sidelines with Mike Bellamy and Frank Hartley

New Coach, New Century

80 yards in the fourth quarter, capped by Griffith's 1-yard touchdown plunge.

Michigan State

Now Illinois was 4-1, 2-0 in the Big 10. A win over Michigan State at East Lansing the next weekend would firmly establish the Illini as serious Rose Bowl contenders.

A national cable television audience got a first-hand look at one of those miracles that the Illini pulled out of the hat. Illinois drove 75 yards on its first possession of the day, keyed by a 53-yard pass play from George to Bellamy.

After that drive, however, the offense sputtered. The Spartans drew even early in the third quarter after returning the kickoff to the Illinois 9-yard line, then went ahead 10-7 on John Langloh's 21-yard fourth-quarter field goal. With time running out, Illinois' offense couldn't move and was forced to give the ball up on downs with just 1:47 left.

On Michigan State's first offensive play, linebacker Brian Williams separated Spartan running back Hyland Hickson from the football and defensive back Quintin Parker pounced on the loose ball at the Spartan 35. Three pass plays later, George and Bellamy hooked up again in the end zone from nine yards out and Illinois was a winner, 14-10.

George called an audible for the clincher.

"Down so close you're going to get some bump and run [coverage] and he just lobbed it over the top on the quick fade," Mackovic explained. "That's where he's good and our team responds to that."

For his part, George earned United Press International's Offensive Player of the Week. Gardner, with 12 tackles, a sack, and a fumble recovery, was again the Associated Press Defensive Player of the Week.

"That game I think the players and coaches will remember for a long time," Mackovic said. "It was such an emotional and hard-hitting game, everyone fought for just a yard."

Wisconsin

There was no lack of excitement the next week in Champaign when the Illini and Wisconsin combined for 15 points and 257 yards in the game's first 53 seconds.

The Badgers' Fred Owens ran the opening kickoff 96 yards for a touchdown, but the Illini blocked the extra point attempt and, under a new NCAA rule, could advance the football. Parker did just that, scrambling an NCAA-record 100 yards for a bizarre two-point defensive conversion that left Illinois trailing 6-2 just 14 seconds into the game.

After the Badgers' kickoff, the Illini needed just two plays to take the lead. George and

1989 Illinois football team

HAIL TO THE ORANGE AND BLUE!

Griffith hooked up on a 45-yard touchdown. Things settled down considerably, however, and the Illini defense allowed only 94 passing yards, 145 rushing, and one more field goal. George, meanwhile, completed 17 of 28 passes for 214 yards and three touchdowns in a 32-9 final.

This time Parker, who also had 13 tackles, a sack, and an interception, was the Associated Press' choice for Defensive Player of the Week.

Iowa

That sent the Illini to Iowa for their first matchup with the Hawkeyes since 1986. A win in Iowa City would set up a Rose Bowl showdown with Michigan the following week.

Nobody scored during the game's first 25 minutes, but the Illini made sure of the showdown, running off 21 points in the first half's final five minutes.

Glasson, who received that week's nod as the Associated Press Defensive Player of the Week with 11 tackles and two interceptions, and his defensive mates held the Hawkeyes scoreless four times after they'd driven inside the 20. The Illini breezed to a 31-7 victory.

Eight games into the season, Illinois was ranked No. 8 in the nation, and a genuine Rose Bowl showdown was in the offing.

Michigan

Sportswriters spent part of the week leading to the game in Barberton, Ohio, getting the scoop from the hometown on both Mackovic and Schembechler. No game had been more eagerly awaited in Champaign-Urbana since Michigan had come to town in 1983.

A crowd of 73,067—largest since 1986—and a national television audience turned out on this unseasonably pleasant November afternoon. A defensive battle was on tap, they all thought, as both teams boasted nationally ranked defensive units. But the Wolverines' Tony Boles dashed 73 yards to the Illinois 1-yard line on the second play from scrimmage, and Michigan scored on its next play.

Undaunted, George directed the Illini on

Moe Gardner

an 85-yard scoring drive on their first possession, capped by Griffith's 3-yard dive. Michigan came back again, eating up 16 plays and nearly eight minutes before J.D. Carlson kicked a 47-yard field goal that put Michigan up 10-7. Back again came the Illini, getting in range for Higgins' 25-yard game-tying field goal. Advantage Michigan again as quarterback Michael Taylor drove the Wolverines 80 yards for a score that put them up 17-10 at halftime.

The Illini came close to getting even again midway through the third quarter, driving inside the Michigan 5-yard line, but on a fourth-and-one attempt, George's pass into the end zone fell incomplete, killing the drive and smothering the Illini's spirit.

In typical Schembechler fashion, the Wolverines, who finished the day with 266 rushing yards, drove all the way downfield before Boles capped the scoring with a 13-yard run and a 24-10 final.

"In the [1988] game, we weren't sure we had an idea how we might win. In this game we played them nose to nose and I think our players understood why we didn't win and what we must do to win that game," Mackovic said. "Now there's no question in the players or coaches' minds how we need to improve and what we expect in the big championship-type games."

Primous and defensive back Luke Petraitis both suffered strained knees and missed the rest of the regular season. The Illini slipped to No. 12 in the Associated Press rankings.

A Citrus Bowl Bid

The Illini had little time to worry about a lost Rose Bowl chance. Victories in their final two regular-season games would virtually assure Illinois of an appearance in a January 1 bowl. The Florida Citrus Bowl would be keenly interested in a 9-2 Big 10 runner-up.

Indiana

Illinois didn't disappoint. The next week Illinois closed its home season by treating a crowd of 53,368 to George's five touchdown passes and Brian Williams' 92-yard interception return for a touchdown in a 41-28 victory over Indiana.

George fired four of his touchdown passes in the first half, strikes of 18 and 21 yards to Bellamy, 38 yards to Wax, and 30 yards to Williams.

Illinois took a 28-14 halftime lead and didn't slow down after intermission as Bellamy, who had an Illinois-record 170 yards in returns, returned the opening kickoff 89 yards to the Hoosiers' 5-yard line where George and Bellamy hooked up for their third scoring connection of the day. Brian Williams' fourth-quarter interception return sealed the verdict.

The Illini defense allowed a second-quarter touchdown pass by Hoosier quarterback Dave Schnell. That broke a string of 49 consecutive quarters that Illinois had not allowed an opposing quarterback a touchdown pass. Also in this game, Indiana All-American Anthony Thompson had a 20-yard touchdown run that made him the NCAA's all-time leading scorer.

Northwestern

Now the Illini would get that Florida Citrus Bowl bid with a win at Northwestern. Michigan's victory over Ohio State earlier in the day ended any hope of a share of the Big 10 championship, but the Illini hardly seemed to notice as they riddled the porous Wildcat defense with 42 first-half points en route to a 63-14 romp.

George hit 15 of 18 first-half passes, good for three touchdowns. The 63 points were the most by an Illinois team since 1944 when the Illini beat Illinois-Normal 79-6, and it was the school's most points in a Big 10 game since it beat Northwestern 64-8 in 1908.

George, who became the tenth Big 10 quarterback to pass for more than 6,000 yards in a career, was Offensive Player of the Week in both wire services' eyes, and the Illini were on their way to Orlando to face Virginia in the 44th Florida Citrus Bowl. But first the accolades.

Gardner, an Outland Trophy finalist, earned first-team All-American recognition from the Walter Camp Football Foundation, AP, Kodak-Coaches, Football Writers Association of America, and *Football News*. He was Illinois' 59th All-American and its first consensus All-American on defense since Butkus. He also led a parade of seven Illini named All-Big 10 first team by the AP. Brownlow, a Butkus Award semifinalist for the second straight year, Primous, Henry Jones, Agee, George, and Lovelace were also honored. Bellamy joined that group on UPI's first team.

For the second straight year, Mackovic was named the league's Coach of the Year. Illinois' nine wins was only the sixth such record in school history—and third since 1951. Its seven Big 10 wins was bettered only by the 1983 championship team.

Although he would have another season of eligibility remaining in 1990, George, who threw 19 touchdown passes in 11 games, would be eligible for the National Football League draft. Would he stay or would he turn pro? That topic of conversation was more widely discussed than even Disney World in Orlando.

But there were other things on the Illini's minds. This was Illinois' fifth postseason appearance of the 1980s, but the Illini had yet to win a bowl game during that span. It was the school's first appearance ever in any New Year's Day game other than the Rose Bowl.

Coach Mackovic accepts an invitation to play in the Citrus Bowl

Victory Over Virginia

Neither George nor anyone else knew for sure if this would be his last game in an Illinois uniform. But it would be one of his best. He delighted a record crowd of 60,016 with a 321-yard, three-touchdown performance, and Illinois dismantled the Atlantic Coast Conference co-champion Cavaliers, 31-21.

The 1990s started on the right foot for the Illini when Virginia fumbled the opening kickoff and Bill Henkel fell on it at the Cavaliers' 36.

Five plays later, George had the first of his scoring passes, a 15-yarder to Steven Williams. Virginia came back to tie 7-7, but the Illini were not to be denied this day. George took the Illini 80 yards for the score that put them on top for good. The drive, triggered by a 68-yard completion to Bellamy, ended when George hit a wide-open tight end Dan Donovan on a fourth-down pass from inside the Cavalier 1-yard line.

A drive late in the second quarter ended with Higgins' 34-yard field goal and a 17-7 halftime lead. The Illini put it out of reach by taking the second-half kickoff and driving 84 yards for a score that gave them a 24-7 lead.

"I felt like we could do anything we wanted," George said afterward. "We marched it up and down the field."

The Illini marched 497 yards this day and probably would have won by more than the 31-21 final score had not they stopped themselves with three fumbles and an interception.

George completed 26 of 38 passes for 321 yards, and Bellamy finished his Illinois career with eight catches and a career-high 166 yards. His last catch was a spectacular end-zone grab that gave Illinois its final score.

Into the Second Century

The Illini's 10-2 finish matched their 1983 total. It was Illinois' first victory of the 1990s, its last victory of its first century, and its first post-season victory since 1964, a drought of 26 years.

Mackovic became the first Illinois coach since Zuppke to lead the Illini to winning seasons in each of his first two years.

"We looked forward to winning 10 games during the season, that was a real motivating factor," Mackovic said. "Our team wanted to be remembered as one of the great teams in Illinois history. And we are."

And Illinois starts its second century with hopes of even greater heights. George would have been a major Heisman Trophy contender, an award no Illinois player has ever won. But on March 20, 1990, he announced his decision to bypass his final season of eligibility to enter the NFL draft. Gardner and Brownlow will be touted for the Outland and Butkus trophies, respectively. The second century could be even better than the first.

"Actually the Citrus Bowl was the start of the next century of football," Mackovic said. "We wanted to get it off to a rousing start.

"Illinois football is today in a position where we enjoy a great deal of prestige and recognition nationally as well as in the Big 10. There is still a lot of work for us to do to establish ourselves as a perennial favorite for the Big 10 crown, but that's one of our objectives. Just as much an objective, though, is to continue in a steadfast manner to see that everyone does graduate, does have the diploma and will look back at their years at the University of Illinois with pride and accomplishment both on and off the field.

"There is something I find good about that."

HAIL TO THE ORANGE AND BLUE!

The decision to stay at the U of I for one more year or to enter the 1990 NFL draft was a very complicated decision. There were many factors to consider . . . I considered heavily some personal goals that I have, also the national championship, the Rose Bowl, and winning the Heisman trophy. Another factor considered was finances. . . I also considered the potential wage scale for rookies in the NFL in the future. Over the last few months I wanted to be absolutely certain that I have spent a great deal of time weighing all the factors of whether to stay for one more year or enter the draft. . . I have decided that it is in my best interest to forego my last year of eligibility at the University of Illinois and petition the NFL to enter the 1990 draft.

Jeff George
March 20, 1990

On April 22, the Indianapolis Colts selected Jeff George as the number one pick in the 1990 NFL draft. He signed a $15 million contract, more than six times the amount George Huff needed to build Memorial Stadium.

20

ILLINI SPIRIT TRADITIONS

The Band

Throughout its long history, Illinois has been at the core of innovation on the football field. That innovation extends to the halftime show. The first University of Illinois band performed in 1872, only four years after the university had first opened its doors. That military band evolved into the first concert band, which gave its first formal concert in 1890.

It was in 1905 that Albert Austin Harding, then a senior, was asked to help direct the Illinois pep band. For the next 43 years, Harding honed and developed a marching band that not only was the pioneer in its field, but also was long recognized as the best. It was so good that in the 1920s, John Philip Sousa called Illinois' the "world's greatest college band."

Harding built the foundation of the modern marching band. He introduced formations and maneuvers to music instead of mere responses to the drum major's whistle. It was he who added accessories to the marching band's uniforms.

Illinois and other universities built large stadiums after World War I, and the football field

328 band members play before Dad's Day crowd, 1929

Illinois band in "State and Nation" formation, 1949

setting was the perfect stage for large band formations.

Harding and Illinois were the pioneers, but marching bands quickly became a national phenomenon. Harding directed Illinois bands until 1948. He was succeeded by Mark Hindsley, who held the post until 1970, when he was succeeded by Dr. Harry Begian.

Today, the Illinois program is the largest in the nation, with as many as 800 participants in at least one of ten ensembles. James Keene has held the post of Director of Bands since 1985. Associate director Gary Smith has led the Marching Illini since 1976.

In 1989 the Marching Illini numbered 242 instrumentalists, 36 flag girls, 28 Illinettes, 3 drum majors, 20 staff members, and Chief Illiniwek. In addition, there are over 1,000 Block I members.

More than 600 students annually turn out for spring and summer auditions; as many as half the members are not music majors. The music and accompanying drills are written especially for the Marching Illini. The band annually produces a cassette tape featuring both Illinois traditional music and halftime feature arrangements. It has also done video tapes of season highlights.

An early Block "I" planning session

The most famous band tradition at Illinois—or perhaps anywhere—is the "Three-in-One." This presentation was created by the Marching Illini in 1926 and remains in its original form. First the band plays "The Pride of the Illini" while marching to the south end zone to pick up Chief Illiniwek. The Chief then enters through the band and dances to the north goalpost.

While he dances, the band spells out "ILLINI" while marching toward midfield. The band ends facing the press box in the "ILLINI" formation with the Chief in the center of the field. Next, with the Chief poised at midfield, the band plays "Hail to the Orange" before the Chief performs his solo dance at the center of the field.

The band performs at all home football games, and at least one road game each season. It also frequently performs at Chicago Bears games, high school games and other functions throughout the state and the nation. Illinois' bands are so respected that in 1983, the Louis Sudler Intercollegiate Marching Band Trophy was awarded to the Marching Illini in recognition of its outstanding achievement.

Rose Bowl hopes from the Block "I"

Block "I" members entertain the crowd

An Illinois drum major puts his heart into his performance

HAIL TO THE ORANGE AND BLUE!

Chief Illiniwek

Since 1926 Chief Illiniwek has served as an enduring and—for the most part—beloved symbol of the University of Illinois athletic teams. Zuppke suggested the name, which means "Chief of Men."

During that year, Ray Dvorak, who was assistant director of bands, thought of the idea of having a Native American war dance performed at halftime of the Illinois-Pennsylvania game in Pittsburgh.

Lester Leutwiler, a student with a keen interest in native lore, was picked to dance. He had a homemade costume complete with a war bonnet made of turkey feathers.

His dance was a big hit, both that October Saturday and subsequently, when Leutwiler performed on the Illinois campus. Leutwiler was Chief Illiniwek until his graduation in 1929.

The Chief's dance might have faded into oblivion except for history major A. Webber Borchers, who picked up the torch.

"I realized the idea of an Indian chief could be turned into a tremendous historical and symbolic advantage for the U. of I.," Borchers wrote in 1984. "I realized that it would be necessary to have certain objects to continue this tradition. If you have a kingdom, there must be, so to speak, a crown, scepter and the regalia to pass down from king to king, chief to chief."

So Borchers, who died in 1989, asked for and received permission from Dvorak to use a temporary costume for the 1929 season. Then he would see about getting permanent, authentic garb for the Chief.

Unfortunately, about the time Borchers wanted to raise money for the project, the Depression gripped the nation and money disappeared. Borchers collected $35 or $40 in con-

First Chief Illiniwek dance, October 30, 1926

Chief Illiniwek bids farewell to first Illini plane trip

tributions, mostly in nickels and dimes, but that didn't come close to covering the cost of suitable attire.

Local businessman Isaac Kuhn offered $500 if Borchers would personally see to it that a proper war suit was made. Soon Borchers, with letters of explanation from Kuhn, Dvorak, and university representative Albert Harding in his pocket, was hitchhiking to the Pine Ridge Reservation in Kadota, South Dakota.

He wanted the colorful regalia of the Sioux for several reasons, not the least of which was that the Indians of Illinois shaved the sides of their heads and he couldn't quite picture himself or any future Chief Illiniwek walking around campus for two or three years with only a scalplock on his head. Also, the Illinois Indians were woodland Indians and did not wear the dramatic war bonnets of the plains Indians.

"I also took other letters of introduction to the Superintendent of Indian Affairs, which at that time was Mr. W.W. Jermark, and explained to him my project," Borchers wrote. "He called in a trader that lived on the reservation and they discussed the matter. They, in turn, called in an old Indian woman and explained to her what I wanted. I wanted the war suit to be made in the old original way. She agreed to undertake the project."

Over a year later, on November 8, 1930, the suit was delivered and ready for Borchers to use during the Illinois-Army game at Yankee Stadium. He quite literally grew attached to it.

"Because of the great number of people on the special train and the great quantity of equipment for the band and team, we were allowed to carry with us only the clothes we had on," Borchers wrote of that trip to New York. "The band, of course, wore their uniforms the entire trip. As Chief Illiniwek, I had to wear the new war suit during the whole trip . . . A few friends and I walked down 5th Avenue to get a milkshake. In the block or so that we walked to the drug store, I had collected behind me a crowd of people that blocked the sidewalk and entrance to the drug store. I am sure from the comments I heard that they thought I was a genuine Indian from the west. The first time this

Chief Illiniwek, 1988

rode around the track in the stadium counter-clockwise. When I reached the south end goal post, and the band had cleared the field, I would ride at full gallop like a bat out of hell to the north goal post, straight down the center of the field, and throw a spear over the goal post while I rode under it. That really brought the crowd to its feet. I then would go back into the team's locker room and change out of the Indian uniform.

"This went on for three or four games, until one day it rained cats and dogs and the ceremonies were delayed during halftime. As I rode at a gallop down the center of the field, mud was flying from the horse's hoofs in every direction. Coach Zuppke and the team had just come out on the field due to the delay and he saw his precious field going up in chunks.

"Everything was quiet in the stadium as all eyes were watching the chief. Zuppke, with his bullhorn voice, must have turned livid with rage. All of a sudden, while at dead gallop I heard his booming voice yell 'get that goddam horse off

war suit was officially worn was when the Illinois band paraded down 5th Avenue before the game. We created a real stir."

Borchers created an equal stir at halftime when, after the Army's mule bucked off two cadets, Chief Illiniwek decided he could stay aboard.

"I took off the war bonnet and the breast-plate, got hold of the halter of the mule, jumped on his back and rode that mule down the field. He did not throw me off—try as he might." The crowd roared.

When Borchers graduated in 1931, he wanted a permanent record of those who would be chief. So, on the tail of the war bonnet, he wrote the names of Lester Leutwiler and himself and their dates of service. Every chief since has added his name to that bonnet.

As a graduate student in the fall of 1931, Borchers came back for an encore as the chief; this time with a twist. He trained a pinto horse to add to his repertoire.

"At the end of the halftime ceremonies, after I had performed the war dance in front of the Illinois side of the stadium, the horse was brought to me. I then jumped on the horse and

Princess Illiniwek, Idelle Stitch, 1943

the field!' I nearly fell off the horse and I missed the throw of the spear over the goal post. That was the last time a horse was ridden on the University of Illinois football field."

Twenty-six men have been Chief Illiniwek, and one woman, Idelle Stitch, served as Princess Illiniwek during the war year of 1943. The costume has been replaced and updated five times.

Borchers established several requirements for Chief candidates. He must have knowledge of the university's history, know Indian dancing and understand that Indian dancing is a religious ceremony, be an eagle scout, be acceptable to university band leaders, maintain a C average, maintain the Chief's

tradition, and never allow that tradition to become, in Borcher's words, clownish or ludicrous.

The Chief tradition was challenged in 1989 by a group of American Indian representatives who charged that the university symbol is offensive to Native Americans.

"My dance is a solemn representation of Indian culture," said Tom Livingston, chief in 1988 and 89. "I don't make commercial appearances, I don't run around the sidelines waving a hatchet."

The flap was settled, and the "Chief of Men," with minor modifications, leads the Fighting Illini into their second century of football excellence.

The Chief Illiniwek tradition once included a horse

The Chiefs

Lester G. Leutwiler, 1926
A. Webber Borchers, 1929-30
William A. Newton, 1931-34
Edward C. Kalb, 1935-38
John Grable, 1939-40
Glen Holthaus, 1941-42
Princess Illiniwek, Idelle Stitch, 1943
Kenneth Hanks, 1944
Robert Bitzer, 1945-46
Robert Bischoff, 1947
James A. Down, 1948-50
William G. Hug, 1951-52
Gaylord Spotts, 1953-55

Ronald S. Kaiser, 1956
John W. Forsyth, 1957-59
Fred Cash, 1964-65
Rick Legue, 1966-67
Gary Simpson, 1968-69
John Bitzer, 1970-73
Mike Gonzalez, 1974-76
Matt Gawne, 1977-79
Pete Marzek, 1980
Scott Christensen, 1981-83
William Forsyth, 1984-85
Michael Rose, 1986-87
Tom Livingston, 1988-89

Kurt Gruben, 1990

EPILOGUE

Huff, Eddleman, Elliott, Mills, Eliot, Zuppke, Mackovic, Lindgren, Fletcher, Ingwersen, Pogue, Chapman, Macomber, Seiler, White, Britton, Carney, Grabowski, Grange, Reitsch, Owens, Bennis, Berry, Beynon, Nitschke, McMillen, Butkovich, Butkus, Agase, Moss, Young, Kasap, Wilson, Lenzini, George, Gardner, Nowack, Eason, Trudeau.

These are names inscribed in memorable chapters of Illinois football history, 1890 to 1990. A hundred years from now there will be other names equally memorable in annals of a second century of the Fighting Illini.

The first hundred years have been captured in this book by Linda Young. They have encompassed millions of football fans, thousands of athletes, and hundreds of coaches and administrators who have guided fortunes of the Fighting Illini through good and bad times.

Remarkable progress in sports as well as in American society and worldwide communications has been recorded since 1890. It was then that a few students and faculty gathered along the sidelines of a dusty fairgrounds and watched canvas-clad players pushing each other up and down seeking to advance a round-looking inflated leather object across a line to achieve that remarkable success called touchdown.

Out-of-town contests were followed by telegraph messages in the window of Western Union, later by a manually-operated grid-graph utilizing a direct wire to some distant playing field. Alumni and followers now file into magnificent stadiums seating 100,000 or more. More playing fields are enclosed, covered, and climate controlled as envisioned by the original architectural sketch of Illinois' Memorial Stadium.

In spite of charter membership in the Intercollegiate Conference of Faculty Representatives (now the Big Ten) in 1896, Illinois was slow to capture broad attention in this new college sport. The game had emanated from the Ivy League in the East, intersectional competition was virtually unheard of, and communications remained in the horse and buggy stage.

It was 1910 when Illinois came to more than local consideration. A team coached by Artie Hall used a heavy line, anchored by 230-pound Fred Twist and a remarkable drop kicker, Otto Seiler, to compile a season never again to be matched—unbeaten, untied, unscored on. That fame was fleeting and George "G" Huff, an Illini player turned athletic director, sought a coach to bring consistency and lasting success to Illinois football.

He found that person in the Little Dutchman, Robert C. Zuppke, a high school mentor at Oak Park. He came to campus in 1912, served as head football coach through 1941, and wrote a history of national championships, the building of Memorial Stadium, and coaching of the greatest football player in Illinois history, Harold E. "Red" Grange. Zup's inventiveness in football, his skill as a painter, and his unique qualities of speech and action gained national, even worldwide attention through the skills of his Boswell, L.M. "Mike" Tobin, athletic publicity director.

Time takes a toll on all human beings. Zup's friend, Director Huff, had passed on in 1936 and the Illinois coach found it difficult to sustain a winning record on the simon-pure basis he believed in. Zup wanted players to come to Illinois to play for him. That was no longer enough. He hated recruiting, but it was now the name of the game. Inter-collegiate football had come to mean major crowds, network radio broadcasts with the Bill Sterns' and Harry Wismers, and the National Football League was beckoning to athletes for post-graduate earnings.

Zup reluctantly stepped aside and one of his proteges came on in 1942. Ray Eliot's debut was a dramatic upset of Minnesota, but the promise gave way to bombs over Europe and the Pacific. World War II superseded football and Illinois' fortunes languished until the conflict ended and survivors of "Ray's boys of 1942" returned.

Eliot's career had many aspects of Zup's—upsets, major championships, two Rose Bowl victories in 1947 and 1952. But Eliot, a man of high ideals, respect for the spirit of amateur athletics, and seeming tireless energies, found that he cared little for mounting pressures. Recruiting became a spectre, alumni emphasis on winning a threat, and demands on ever-increasing athletic budgets an unwanted care. So, the first Illinois coach to fly a football team to an away game, the first to direct a team in the Rose Bowl, accepted an administrative chair until his death.

Pete Elliott, Bob Blackman, Gary Moeller, and Mike White followed in the paths of Zup's and Eliot's footsteps. Elliott's abilities to attract young players brought the Illini back into the limelight with a third Rose Bowl victory. White took a team to Pasadena that had beaten every other Big Ten school, Illinois fell that New Year's day to UCLA. Both Elliott and White saw coaching careers virtually ended by NCAA investigations.

John Mackovic, currently the head football coach and director of athletics, first provided his magic on the gridiron, again putting the Illini into conference and post-season contention. Illinois' victory over Virginia in the January 1 Citrus Bowl this year could well be prophetic.

Those of us who have witnessed a major portion of the Illini's first 100 years can ponder what lies ahead. We have marvelled at improvements of equipment and facilities for physical conditioning.

Television and instant replay have revolutionized many aspects of the game. Multi-million dollar budgets and intense recruiting, some on an international basis, have brought forth dangers of over-commercialization and diminution of the academic aspects of college life. The threat that an in-bred organization, the NCAA, will consume itself in its own fires must demand attention across the land.

The Fighting Illini have stood proud over the last century. The foundations of academic structure and athletic programs are firm and lasting. That stability, that strength will carry the Orange and Blue on to greater achievements as the years roll by until 2090.

Charles Flynn
1990

HAIL TO THE ORANGE AND BLUE!

APPENDICES

ILLINOIS

1
8
9
0

1
9
9
0

FOOTBALL
100 YEARS OF TRADITION

ALL-AMERICAN HONORS

F.C. Van Hook, guard	1906,07,08
J. F. Twist, center	1910
G. D. Butzer, guard	1910
Otto Seiler, quarterback	1910
Ralph Chapman, guard	1914
Perry Graves, end	1914
Harold Pogue, halfback	1914
Bart Macomber, halfback	1915
C. K. Squier, end	1915
J. W. Watson, center	1915
John Depler, center	1918
C. O. Applegran, guard	1919
Burt Ingwersen, tackle	1919
Charles Carney, end	1920
Jack Crangle, fullback	1920
Jim McMillen, guard	1923
Harold "Red" Grange, halfback	1923,24,25
C. E. Kassel, end	1925
Bernie Shively, guard	1926
Russ Crane, guard	1927
Robert Reitsch, center	1927
A.J. "Butch" Nowack, tackle	1928
J.A. Timm, halfback	1928
Leroy Wietz, guard	1928
Lou Gordon, tackle	1929
Gilbert Berry, halfback	1932
Lester Lindberg, halfback	1935
James McDonald, center	1938
Jim Reeder, tackle	1939
Alex Agase, guard	1942,43,46

Claude "Buddy" Young, halfback	1944
Ralph Serpico, guard	1944
Ike Owens, end	1947
Richard Raklovits, fullback	1950
William Vohaska, center	1950
Albert Tate, tackle	1950
Al Brosky, safety	1951
Johnny Karras, halfback	1951
Charles Ulrich, tackle	1951
Charles Boerio, linebacker	1951
Tommy O'Connell, quarterback	1952
J. C. Caroline, halfback	1953
Rich Kreitling, end	1958
Bill Burrell, guard	1959
Joe Rutgens, tackle	1959,60
Dick Butkus, center	1963,64
Archie Sutton, tackle	1964
George Donnelly, safety	1964
Jim Grabowski, fullback	1964,65
Tab Bennett, tackle	1971
Scott Studwell, linebacker	1976
Dan Beaver, placekicker	1976
Mike Bass, placekicker	1982
Tony Eason, quarterback	1982
Jim Juriga, tackle	1983
Craig Swoope, safety	1983
Don Thorp, tackle	1983
David Williams, wide receiver	1984,85
Moe Gardner, nose tackle	1989
Mike Bellamy, return specialist	1989

MOST VALUABLE PLAYERS

1930-Stan Bodman, G
1931-Fred Frink, E
1932-Gil Berry,HB
1933-Dave Cook, FB
1934-Les Lindberg, HB
1935-Ed Gryboski, G
1936-Cliff Kuhn, G
1937-Jack Berner, QB
1938-James Hodges, G
1939-Bill Lenich, D
1940-George Bernhardt, FB
1941-Nate Johnson, T
1942-Elmer Engle, E
1943-Eddie Bray, HB
1944-Buddy Young, HB
1945-Mac Wenskunas, C
1946-Alex Agase, G
1947-Ike Owens, E
1948-James Valek, E
1949-John Karras, HB
1950-Tony Klimek, E
1951-Charles Boerio, LB
1952-Al Brosky, HB
1953-Don Ernst, T
1954-Jack Chamblin, C
1955-Em Lindbeck, QB
1956-Dave Walker, G
1957-Ron Hanson, E
1958-Gene Cherney, C
1959-Bill Burrell, G
1960-Joe Rutgens, T
1961-Tony Parrilli, G
1962-Ken Zimmerman, HB
1963-Dick Butkus, C
1964-Dick Butkus, C
1965-Jim Grabowski, FB

1966-Ron Guenther, G
1967-John Wright, E
1968-Rich Johnson, FB
1969-Doug Dieken, E
1970-Doug Dieken, E
1971-Terry Masar, P-HB
1972-Larry McCarren, C
    Larry Allen, DE
1973-Eddie Jenkins, HB
    Octavus Morgan, DE
1974-Tom Hicks, LB
    Jeff Hollenbach, QB
1975-Stu Levenick, OT
    Bruce Beaman, DB
1976-Jerry Finis, OT
    Scott Studwell, LB
1977-John Sullivan, LB
    James Coleman, TB
1978-John Sullivan, LB
    Randy Taylor, C
1979-Lawrence McCullough, QB
1980-Dave Wilson, QB
1981-Tony Eason, QB
    Kelvin Atkins, OLB
    Ron Ferrari, OLB
    Dan Gregus, DT
    Mike Bass, K
1982-Tony Eason, QB
1983-Don Thorp, DT
1984-David Williams, WR
1985-David Williams, WR
1986-Keith Jones, RB
1987-Darryl Usher, WR
1988-Keith Jones, RB
1989-Mike Bellamy, WR
    Moe Gardner, NT

FOOTBALL CAPTAINS

1890-Scott Williams, QB
1891-R. W. Hart, FB
1892-R. W. Hart, FB
1893-George H. Atherton, E
1894-J.E. Pfeffer,T
1895-Robert J. Hotchkiss, FB
1896-Charles D. Beebe,G
1897-Don Sweney, T
1898-A. R. Johnston, FB
1899-E.C. McLane, C
1900-Arthur R. Hall, E-HB
1901-Justa M. Lindgren, T
1902-Garland (Jake) Stahl, T
1903-Claude J. Rothgeb, G-E
1904-C. A. Fairweather, G
1905-C. J. Moynihan, T-HB
1906-Ira T. Carrithers, HB
1907-Lion Gardiner, HB
1908-F. C. VanHook, G
1909-Benjamin F. Baum, E
1910-G. D. Butzer, G
1911-Chester C. Roberts, HB
1912-William Woolston, FB-HB
1913-Enos M. Rowe, FB
1914-Ralph D. Chapman, G
1915-John W. Watson, C
1916-Frank B. Macomber, QB
1917-Reynold R. Kraft, E
1918-Bert Ingwersen, T (Acting)
1919-William K. Kopp, FB
1920-J. C. Depler, C
1921-L. W. Walquist, HB
1922-David D. Wilson, E
1923-James W. McMillen, G
1924-Frank E. Rokusek, E-T
1925-Harold (Red) Grange, HB
1926-Charles E. Kassel, E
1927-Robert Reitsch, C
1928-Albert J. Nowack, T
1929-Russell J. Crane, G
1930-Olaf E. Robinson, FB
1931-Gilbert Berry, HB
1932-Gilbert Berry, QB
1933-Herman Walser, FB
1934-Charles Bennis,G
    Jack Beynon, QB
1935-Charles S. Galbreath, T

1936-Elvin C. Sayre, C
1937-Lowell Spurgeon, HB
1938-James W. McDonald, C
1939-Melvin Brewer, G
1940-Thomas J. Riggs, T
1941-Selected each game
1942-James Smith, FB
1943-Selected each game
1944-Selected each game
1945-Ralph Serpico, T
1946-Mac Wenskunas, C
1947-Art Duffelmeier, HB
1948-Herb Siegert,G
1949-Lyle Button, T
1950-Bill Vohaska, C
1951-Charles Studley, G
1952-Alfred Brosky, HB
1953-Robert Lensini,T
1954-Jan Smid, G
1955-Selected each game
1956-James Minor, C
1957-Dale Smith, HB
1958-Jack Delveaux, FB
1959-Bill Burrell, G
1960-Bill Brown, FB
1961-Gary Brown, T
1962-Bob Scharbert, T
    Ken Zimmerman, HB
1963-Mike Taliaferro, QB
    Dick Deller, G
1964-Dick Butkus, C
    George Donnelly, HB
1965-Jim Grabowski, FB
    Don Hansen, LB
1966-Bo Batchelder, E
    Kai Anderson, C
1967-Ron Bess, HB
    Ken Kmiec, E
1968-Carson Brooks, E
    Tony Pleviak, T
1969-Doug Redmann, G
    Bruce Erb, LB
1970-Kirk McMillin, G
    Doug Dieken, E
1971-Glen Collier, E
    Larry McCarren, C
1972-Larry McCarren, C

    John Wiza, LB
1973-John Gann, G
    Ken Braid, LB
1974-Ty McMillin, LB
    Revie Sorey, G
1975-Dean March, DE
    Stu Levenick, OT
1976-Dean March, DE
    Scott Studwell, LB
    Marty Friel, TE
1977-Kurt Steger, QB
    Rickie Mitchem, W
1978-John Sullivan, LB
    Randy Taylor, C
1979-Lawrence McCullough,
    QB
    Stanley Ralph, DT
1980-Dave Dwuer, DT
    Ron Ferrari, Spec. T
    Dave Wilson, QB
1981-Greg Boeke, C
    Ron Ferrari, OLB
    Jack Squirek, MLB
1982-Mike Bass, K
    Dan Gregus, DT
    Mike Martin, WR
1983-Don Thorp, DT
    Tim Brewster, TE
    Joe Miles, FB
1984-David Edwards, DB
    Rick Schulte, OG
1985-Jack Trudeau, QB
    Craig Swoope, DB
    Chris White, K
1986-Scott Davis, DE
    Mark Dennis, OT
    Sam Ellsworth, LB
    Shane Lamb, QB
1987-Mike Scully, OG
    Mike Piel, DE
    Darrick Brownlow, LB
1988-Glenn Cobb, S
    Mark McGowan, OT
1989-Craig Schneider, OT
    Mike Bellamy, WR
    Steve Glasson, LB
    Moe Gardner, NT

HAIL TO THE ORANGE AND BLUE!

ILLINI HEAD COACHES' RECORDS

	Years	Won	Lost	Ties	Pct.
Scott Williams	1890	1	2	0	.333
Robert Lackey	1891	6	0	0	1.000
E.K. Hall	1892-93	12	5	5	.706
Louis D. Vail	1894	5	3	0	.625
George Huff	1895-99	21	16	3	.563
Fred L. Smith	1900	7	3	2	.667
Edgar G. Holt	1901-2	18	4	1	.818
George Woodruff	1903	8	6	0	.571
Alumni*	1904	9	2	1	.818
Fred Lowenthal	1905	5	4	0	.556
Justa Lindgren	1906	1	3	1	.250
Arthur R.Hall	1907-1912	27	10	3	.730
Robert C. Zuppke	1913-41	131	81	13	.618
Ray Eliot	1942-59	83	73	11	.532
Pete Elliott	1960-66	31	34	1	.477
Jim Valek	1967-70	8	32	0	.200
Bob Blackman	1971-76	29	36	1	.439
Gary Moeller	1977-79	6	24	3	.227
Mike White	1980-87	47	41	3	.533
John Mackovic	1988-	16	7	1	.688
Totals	100 years	471	386	49	.547

*Arthur R. Hall, Justa Lindgren, Fred Lowenthal, Clyde Matthews

ASSISTANT COACHES

(Since 1925)

Adolph, Dave (1973-76)
Agase, Lou (1950-54)
Anderson, Ross (1946-47)
Anderson, Walt (1971-76)
Anderson, Wright (1977-78)
Andros, Dee (1960-61)
Axman, Steve (1979)
Baer, Charles (1942-44)
Baker, Bob (1973)
Baker, Lou (1964-70)
Bennis, Chuck (1939-40)
Bernstein, Steve (1988-)
Beynon, Jack (1936-37)
Blazine, Tony (1942-46)
Boerio, Chuck (1958)
Brewer, Mel (1947-59)
Brown, Jim (1962-70)
Callahan, Bill (1983-86)
Caroline, J.C. (1967-76)
Carr, Lloyd (1978-79)
Childress, Brad (1981-84)
Colby, Greg (1988-)
Coletta, Mike (1978)
Cosgrove, Kevin (1983-87)
Crawford, Walter (1941)
Dahlquist, Gene (1988-)
Daniels, Art (1939-40)
Deal, Mike (1989-)
Durchik, Gary (1979)
Easterbrook, John (1967-70)
Eliot, Ray (1937-41)
Engel, Elmer (1947-49)
Fletcher, Ralph (1942-63)
Fraser, Jim (1976)

Gambold, Bob (1983-)
George, Rick (1984-86)
Godbolt, Michael (1988-)
Golden, Gary (1971-74)
Harkness, Tim (1987-)
Harris, Walt (1980-82)
Hart, Jack (1964-67)
Herndon, Bob (1960-66)
Hoener, Peter (1987)
Hoffman, Bruce (1974-77)
Holton, Larry (1983-86)
Horton, Gary (1980-82)
Hudson, Ron (1987)
Ingwersen, Burt (1946-1965)
Jackson, John (1971-75)
Johnson, Leo (1937, 1942-56)
Karmelowicz, Bob (1983-86)
King, Robert (1947-57)
Kollar, Bill (1986-87)
Krueger, Phil (1971-72)
Law, Glenn (1943-44)
Lewis, Terry (1977-78)
Lindgren, Justa (1904-43)
Malone, Red (1980)
Marcin, Denny (1988-)
Mason, Glenn (1977)
McCartney, Max (1980-85)
McClure, W. E. (1932)
McPhail, Buck (1960-66)
McPherson, Dick (1959)
Meyer, Carl (1971-76)
Mills, Doug (1936-41)
Monsson, Doug (1935-37)
Morand, Elroy (1976)

Myers, Chip (1980-82)
Nelson, John (1971-75)
Novak, Joe (1977-79)
O'Connell, Tommy (1958)
Olander, Milt (1924-34)
Painter, Dwain (1987)
Parker, Norm (1977-79)
Purvis, Chuck (1949-57)
Rainsberger,Ellis (1967-72)
Rehfield, John (1980)
Robinson, Jack (1968-70)
Sabo, J.P. (1932)
Smith, Bob (1978-83, 88)
Solomon, Rich (1980-86)
Stauber, Gene (1960-70)
Studley, Chuck (1955-59)
Sucic, Steve (1958-59)
Sutton, Bob (1977-79)
Tarwain, John (1941,1945-46)
Tate, Bill (1959-63)
Taylor, Bill (1960-66)
Teerlinck, John (1980-82)
Tepper, Lou (1988-)
Tippett, Howard (1987)
Townsend, John (1979)
Valek, Jim (1959-1960)
Venturi, Rick (1977)
Wallace, Bob (1987)
Watson, Shawn (1985-86)
Watt, John (1937)
Westen, Brodie (1968-70)
Wilson, Wendell (1935-37)
Williams, Wayne (1975-76)

HAIL TO THE ORANGE AND BLUE!

ILLINI SCORES THROUGH THE YEARS

National Championships: 1914 (tied with Army); 1919 (tied with Harvard and Notre Dame); 1923; 1927. Authority, Parke H. Davis in Spalding's Guides. Rose Bowl Appearances: 1947, 1952, 1964,1984.

•Games at Champaign-Urbana
Illini Scores First

Coach Scott Williams
(1 year, 1-2-0)
1890
Captain: Scott Williams

O	2	0	Ill. Wesleyan	16
N	22	0	Purdue	62
•N	27	12	Ill. Wesleyan	6
	12	(1-2-0)		84

Coach Robert Lackey
(1 year, 6-0-0)
1891
Captain: Robert W. Hart

@O	1	0	Lake Forest	8
•O	17	26	Bloomington Swifts	0
•N	7	40	Eureka College	0
•N	13	44	Ill. Wesleyan	4
•N	21	12	Knox College	0
N	26	20	Bloomington	12
		142	(6-0-0)	24

@Lake Forest later forfeited game for using ineligible players. Illinois was champion of Illinois Intercollegiate Football League.

Coach E.K. Hall
(2 years, 12-5-5)
1892
Captain: Robert W. Hart

•O	8	6	Purdue	12
•O	12	16	Northwestern	16
O	21	22	Washington (St. Louis)	0
O	22	20	Doane College (Omaha)	0
O	24	0	Nebraska	6
O	26	26	Baker U. (Baldwin, KS)	10
O	27	4	Kansas	26
O	29	42	Kansas City A.C.	0
•N	1		Wisconsin (forfeited)	
•N	5	38	Englewood H.S. (Chicago)	0
N	16	4	Chicago	4
N	17		Beloit (Forfeited)	

•N	18	34	DePauw	0
•N	24	28	Chicago	12
	240	(9-3-2)		86

1893
Captain: George H. Atherton

•S	30	60	Wabash	6
O	7	14	DePauw	4
O	21	0	Northwestern	0
•O	28	4	Chi. Ath. Assn.	10
•N	6	24	Oberlin	34
@N	11	18	Pastime Ath. Club	16
N	25	26	Purdue	26
•N	30	10	Lake Forest	10
	156	(3-2-3)		106

@At St. Louis, MO

Coach Louis D. Vail
(1 year, 5-3-0)
1894
Captain: J. E. Pfeffer

O	6	36	Wabash	6
O	13	0	Chicago A.C.	14
•O	20	54	Lake Forest	6
•N	3	66	Northwestern	0
•N	17	2	Purdue	22
N	21		Chicago (forfeit)	
•N	24	14	Indianapolis Artillery	18
@N	29	10	Pastime Ath. Club	0
	182	(5-3-0)		66

@at St. Louis, MO

Coach George A. Huff
(5 years, 21-16-3)
1985
Captain: R. J. Hotchkiss

•O	5	48	Wabash	0
O	12	0	Chicago A.C.	8
•O	19	79	Illinois Coll.	0
O	26	10	Wisconsin	10
•N	2	38	Rush-Lake Forest	0
•N	23	38	Northwestern	4
N	28	2	Purdue	6
	215	(4-2-1)		28

1896
Captain C.D. Beebe

•O	3	38	Lake Forest	0
•O	10	70	Knox	4
@O	17	10	Missouri	0
•O	21	22	Oberlin	6
O	31	0	Chicago	12
•N	7	4	Northwestern	10
N	26	4	Purdue	4
		148	(4-2-1)	36

@at St. Louis, MO

1897
Captain: Don Sweney

•O	2	26	Eureka	0
•O	9	6	Physicians-Surgeons	0
•O	16	36	Lake Forest	0
•O	23	34	Purdue	4
•O	30	12	Chicago	18
•N	12	64	Knox	0
@•N	20	6	Carlisle Indians	23
+N	25	6	Eureka	0
		190	(6-2-0)	45

@at Chicago Coliseum in first night and indoor game
+at Peoria

1898
Captain: A.R. Johnston

•S	28	18	Ill. Wesleyan	0
•O	1	6	Physicians-Surgeons	11
•O	8	0	Notre Dame	5
•O	15	16	DePauw	0
•O	22	10	Alumni	6
•N	4	17	Alumni	23
@N	12	5	Michigan	12
+N	19	0	Carlisle Indians	11
N	24	11	Minnesota	10
		83	(4-5-0)	78

@at Detroit
+at Chicago

1899
Captain: E.C. McLane

•S	30	6	Ill. Wesleyan	0
O	7	5	Knox	0
•O	14	0	Indiana	5
•O	28	0	Michigan	5
•N	6	0	Alumni	0
@N	11	0	Wisconsin	23
N	22	0	Purdue	5
N	25	29	St. Louis U.	0
+N	30	0	Iowa	58
		40	(3-5-1)	96

@at Milwaukee
+at Rock Island

Coach Fred L. Smith
(1 year, 7-3-2)
1900
Captain: A.R. Hall

•S	29	26	Rose Poly	0
•O	3	63	DePauw	0
•O	6	21	Ill Wesleyan	0
•O	10	6	Physicians-Surgeons	0
•O	13	16	Knox	0
•O	16	35	Lombard	0
O	20	0	Northwestern	0
@O	27	0	Michigan	12
•N	3	17	Purdue	5
N	10	0	Minnesota	23
+N	17	0	Indiana	0
N	24	0	Wisconsin	27
		184	(7-3-2)	67

@at Chicago
+at Indianapolis

Coach Edgar G. Holt
(2 years, 18-4-1)
1901
Captain: J.M. Lindgren

•S	28	39	Englewood HS	0
•O	5	52	Marion Sims	0
•O	11	23	Physicians-Surgeons	0
•O	12	21	Washington (St. Louis)	0
O	19	24	Chicago	0
•O	26	11	Northwestern	17
@N	2	18	Indiana	0
N	9	27	Iowa	0
N	16	28	Purdue	6
•N	28	0	Minnesota	16
		243	(8-2-0)	39

@at Indianapolis

1902
Captain: Garland Stahl

•S	20	34	North Div.	6
•S	27	45	Englewood HS	0
•O	1	22	Osteopaths	0
•O	4	33	Monmouth	0

			Haskell	10
•O	8	24	Haskell	10
•O	11	44	Washington (St. Louis)	0
*O	18	29	Purdue	5
O	25	0	Chicago	6
•N	1	47	Indiana	0
N	8	5	Minnesota	17
N	15	0	Ohio State	0
N	22	17	Northwestern	0
•N	27	80	Iowa	0
		380	(10-2-1)	44

Coach George Woodruff
(1 year, 8-6-0)
1903
Captain: C.J. Rothgeb

•S	19	45	Englewood HS	5
•S	26	43	Lombard	0
•S	30	36	Osteopaths	0
•O	3	29	Knox	5
•O	7	40	Physicians-Surgeons	0
•O	10	64	Rush	0
•O	14	54	Chicago Dentistry	0
O	17	24	Purdue	0
O	24	6	Chicago	18
•O	31	11	Northwestern	12
N	6	0	Indiana	17
•N	14	0	Minnesota	32
N	21	0	Iowa	12
N	26	0	Nebraska	16
		352	(8-6-0)	117

Alumni
(1 year, 9-2-1)
1904
Captain: C.A.Fairweather

•S	24	10	Northwestern College	0
•S	28	23	Wabash	2
•O	1	11	Knox	0
•O	5	26	Physicians-Surgeons	0
O	8	31	Washington (St. Louis)	0
•O	15	10	Indiana	0
O	22	24	Purdue	6
O	29	6	Chicago	6
N	5	46	Ohio State	0
N	12	6	Northwestern	12
•N	19	29	Iowa	0
N	24	10	Nebraska	16
		232	(9-2-1)	42

Coach Fred Lowenthal
(1 year, 5-4-0)
1905
Captain: C.J. Moynihan

•S	30	6	Knox	0
•O	4	6	Wabash	0
•O	7	24	Northwestern College	0
•O	14	12	St. Louis	6
•O	21	0	Purdue	29
•O	28	30	Physicians-Surgeons	0
•N	4	0	Michigan	33
N	18	0	Chicago	44
N	30	6	Nebraska	24
		84	(5-4-0)	136

Coach Justa Lindgren
(1 year, 1-3-1)
1906
Captain: I.T. Carrithers

•O	13	0	Wabash	0
O	27	9	Michigan	28
•N	10	6	Wisconsin	16
N	17	0	Chicago	63
N	24	5	Purdue	0
		20	(1-3-1)	107

Coach Arthur R. Hall
(6 years, 27-10-3)
1907
Captain: Lion Gardiner

•O	19	6	Chicago	42
O	26	15	Wisconsin	4
•N	2	21	Purdue	4
N	9	12	Iowa	25
N	22	10	Indiana	6
		64	(3-2-0)	81

1908
Captain: F. C. Van Hook

•O	3	17	Monmouth	6
•O	10	6	Marquette	6
O	17	6	Chicago	11
•O	31	10	Indiana	0
•N	7	22	Iowa	0
N	14	15	Purdue	6
•N	21	64	Northwestern	8
		140	(5-1-1)	37

1909
Captain: B.F. Baum

•O	2	23	Millikin	0
•O	9	2	Kentucky	6

O	16	8	Chicago	14
•O	30	24	Purdue	6
•N	6	6	Indiana	5
N	13	35	Northwestern	0
N	20	17	Syracuse	8
		115	(5-2-0)	39

1910
Captain: G.D. Butzer

•O	1	13	Millikin	0
•O	8	29	Drake	0
@•O	15	3	Chicago	0
O	29	11	Purdue	0
N	5	3	Indiana	0
N	12	27	Northwestern	0
•N	19	3	Syracuse	0
		89	(7-0-0)	0

@First College Homecoming
First Western Conference title, undefeated, untied, and unscored upon

1911
Captain: C.C.Roberts

•O	7	33	Millikin	0
•O	14	9	St. Louis	0
O	21	0	Chicago	24
•N	4	12	Purdue	3
N	11	0	Indiana	0
•N	18	27	Northwestern	13
•N	25	0	Minnesota	11
		81	(4-2-1)	51

1912
Captain: W.H. Woolston

•O	5	87	Ill. Wesleyan	3
•O	12	13	Washington (St. Louis)	0
•O	19	13	Indiana	7
N	2	0	Minnesota	13
N	9	9	Purdue	9
•N	16	0	Chicago	10
N	23	0	Northwestern	6
		122	(3-3-1)	48

Coach Robert C. Zuppke
(29 years, 131-81-13)
1913
Captain: E.M. Rowe

•O	4	21	Kentucky	0
•O	11	24	Missouri	7
•O	18	37	Northwestern	0
O	25	10	Indiana	0
N	1	7	Chicago	28
•N	15	0	Purdue	0
•N	22	9	Minnesota	19
		108	(4-2-1)	54

1914
Captain: R.D.Chapman

•O	3	37	Christian Bros.	0
•O	10	51	Indiana	0
•O	17	37	Ohio State	0
O	24	33	Northwestern	0
O	31	21	Minnesota	6
•N	14	21	Chicago	7
N	21	24	Wisconsin	9
		224	(7-0-0)	22

1915
Captain: J.W. Watson

•O	2	36	Haskell Indians	0
•O	9	75	Rolla Mines	7
O	16	3	Ohio State	3
•O	23	36	Northwestern	6
•O	30	6	Minnesota	6
•N	13	17	Wisconsin	3
N	20	10	Chicago	0
		183	(5-0-2)	25

1916
Captain: F.B. Macomber

•O	7	30	Kansas	0
•O	14	3	Colgate	15
•O	21	6	Ohio State	7
O	28	14	Purdue	7
N	4	14	Minnesota	9
•N	18	7	Chicago	20
N	25	0	Wisconsin	0
		74	(3-3-1)	58

1917
Captain: R.R. Kraft

•O	6	22	Kansas	0
•O	13	44	Oklahoma	0
•O	20	7	Wisconsin	0
•O	27	27	Purdue	0
N	3	0	Chicago	0
N	17	0	Ohio State	13
•N	24	6	Minnesota	27
N	29	28	Camp Funston Kansas	0
		134	(5-2-1)	40

1918
Captains: E.C. Sternaman, B.A. Ingwersen

O	4	3	Chanute Field	0
•O	12	0	Great Lakes	7
•O	26	0	Municipal Pier	7
N	2	19	Iowa	0
N	9	22	Wisconsin	0
•N	16	13	Ohio State	0
N	23	29	Chicago	0
		86	(5-2-0)	14

1919
Captain: W.K. Kopp

O	11	14	Purdue	7
•O	18	9	Iowa	7
•O	25	10	Wisconsin	14
•N	1	10	Chicago	0
N	8	10	Minnesota	6
•N	15	29	Michigan	7
N	22	9	Ohio State	7
		91	6-1-0	48

1920
Captain: J.C. Depler

•O	9	41	Drake	0
•O	16	20	Iowa	3
•O	23	7	Michigan	6
•O	30	17	Minnesota	7
N	6	3	Chicago	0
N	13	9	Wisconsin	14
@•N	20	0	Ohio State	7
		97	(5-2-0)	37

@First College Dad's Day

1921
Captain: L.W. Walquist

•O	8	52	South Dakota	0
O	15	2	Iowa	14
•O	22	0	Wisconsin	20
•O	29	0	Michigan	3
•N	5	21	DePauw	0
•N	12	6	Chicago	14
N	19	7	Ohio State	0
		88	(3-4-0)	51

1922
Captain: D.D.Wilson

•O	14	7	Butler	10
•O	21	7	Iowa	8
O	28	0	Michigan	24
•N	4	6	Northwestern	3
N	11	3	Wisconsin	0
N	18	0	Chicago	9
•N	25	3	Ohio State	6
		26	(2-5-0)	60

1923
Captain: J.W. McMillen

•O	6	24	Nebraska	7
•O	13	21	Butler	7
O	20	9	Iowa	6
@O	27	29	Northwestern	0
•+N	3	7	Chicago	0
•N	10	10	Wisconsin	0
•N	17	27	Miss. A & M	0
N	24	9	Ohio State	0
		136	(8-0-0)	20

@at Chicago
+First game played at Memorial Stadium

1924
Captain: F.E. Rokusek

O	4	9	Nebraska	6
•O	11	40	Butler	10
•@O	18	39	Michigan	14
•O	25	45	DePauw	0
•N	1	36	Iowa	0
N	8	21	Chicago	21
N	15	7	Minnesota	20
•N	22	7	Ohio State	0
		204	(6-1-1)	71

@Memorial Stadium dedicated

1925
Captain: H.E. Grange

•O	3	0	Nebraska	14
•O	10	16	Butler	13
O	17	10	Iowa	12
•O	24	0	Michigan	3
O	31	24	Pennsylvania	2
•N	7	13	Chicago	6
•N	14	21	Wabash	0
N	21	14	Ohio State	9
		98	(5-3-0)	59

1926
Captain: C.E. Kassel

•O	2	27	Coe	0
•O	9	38	Butler	7
•O	16	13	Iowa	6
O	23	0	Michigan	13
•O	30	3	Pennsylvania	0
N	6	7	Chicago	0
•N	13	27	Wabash	13
•N	20	6	Ohio State	7
		121	(6-2-0)	46

1927
Captain: Robert Reitsch

•O	1	19	Bradley	0
•O	8	58	Butler	0
•O	15	12	Iowa State	12
O	22	7	Northwestern	6
•O	29	14	Michigan	0
N	5	14	Iowa	0
•N	12	15	Chicago	6
N	19	13	Ohio State	0
		152	(7-0-1)	24

1928
Captain: A.J. Nowack

•O	6	33	Bradley	6
•O	13	31	Coe	0
•O	20	13	Indiana	7
•O	27	6	Northwestern	0
N	3	0	Michigan	3
N	10	14	Butler	0
N	17	40	Chicago	0
•N	24	8	Ohio State	0
		145	(7-1-0)	16

1929
Captain: R.J. Crane

•O	5	25	Kansas	0
•O	12	45	Bradley	0
O	19	7	Iowa	7
•O	26	14	Michigan	0
N	2	0	Northwestern	7
•N	9	17	Army	7
•N	16	20	Chicago	6
N	23	27	Ohio State	0
		155	(6-1-1)	27

1930
Captain: O.E. Robinson

•O	4	7	Iowa State	0
•O	11	27	Butler	0
•O	18	0	Northwestern	32
O	25	7	Michigan	15
•N	1	0	Purdue	25
@N	8	0	Army	13
N	15	28	Chicago	0
•N	22	9	Ohio State	12
		78	(3-5-0)	97

@at New York

1931
Captain: Gil Berry

•O	3	20	St. Louis	6
O	10	0	Purdue	7
•O	17	20	Bradley	0
•O	24	0	Michigan	35
O	31	6	Northwestern	32
•N	7	6	Wisconsin	7
•N	14	6	Chicago	13
N	21	0	Ohio State	40
N	26	0	Indiana	0
		58	(2-6-1)	140

1932
Captain: Gil Berry

#•O	1	20	Miami of Ohio	7
#•O	1	13	Coe	0
•O	8	20	Bradley	0
•O	15	0	Northwestern	26
O	22	0	Michigan	32
O	29	13	Chicago	7
N	5	12	Wisconsin	20
•N	12	18	Indiana	6

•N	19	0	Ohio State		3
		96	(5-4-0)		101

#Doubleheader

1933
Captain: H. Walser

•S	30	13	Drake		6
O	7	21	Washington (St. Louis)		6
•O	14	21	Wisconsin		0
@O	21	0	Army		6
•N	4	6	Michigan		7
N	11	3	Northwestern		0
•N	18	7	Chicago		0
N	25	6	Ohio State		7
		77	(5-3-0)		32

@at Cleveland

1934
Captains: C. Bennis, J. Beynon

•S	29	40	Bradley		7
O	6	12	Washington (St. Louis)		7
•O	13	14	Ohio State		13
O	27	7	Michigan		6
•N	3	7	Army		0
N	10	14	Northwestern		3
N	17	3	Wisconsin		7
N	24	6	Chicago		0
		103	(7-1)		43

1935
Captain: Charles S. Galbreath, Jr.

•S	28	0	Ohio Univ.		6
•O	5	28	Washington (St. Louis)		6
O	12	19	Southern Cal.		0
•O	26	0	Iowa		19
N	2	3	Northwestern		10
•N	9	3	Michigan		0
N	16	0	Ohio State		6
•N	23	6	Chicago		7
		59	(3-5-0)		54

1936
Captain: Elvin C. Sayre

•S	26	9	DePaul		6
•O	3	13	Washington (St. Louis)		7
•O	10	6	Southern Cal.		24
O	17	0	Iowa		0

•O	24	2	Northwestern		13
O	31	9	Michigan		6
•N	14	0	Ohio State		13
N	21	18	Chicago		7
		57	(4-3-1)		76

1937
Captain: Lowell Spurgeon

•S	25	20	Ohio Univ.		6
•O	2	0	DePaul		0
•O	9	0	Notre Dame		0
O	16	6	Indiana		13
•O	30	6	Michigan		7
N	6	6	Northwestern		0
N	13	0	Ohio State		19
N	20	21	Chicago		0
		59	(3-3-2)		45

1938
Captain: James W. McDonald

•S	24	0	Ohio Univ.		6
•O	1	44	DePaul		7
•O	8	12	Indiana		2
O	15	6	Notre Dame		14
•O	22	0	Northwestern		13
O	29	0	Michigan		14
•N	12	14	Ohio State		32
N	19	34	Chicago		0
		110	(3-5-0)		88

1939
Captain: Melvin C. Brewer

•S	30	0	Bradley		0
O	14	0	Southern Cal.		26
•O	21	6	Indiana		7
O	28	0	Northwestern		13
•N	4	16	Michigan		7
•N	11	7	Wisconsin		0
N	18	0	Ohio State		21
N	25	46	Chicago		0
		75	(3-4-1)		74

1940
Captain: Thomas J. Riggs

•O	5	31	Bradley		0
•O	12	7	Southern Cal.		13
O	19	0	Michigan		28
•O	26	0	Notre Dame		26

N	2	6	Wisconsin	13
N	9	14	Northwestern	32
•N	16	6	Ohio State	14
N	25	7	Iowa	18
		71	(1-7-0)	144

1941
Captain: Selected each game

•O	4	45	Miami of Ohio	0
O	11	6	Minnesota	34
•O	18	40	Drake	0
O	25	14	Notre Dame	49
•N	1	0	Michigan	20
•N	8	0	Iowa	21
N	15	7	Ohio State	12
N	22	0	Northwestern	27
		112	(2-6-0)	163

Coach Ray Eliot
(18 years, 83-73-11)
1942
Captain: James Smith

•S	26	46	South Dakota	0
•O	3	67	Butler	0
•O	10	20	Minnesota	13
O	17	12	Iowa	7
•O	24	14	Notre Dame	21
O	31	14	Michigan	28
N	7	14	Northwestern	7
@N	14	20	Ohio State	44
•N	21	0	Great Lakes	6
+N	28	20	Camp Grant	0
		227	(6-4-0)	126

@at Cleveland
+at Rockford

1943
Captain: Selected each game

•S	11	0	Camp Grant	23
•S	18	18	Iowa Seahawks	32
O	2	21	Purdue	40
O	9	25	Wisconsin	7
•O	16	33	Pittsburgh	25
O	23	0	Notre Dame	47
•O	30	6	Michigan	42
N	6	19	Iowa	10
N	13	26	Ohio State	29
N	20	6	Northwestern	53
		154	(3-7-0)	308

1945
Captain: Ralph Serpico

•S	22	23	Pittsburgh	6
S	29	0	Notre Dame	7
•O	6	0	Indiana	6
O	20	7	Wisconsin	7
•O	27	0	Michigan	19
•N	3	6	Great Lakes	12
•N	10	48	Iowa	7
N	17	2	Ohio State	27
N	24	7	Northwestern	13
		93	(2-6-1)	104

1946
Captain: Mac Wenskunas

S	21	33	Pittsburgh	7
•S	28	6	Notre Dame	26
•O	5	43	Purdue	7
O	12	7	Indiana	14
•O	19	27	Wisconsin	21
O	26	13	Michigan	9
N	2	7	Iowa	0
•N	16	16	Ohio State	7
N	23	20	Northwestern	0
@J	1	45	UCLA	14
		217	(8-2-0)	105

@1947 Rose Bowl

1947
Captain: Art Dufelmeier

•S	27	14	Pittsburgh	0
O	4	35	Iowa	12
@O	11	0	Army	0
•O	18	40	Minnesota	13
O	25	7	Purdue	14
•N	1	7	Michigan	14
•N	8	60	W. Michigan	14
N	15	28	Ohio State	7
•N	22	13	Northwestern	28
		204	(5-3-1)	102

@at NY City's Yankee Stadium

1948
Captain: Herbert Siegert

•S	25	40	Kansas State	0
O	2	16	Wisconsin	20
•O	9	21	Army	26
O	16	0	Minnesota	6
•O	23	10	Purdue	6
O	30	20	Michigan	28

•N	6	14	Iowa	0
•N	13	7	Ohio State	34
N	20	7	Northwestern	20
		135	(3-6-0)	140

1949
Captain: Lyle Button

•S	24	20	Iowa State	20
•O	1	13	Wisconsin	13
O	8	20	Iowa	14
•O	15	20	Missouri	27
O	22	19	Purdue	0
•O	29	0	Michigan	13
•N	5	33	Indiana	14
N	12	17	Ohio State	30
•N	19	7	Northwestern	9
		149	(3-4-2)	140

1950
Captain: William Vohaska

•S	30	28	Ohio Univ.	2
•O	7	6	Wisconsin	7
O	13	14	UCLA	6
•O	21	20	Washington	13
•O	28	20	Indiana	0
N	4	7	Michigan	0
N	11	21	Iowa	7
•N	18	14	Ohio	7
N	25	7	Northwestern	14
		137	(7-2-0)	56

1951
Captain: Charles Studley

•S	29	27	UCLA	13
•O	6	14	Wisconsin	10
O	13	41	Syracuse	20
O	20	27	Washington	20
O	27	21	Indiana	0
•N	3	7	Michigan	0
•N	10	40	Iowa	13
N	17	0	Ohio State	0
N	24	3	Northwestern	0
@J	1	40	Stanford	7
		220	(9-0-1)	83

@1952 Rose Bowl

1952
Captain: Alfred Brosky

*S	27	33	Iowa State	7
O	4	6	Wisconsin	20
•O	11	48	Washington	14
O	18	7	Minnesota	13
•O	25	12	Purdue	40
N	1	22	Michigan	13
N	8	33	Iowa	13
•N	15	7	Ohio State	27
•N	22	26	Northwestern	28
		194	(4-5-0)	175

1953
Captain: Robert Lenzini

•S	26	21	Nebraska	21
•O	3	33	Stanford	21
O	10	41	Ohio State	20
•O	17	27	Minnesota	7
•O	24	20	Syracuse	13
•O	31	21	Purdue	0
•N	7	19	Michigan	3
N	14	7	Wisconsin	34
N	21	39	Northwestern	14
		228	(7-1-1)	133

1954
Captain: Jan Smid

•S	25	12	Penn State	14
O	2	2	Stanford	12
•O	9	7	Ohio State	40
O	16	6	Minnesota	19
•O	23	34	Syracuse	6
O	30	14	Purdue	28
N	6	7	Michigan	14
•N	13	41	Wisconsin	27
•N	20	7	Northwestern	20
		103	(1-8-0)	180

1955
Captain: J.C. Caroline

S	24	20	California	13
•O	1	40	Iowa State	0
O	8	12	Ohio State	27
•O	15	21	Minnesota	13
O	22	7	Michigan State	21
•O	29	0	Purdue	13
•N	5	25	Michigan	6

N	12	17	Wisconsin	14
N	19	7	Northwestern	7
		149	(5-3-1)	114

1956
Captain: James Minor

•S	29	32	California	20
O	6	13	Washington	28
•O	13	6	Ohio State	26
O	20	13	Minnesota	16
•O	27	20	Michigan State	13
N	3	7	Purdue	7
N	10	7	Michigan	17
•N	17	13	Wisconsin	13
N	24	13	Northwestern	14
		124	(2-5-2)	154

1957
Captain: Dale Smith

S	27	6	UCLA	16
•O	5	40	Colgate	0
O	12	7	Ohio State	21
•O	19	34	Minnesota	13
O	26	14	Michigan State	19
•N	2	6	Purdue	21
•N	9	20	Michigan	19
N	16	13	Wisconsin	24
•N	23	27	Northwestern	0
		167	(4-5-0)	133

1958
Captain: Jack Delveaux

•S	27	14	UCLA	18
O	4	13	Duke	15
•O	11	13	Ohio State	19
O	18	20	Minnesota	8
•O	25	16	Michigan State	0
N	1	8	Purdue	31
N	8	21	Michigan	8
•N	15	12	Wisconsin	31
•N	22	28	Northwestern	27
		145	(4-5-0)	157

1959
Captain: William Burrell

S	26	0	Indiana	20
•O	3	20	Army	14
O	10	9	Ohio State	0

•O	17	14	Minnesota	6
@O	24	9	Penn State	20
•O	31	7	Purdue	7
•N	7	15	Michigan	20
N	14	9	Wisconsin	6
•N	21	28	Northwestern	0
		111	(5-3-1)	93

@at Cleveland

Coach Pete Elliott
(7 years, 31-34-1)
1960
Captain: William Brown

•S	24	17	Indiana	6
•O	1	33	West Virginia	0
•O	8	7	Ohio State	34
O	15	10	Minnesota	21
•O	22	10	Penn State	8
O	29	14	Purdue	12
N	5	7	Michigan	8
•N	12	35	Wisconsin	14
N	19	7	Northwestern	14
		140	(5-4-0)	117

1961
Captain: Gary Brown

•S	30	7	Washington	20
•O	7	7	Northwestern	28
O	14	0	Ohio State	44
*O	21	0	Minnesota	33
O	28	10	Southern Cal.	14
•N	4	9	Purdue	23
•N	11	6	Michigan	38
N	18	7	Wisconsin	55
N	25	7	Michigan State	34
		53	(0-9-0)	289

1962
Captains: Bob Scharbert, Ken Zimmerman

S	29	7	Washington	28
O	6	0	Northwestern	45
•O	13	15	Ohio State	51
O	20	0	Minnesota	17
•O	27	16	Southern Cal.	28
N	3	14	Purdue	10
N	10	10	Michigan	14
•N	17	6	Wisconsin	35
•N	24	7	Michigan State	6
		75	(2-7-0)	234

1963
Captains: Mike Taliaferro, Dick Deller

•S	28	10	California	0
•O	5	10	Northwestern	9
O	12	20	Ohio State	20
•O	19	16	Minnesota	6
O	25	18	UCLA	12
•N	2	41	Purdue	21
•N	9	8	Michigan	14
N	16	17	Wisconsin	7
N	28	13	Michigan State	0
@J	1	17	Washington	7
		170	(8-1-1)	96

@1964 Rose Bowl

1964
Captains: Dick Butkus, George Donnelly

S	26	20	California	14
O	3	17	Northwestern	6
•O	10	0	Ohio State	26
O	17	14	Minnesota	0
•O	24	26	UCLA	7
O	31	14	Purdue	26
N	7	6	Michigan	21
•N	14	29	Wisconsin	0
•N	21	16	Michigan State	0
		142	(6-3-0)	100

1965
Captains: Jim Grabowski, Don Hansen

•S	18	10	Oregon State	12
•S	25	42	SMU	0
O	2	12	Michigan State	22
O	9	14	Ohio State	28
*O	16	34	Indiana	13
•O	23	28	Duke	14
•O	30	21	Purdue	0
•N	6	3	Michigan	23
N	13	51	Wisconsin	0
N	20	20	Northwestern	6
		235	(6-4-0)	118

1966
Captains; Kai Anderson, Bo Batchelder

S	17	7	SMU	26
•S	24	14	Missouri	21
•O	1	10	Michigan State	26
•O	8	10	Ohio State	9
O	15	24	Indiana	10
•O	22	3	Stanford	6
O	29	21	Purdue	25
N	5	28	Michigan	21
•N	12	49	Wisconsin	14
N	19	7	Northwestern	35
		173	(4-6-0)	193

Coach Jim Valek
(4 years, 8-32-0)
1967
Captains: Ken Kmiec, Ron Bess

S	23	0	Florida	14
•S	30	34	Pittsburgh	6
•O	7	7	Indiana	20
•O	14	7	Minnesota	10
•O	21	7	Notre Dame	47
O	28	17	Ohio State	13
•N	4	9	Purdue	42
•N	11	14	Michigan	21
N	18	27	Northwestern	21
N	25	21	Iowa	19
		143	(4-6-0)	213

1968
Captains: Carson Brooks, Tony Pleviak

•S	21	7	Kansas	47
•S	28	0	Missouri	44
O	5	14	Indiana	28
O	12	10	Minnesota	17
O	19	8	Notre Dame	58
•O	26	24	Ohio State	31
N	2	17	Purdue	35
N	9	0	Michigan	36
•N	16	14	Northwestern	0
•N	23	13	Iowa	37
		107	(1-9-0)	333

1969
Captains:Bruce Erb, Doug Redmann

•S	20	18	Washington St.	19
S	27	6	Missouri	37
O	4	20	Iowa State	48
•O	11	6	Northwestern	10
O	18	20	Indiana	41
O	25	0	Ohio State	41
•N	1	22	Purdue	49
•N	8	0	Michigan	57
N	15	14	Wisconsin	55
•N	22	0	Iowa	40
		106	(0-10-0)	397

1970
Captains: Doug Dieken, Kirk McMillin

•S	19	20	Oregon	16
•S	26	9	Tulane	23
•O	3	27	Syracuse	0
O	10	0	Northwestern	48
•O	17	24	Indiana	30
•O	24	29	Ohio State	48
O	31	23	Purdue	21
N	7	0	Michigan	42
•N	14	17	Wisconsin	29
N	21	16	Iowa	22
		165	(3-7-0)	279

Coach Bob Blackman
(6 years, 29-36-1)
1971
Captains: Glenn Collier, Larry McCarren

S	11	0	Michigan State	10
•S	18	0	North Carolina	27
S	25	0	Southern Cal.	28
•O	2	14	Washington	52
•O	9	10	Ohio State	24
O	16	6	Michigan	35
•O	23	21	Purdue	7
•O	30	24	Northwestern	7
N	6	22	Indiana	21
N	13	35	Wisconsin	27
•N	20	31	Iowa	0
		163	(5-6-0)	238

1972
Captains:Larry McCarren, John Wiza

•S	16	0	Michigan State	24
•S	23	20	Southern Cal.	55
S	30	11	Washington	31
•O	7	17	Penn State	35
O	14	7	Ohio State	26
•O	21	7	Michigan	31
O	28	14	Purdue	20
N	4	43	Northwestern	13
•N	11	37	Indiana	20
•N	18	27	Wisconsin	7
N	25	14	Iowa	15
		197	(3-8-0)	277

1973
Captains: Ken Braid, John Gann

S	15	28	Indiana	14

S	22	27	California	7
•S	29	10	W. Virginia	17
•O	6	0	Stanford	24
•O	13	15	Purdue	13
O	20	6	Michigan State	3
•O	27	50	Iowa	0
•N	3	0	Ohio State	30
N	10	6	Michigan	21
•N	17	16	Minnesota	19
N	24	6	Northwestern	9
		164	(5-6-0)	157

1974
Captains: Ty McMillin, Revie Sorey

•S	14	16	Indiana	0
S	21	41	Stanford	7
•S	28	21	Washington St.	19
•O	5	14	California	31
O	12	27	Purdue	23
@•O	19	21	Michigan State	21
O	26	12	Iowa	14
N	2	7	Ohio State	49
•N	9	6	Michigan	14
N	16	17	Minnesota	14
N	23	28	Northwestern	14
		210	(6-4-1)	206

@Memorial Stadium's Golden Anniversary Game

1975
Captains: Dean March, Stu Levenick

S	13	27	Iowa	12
•S	20	20	Missouri	30
S	27	13	Texas A & M	43
•O	4	27	Washington St.	21
•O	11	42	Minnesota	23
•O	18	24	Purdue	26
O	25	21	Michigan State	19
N	1	9	Wisconsin	18
•N	8	3	Ohio State	40
•N	15	15	Michigan	21
N	22	28	Northwestern	7
		229	(5-6-0)	260

1976
Captains: Marty Friel, Dean March, Scott Studwell

•S	11	24	Iowa	6
S	18	31	Missouri	6
•S	25	19	Baylor	34
•O	2	7	Texas A & M	14
O	9	14	Minnesota	29

O	16	21	Purdue	17
•O	23	23	Michigan State	31
•O	30	31	Wisconsin	25
N	6	10	Ohio State	42
N	13	7	Michigan	38
•N	20	48	Northwestern	6
		235	(5-6-0)	248

Coach Gary Moeller
(3 years, 6-24-3)
1977
Captains: Rickie Mitchem, Kurt Steger

•S	10	9	Michigan	37
•S	17	11	Missouri	7
S	24	24	Stanford	37
•O	1	20	Syracuse	30
O	8	0	Wisconsin	26
O	15	29	Purdue	22
•O	22	21	Indiana	7
O	29	20	Michigan State	49
•N	5	0	Ohio State	35
•N	12	0	Minnesota	21
N	19	7	Northwestern	21
		141	(3-8-0)	292

1978
Captains: John Sullivan, Randy Taylor

•S	9	0	Northwestern	0
S	16	0	Michigan	31
•S	23	10	Stanford	35
S	30	28	Syracuse	14
O	7	3	Missouri	45
•O	14	20	Wisconsin	20
•O	21	0	Purdue	13
O	28	10	Indiana	31
•N	4	19	Michigan State	59
N	11	7	Ohio State	45
N	18	6	Minnesota	24
		103	(1-8-2)	317

1979
Captains: Lawrence McCullough, Stanley Ralph

S	8	16	Michigan State	33
•S	15	6	Missouri	14
S	22	27	Air Force	19
•S	29	12	Navy	13
•O	6	7	Iowa	13
O	13	14	Purdue	28
•O	20	7	Michigan	27
O	27	17	Minnesota	17
•N	3	7	Ohio State	44
•N	10	14	Indiana	45
N	17	29	Northwestern	13
		156	(2-8-1)	266

Coach Mike White
(8 years, 47-41-3)
1980
Captains: Dave Dwyer, Ron Ferrari, Dave Wilson

•S	6	35	Northwestern	9
•S	13	20	Michigan State	17
S	20	7	Missouri	52
•S	27	20	Air Force	20
•O	4	21	Mississippi St.	28
O	11	20	Iowa	14
•O	18	20	Purdue	45
O	25	14	Michigan	45
•N	1	18	Minnesota	21
N	8	42	Ohio State	49
N	15	24	Indiana	26
		241	(3-7-1)	326

1981
Captains: Greg Boeke, Ron Ferrari, Jack Squirek

S	5	6	Pittsburgh	26
S	12	27	Michigan State	17
•S	19	17	Syracuse	14
•O	3	38	Minnesota	29
O	10	20	Purdue	44
O	17	27	Ohio State	34
•O	24	23	Wisconsin	21
•O	31	24	Iowa	7
N	7	21	Michigan	70
•N	14	35	Indiana	14
N	21	49	Northwestern	12
		287	(7-4-0)	288

1982
Captains: Mike Bass, Dan Gregus, Mike Martin

@•S	4	49	Northwestern	13
•S	11	23	Michigan State	16
S	18	47	Syracuse	10
•S	25	3	Pittsburgh	20
O	2	42	Minnesota	24
•O	9	38	Purdue	34
•O	16	21	Ohio State	26
O	23	29	Wisconsin	28
O	30	13	Iowa	14

•N	6	10	Michigan	16
N	13	48	Indiana	7
#D	29	15	Alabama	21
		338	(7-5-0)	229

@First night game in Memorial Stadium
#Liberty Bowl, Memphis, TN

1983
Captains: Tim Brewster, Joe Miles, Don Thorp

S	10	18	Missouri	28
•S	17	17	Stanford	7
S	24	20	Michigan State	10
•O	1	33	Iowa	0
O	8	27	Wisconsin	15
•O	15	17	Ohio State	13
O	22	35	Purdue	21
•O	29	16	Michigan	6
N	5	50	Minnesota	23
•N	12	49	Indiana	21
N	19	56	Northwestern	24
@J	2	9	UCLA	45
		347	(10-2-0)	213

@1984 Rose Bowl

1984
Captains: Rick Schulte, David Edwards

•S	1	24	Northwestern	16
•S	8	30	Missouri	24
S	15	19	Stanford	34
•S	22	40	Michigan State	7
S	29	16	Iowa	21
•O	6	22	Wisconsin	6
O	13	38	Ohio State	45
•O	20	34	Purdue	20
O	27	18	Michigan	26
•N	3	48	Minnesota	3
#N	10	34	Indiana	7
		323	(7-4-0)	209

#at Hoosier Dome, Indianapolis

1985
Captains: Jack Trudeau, Craig Swoope, Chris White

•S	7	10	Southern Cal.	20
•S	14	28	So. Illinois	25
S	21	25	Nebraska	52
•O	5	31	Ohio State	28
O	12	24	Purdue	30
O	19	30	Michigan State	17
•O	26	38	Wisconsin	25

•N	2	3	Michigan	3
N	9	0	Iowa	59
•N	16	41	Indiana	24
N	23	45	Northwestern	20
@D	31	29	Army	31
		304	(6-5-1)	334

@Peach Bowl, Atlanta, GA

1986
Captains: Scott Davis, Sam Ellsworth, Mark Dennis, Shane Lamb

•S	6	23	Louisville	0
S	13	16	Southern Cal.	31
•S	20	14	Nebraska	59
O	4	0	Ohio State	14
•O	11	34	Purdue	27
•O	18	21	Michigan State	29
O	25	9	Wisconsin	15
N	1	13	Michigan	69
•N	8	20	Iowa	16
N	15	21	Indiana	16
•N	22	18	Northwestern	23
		189	(4-7-0)	299

1987
Captains: Mike Scully, Mike Piel, Darrick Brownlow

S	5	14	North Carolina	34
•S	12	7	Arizona State	21
•S	19	20	East Carolina	10
•O	3	6	Ohio State	10
O	10	3	Purdue	9
•O	17	16	Wisconsin	14
O	24	14	Michigan State	14
•O	31	27	Minnesota	17
N	7	22	Indiana	34
•N	14	14	Michigan	17
N	21	10	Northwestern	28
		153	(3-7-1)	208

Coach John Mackovic
(2 years, 16-7-1)
1988
Captains: Glenn Cobb, Mark McGowan

•S	3	7	Washington St.	44
S	10	16	Arizona State	21
•S	17	35	Utah	24
O	1	31	Ohio State	12
•O	8	20	Purdue	0
O	15	34	Wisconsin	6

•O	22	21	Michigan State	28
O	29	27	Minnesota	27
•N	5	21	Indiana	20
N	12	9	Michigan	38
•N	19	14	Northwestern	9
#D	29	10	Florida	14
		245	(6-5-1)	243

#All American Bowl, Birmingham, Alabama

1989
Captains: Craig Schneider, Steve Glasson, Mike Bellamy and Moe Gardner

S	4	14	Southern Cal	13
S	16	7	Colorado	38
•S	23	41	Utah State	2
•O	7	34	Ohio State	14
O	14	14	Purdue	2
O	21	14	Michigan State	10
•O	28	32	Wisconsin	9
N	4	31	Iowa	7
•N	11	10	Michigan	24
•N	18	41	Indiana	28
N	25	63	Northwestern	14
#J	1	31	Virginia	21
		332	(10-2-0)	182

#Florida Citrus Bowl, Orlando, FL

ALL-TIME ILLINI FOOTBALL LETTERWINNERS

A

Abraham, Geo. E., 1932
Acks, Ron, 1963, 64, 65
Adams, Earnest, 1977, 78, 79, 80
Adams, Paul, 1956, 57
Adsit, Bertram, W., 1898, 99, 1900
Agase, Alex, 1941, 42, 46
Agase, Louis, 1944, 45, 46, 47
Agee, Mel, 1987, 88, 89
Agnew, Lester P., 1922
Aina, David F., 1984, 85
Allen, Larry, 1970, 71, 72
Allen, Lawrence, T., 1903
Allen, Robert, 1956, 57, 58
Allen, Steve, 1969
Allen, William M., 1965
Allie, Glen, 1967
Amaya, Doug, 1987, 88
Anders, Alphonse, 1939
Anderson, Harold, B., 1909
Anderson, Kai, 1965, 66
Anderson, Neal, 1961, 62
Anderson, Paul T., 1921
Anderson, Wm. W., 1915, 16
Antilla, Arvo A., 1933, 34, 35
Antonacci, Rich, 1977
Applegate, Frank G., 1903
Applegran, Clarence O., 1915, 19
Archer, Arthur E., 1948
Armstead, Charles, 1981, 82
Armstrong, James W., 1891, 92
Armstrong, Lennox F., 1913, 14
Arvanitis, George, 1984
Ash, David, 1957, 58, 59
Ashley, Richard Jr., 1892
Ashlock, Dennis, 1976, 77
Astroth, Lavere L., 1939, 40, 41
Atherton, Geo. H., 1891, 92, 93
Atkins, Kelvin, 1979, 80, 81
Avery, Galen, 1972
Avery, Todd D., 1984, 85
Ayres, John, 1983, 84

B

Babyar, Chris, 1981, 82, 83, 84
Bachouros, Peter F., 1950, 51, 52
Badal, Herbert, 1954
Baietto, Robert E., 1954, 55
Bailey, Gordon R., 1931
Baker, Clarence, 1977
Bareither, Charles, 1967, 68, 69

Bargo, Ken, 1967, 68, 69
Barker, John K., 1891
Barnes, Jeff, 1978
Barter, Harold H., 1903
Baskin, Neil, 1969
Bass, Mike, 1980, 81, 82
Bassett, Denman J., 1947
Bassey, Ralph C., 1943
Batchelder, Robt. (Bo), 1964, 65, 66
Bateman, James M., 1905
Bates, Melvin B., 1953, 54, 55
Bauer, John A., 1930
Bauer, John R., 1951, 52, 53
Baughman, James, 1951
Baum, Benjamin F., 1907, 08, 09
Baum, Harry, W., 1893, 94, 95
Bauman, Frank, 1946
Baumgart, Tom, 1970, 72
Beadle, Thomas B., 1895, 97
Beaman, Bruce, 1972, 73, 74, 75
Beaver, Daniel, 1973, 74, 75, 76
Beckmann, Bruce, 1958, 59
Bedalow, John, 1970, 71, 72
Beebe, Charles, D., 1894, 95, 96
Beers, Harley, 1902, 03
Bell, Frank E., 1936, 37
Bell, Kameno, 1989
Bellamy, Mike, 1988, 89
Bellephant, Joe F., 1957
Belmont, Lou, 1980, 81
Belting, Charles H., 1910, 11
Belting, Paul E., 1911
Bennett, Caslon K., 1930
Bennett, James, 1985
Bennett, Ralph E., 1937, 38, 39
Bennett, Tab, 1970, 71, 72
Bennis, Charles W., 1932, 33, 34
Bennis, William, 1937
Benson, Cam, 1980, 81, 82, 83
Bergeson, C. H., 1928
Berner, John R., 1935, 36, 37
Bernhardt, Geo. W., 1938, 39, 40
Bernstein, Louis S., 1909, 10
Berry, Gilbert I., 1930, 31, 32
Berschet, Marvin, 1951
Bess, Bob, 1968, 69
Bess, Ronald W., 1965, 66, 67
Beverly, Dwight, 1982, 83
Beynon, Jack T., 1932, 33, 34
Bias, Mo, 1982, 83
Bieszczad, Bob, 1968, 69
Bingaman, Lester A., 1944, 45, 46, 47

Birky, David A., 1984, 85
Bishop, Dennis, 1981, 82
Bishop, Robert E., 1952, 53
Blackaby, Ethan, 1959, 60
Blakely, David A., 1977
Blondell, Jim, 1985, 86, 87
Bloom, Robert J., 1932, 33
Boatright, David, 1983, 84, 85
Bodman, Alfred E., 1930, 31, 32
Bodman, Stanley L., 1930
Boeke, Greg, 1978, 80, 81
Boeke, Leroy, 1977, 78, 79, 80
Boerio, Charles, 1950, 51
Bohm, Ron, 1983, 84, 85, 86
Bonner, Bonjiovanna, 1978, 79
Bonner, Lory T., 1957, 58
Booze, MacDonald C., 1912
Borman, Herbert R., 1951, 52, 53
Boso, Cap, 1984, 85
Bostrom, Kirk, 1979, 80
Boughman, James A., 1951
Bourke, Timothy E., 1984, 85, 86, 87
Bowen, Herbert L., 1890
Bowlay-Williams, Victor, 1988, 89
Boysaw, Greg, 1986, 88, 89
Bradley, John J., 1905, 06
Bradley, Kendall R., 1935
Bradley, Theron A., 1943
Brady, Ed., 1980, 81, 82, 83
Braid, Ken, 1971, 72, 73
Branch, James M., 1894, 95, 96
Bray, Edward C., 1943, 44, 45
Brazas, Steven E., 1984
Bremer, Lawrence H., 1908
Breneman Amos L., 1915
Brennan, Rich, 1969, 70
Brewer, Melvin C., 1937, 38, 39
Brewster, Tim, 1982, 83
Brice, Romero, 1987, 88, 89
Briggs, Claude P., 1900
Briley, Norman P., 1899
Britton, Earl T., 1923, 24, 25
Broerman, Richard, 1952
Brokemond, Geo. R., 1958
Bronson, Geo. D., 1902
Brookins, Mitchell, 1980, 82, 83

HAIL TO THE ORANGE AND BLUE!

Brooks, Carson C., 1966, 67, 68
Brooks, Richard A., 1906
Brosky, Alfred E., 1950, 51, 52
Brown, Charles A., 1923, 24, 25
Brown, Charles E., 1948, 49, 50
Brown, Darrin I., 1984, 85, 86
Brown, Gary W., 1959, 60, 61
Brown, Horace T., 1909
Brown, James E., 1958, 59, 60
Brown, Joseph A., 1937
Brown, Julyon, 1988, 89
Brown, William D., 1958, 59, 60
Brownlow, Darrick, 1987, 88, 89
Brundage, Martin D., 1901
Brzuszkiewicz, Michael, 1976
Bucheit, George C., 1918
Bucklin, Robert, 1969, 70, 71
Bujan, George P., 1943, 44, 45
Bulow, Dan, 1977
Bundy, Herman W., 1901, 02
Burchfield, Brian, 1986, 87
Burdick, Lloyd S., 1927, 28, 29
Burgard, Peter, 1980, 81, 82
Burkland, Theo. L., 1896
Burlingame, Keith, 1978
Burman, Jon, 1988
Burns, Bob, 1968, 69, 70
Burrell, William G., 1957, 58, 59
Burris, Merlyn G., 1938
Burroughs, Wilbur C., 1904, 05, 06
Buscemi, Joseph A., 1946, 47
Bush, Arthur W., 1891
Butkovich, Anthony J., 1941, 42
Butkovich, William, 1943, 44, 45
Butkus, Dick M., 1962, 63, 64
Butkus, Mark, 1980, 81, 82, 83
Butler, Charles, 1954, 56
Button, Lyle A., 1947, 48, 49
Butzer, Glenn D., 1908, 09, 10
Byrd, Darryl, 1981, 82

C

Cabell, Kevin, 1976
Cahill, Leo H., 1948, 49, 50
Callaghan, Richard T., 1962, 63, 64
Campbell, Robert A., 1939
Campbell, Tracy, 1973, 74
Campos, Lou, 1984, 85, 86, 87
Cantwell, Francis R., 1934, 35
Capel, Bruce, 1962, 63, 64
Capen, B. C., 1902
Carbonari, Gerald M., 1965, 66
Carlini, Perry, 1983, 84
Carmien, Tab, 1978, 80
Carney, Charles R., 1918, 19, 20, 21

Caroline, J. C., 1953, 54
Carpenter, Chris, 1986
Carr, Chris, 1979
Carr, H. Eugene Jr., 1958
Carrington, Michael, 1978, 79, 80, 81
Carrithers, Ira T., 1904
Carson, Howard W., 1934, 37
Carson, Paul H., 1931
Carter, Archie, 1982, 83
Carter, Donald H., 1911
Carter, Vincent, 1978
Cast, Dick L., 1961
Castelo, Robert E., 1936, 37, 38
Catlin, James M., 1952
Cerney, Bill, 1974, 75, 76
Chalcraft, Kenneth G., 1961
Chamblin, William J., 1953, 54
Chapman, Ralph D., 1912, 13, 14
Charle, William W., 1936
Charpier, Leonard L., 1916, 17
Chattin, Ernest P., 1930
Cheeley, Kenneth D., 1940, 41
Cherney, Eugene K., 1957, 58
Cherry, Robert S., 1940, 41
Chester, Guy S., 1894
Christensen, Paul G., 1916
Chronis, Tony, 1973
Chrystal, Jeff, 1973, 74, 75
Cies, Jerry B., 1944, 45
Ciszek, Ray A. C., 1943, 44, 45, 46
Clark, George, 1914, 15
Clark, Robert, 1922
Clark, Ronald, 1949, 50
Clarke, Curtis, 1983, 85
Clarke, Edwin B., 1890
Clarke, Frederick W., 1890
Clayton, Clark M., 1898, 99
Clear, Samuel, 1979, 80
Clements, John H., 1930
Clements, Tony, 1968, 69
Clinton, Edgar M., 1896
Coady, Tom, 1979, 80
Cobb, Glenn, 1987, 88
Coffeen, Harry C., 1896, 97
Colby, Greg, 1971, 72, 73
Cole, E. Joseph, 1949, 50, 51
Cole, Jewett, 1935, 36
Cole, Jerry, 1969, 70
Cole, Terry, 1980, 81, 82, 83
Coleman, DeJustice, 1957, 58, 59
Coleman, James, 1976, 77
Coleman, Roger, 1973, 74
Colement, Norris, 1969
Collier, Glenn, 1969, 70, 71
Collier, Steve, 1982
Collins, John J., 1962

Collins, Michael E., 1976
Conover, Robert J., 1930
Conradt, Greg, 1988
Cook, David F., 1931, 33
Cook, James F., 1898, 1900, 01, 02
Cook, James W., 1891, 92
Cooledge, Marshall M., 1925
Cooper, Norm, 1970
Cooper, Paul H. Jr., 1893, 94, 95
Correll, Walter K., 1941, 42
Counts, John E., 1959
Coutchie, Stephen A., 1922, 23
Covington, Jim, 1981
Cozen, Douglas, 1978, 79
Crangle, Walter F., 1919, 20, 21
Cramer, Willard M., 1937, 38
Crane, Russell J., 1927, 28, 29
Craven, Forest, I., 1932
Cravens, Robert D., 1961
Crawford, Walter C., 1923
Crum, Tom, 1968
Cruz, Ken, 1983, 84
Cummings, Barton A., 1932, 33, 34
Cunz, Robert W., 1945, 46, 47
Curry, Jack C., 1943
Curtis, Joe, 1980, 81, 82
Custardo, Fred, 1963, 64, 65

D

D'Ambrosio, Arthur L., 1925, 26, 27
Dadant, M. G., 1907
Dahl, Andres W., 1934
Dallenbach, M. Karl, 1909
Damos, Donn, 1970
Damron, Tim, 1981, 82
Daniel, Cullen, 1980
Danosky, Anthony J., 1958
Dardano, Rusty, 1981
Darlington, Dan, 1969, 70, 71
Daugherity, Russell S., 1925, 26
Davis, Chester W., 1910, 11
Davis, John, 1966, 67
Davis, Scott, 1983, 85, 86, 87
Dawson, Bobby, 1986, 87
Dawson, George, 1922
DeDecker, Darrel, 1959, 60
DeFalco, Steven, 1976
Deimling, Keston J., 1927, 28
de la Garza, Gabriel, 1987
Delaney, Robert F., 1956, 57

Geraci, Joseph L., 1959
Gerometta, Arthur L., 1943
Gibbs, Robert, 1940, 42
Gibson, Alec, 1984, 85
Giddings, Mike W., 1984, 85
Gillen, John, 1977, 78, 79, 80
Gillen, Ken, 1979, 80, 82
Glasson, Steve, 1986, 87, 88, 89
Glauser, Glenn L., 1961
Glazer, Herbert, 1935
Glielmi, Rob, 1982, 83, 84, 85
Glosecki, Andy R., 1936
Gnidovic, Donald J., 1950, 51
Goelitz, Walter A., 1917
Golaszewski, Paul P., 1961
Goldberg, Jeff, 1976
Golden, Scott, 1981, 82, 83
Gongala, Robert B., 1952, 54
Good, Richard, J., 1940, 41, 42
Gordon, James, 1986, 87
Gordon, Louis J., 1927, 28, 29
Gordon, Stephen M., 1976
Gorenstein, Sam, 1931
Gosier, Harry, 1983
Gottfried, Charles, 1946, 47, 48, 49
Gould, Dennis C., 1961
Gould, Maurice, 1941
Gow, Mike, 1972, 73, 74
Grable, Leonard M., 1925, 26, 27
Grabowski, Jim S., 1963, 64, 65
Graeff, Robert E., 1955
Gragg, Elbert R., 1932, 33
Graham, John, 1970, 71
Graham, Walter, 1976
Grange, Garland A., 1927
Grange, Harold E. (Red), 1923, 24, 25
Grant, African, 1985, 86, 87
Grant, Randy, 1983, 84
Graves, Perry H., 1913, 14
Greathouse, Forrest E., 1925
Greco, Dale, 1964, 65
Green, Chris, 1987, 88, 89
Green, Gordon, 1985
Green, Howard S., 1906, 07
Green, Robert K., 1932
Green, Stanley C., 1946
Green, Vivian J., 1922, 23
Green, William, J., 1924, 25
Greene, Earl B., 1921
Greene, Steve, 1972, 73, 74, 75
Greenwood, Donald G., 1943, 44
Gregus, Dan, 1980, 81, 82
Gregus, Kurt, 1986, 87, 88, 89
Gremer, John A., 1955, 59
Grierson, Ray G., 1941, 42, 46

Grieve, Robert S., 1935, 36
Griffin, Donald D., 1941, 42
Griffith, Howard, 1987, 88, 89
Grimmett, Richard, 1977
Grothe, Don, 1953, 57, 58
Gryboski, Edward, 1933, 34, 35
Guard, Jason, 1986, 87, 88, 89
Guenther, Ron, 1965, 66
Gumm, Percy E., 1908, 09

H

Hadsall, H. Harry, 1895
Hairston, Ray, 1984, 85, 86
Halas, George S., 1917
Hall, Albert L., 1911
Hall, Arthur R., 1898, 99, 1900
Hall, Charles V., 1928, 30
Hall, Harry A., 1923, 24, 25
Hall, Joseph W., 1950, 52
Hall, Orville, E., 1944
Hall, Richard L., 1923, 24
Haller, Thomas, F., 1956, 57
Halstrom, Bernard C., 1915
Hamner, Jerry, 1987, 88, 89
Hannum, Philip E., 1903
Hanschmann, Fred R., 1915, 18
Hansen, Don, 1963, 64, 65
Hanson, Martin E., 1900
Hanson, Rodney, 1955, 56, 57
Happenney, J. Clifford, 1922
Harbour, Dave, 1986, 87
Hardy, Dale G., 1976, 77 78
Harford, Doug, 1965, 66
Harkey, Lance, 1985, 86
Harmon, Ivan G., 1903
Harms, Frederick E., 1965, 66, 67
Harper, William, 1965
Hart, R. W., 1890, 91, 92
Hartley, Frank, 1988, 89
Haselwood, John M., 1903, 04
Hatfield, Joe, 1972, 73, 74
Hathaway, Ralph W., 1938, 39
Hauser, Bob, 1979
Hayer, Joseph C., 1949
Hayes, Bob, 1972
Haynes, Clint, 1982, 83
Hazelett, John, 1943
Heaven, Mike, 1981, 82, 83, 84
Hedtke, William A., 1931
Heinrich, Mick, 1972, 73
Heiss, William C. Jr., 1944, 45, 46
Helbling, James L., 1943
Helle, Mark, 1980, 81, 82
Hellstrom, Norton E., 1920
Hembrough, Gary, 1959, 60, 61

Henderson, William R., 1956, 57, 58
Hendrickson, Richard W., 1957
Henkel, Bill, 1987, 88, 89
Henry, Wilbur, L., 1934, 35, 36
Herr, Rich, 1989
Hickey, Robert, 1957, 58, 59
Hickman, Robert Z., 1928
Hicks, Tom, 1972, 73, 74
Higgins, Albert, G., 1890
Higgins, Doug, 1987, 88, 89
Hill, Sam C., 1922
Hill, Stanley, 1912
Hill, W. Leron, 1957, 58
Hills, Otto R., 1928, 29, 30
Hinkle, Robert, 1947
Hinsberger, Mike, 1973
Hodges, James D., 1937, 38
Hoeft, Julius, 1932
Hofer, Lance, 1980
Hoffman, James H., 1966
Hoffman, Robert W., 1912
Hogan, Mickey, 1967, 68
Hogan, Richard, 1982
Hollenbach, Jeff, 1973, 74
Holmes, Mike, 1979, 80
Hopkins, Mike, 1988, 89
Horsely, Robert E., 1931
Hotchkiss, R. J., 1894, 95
Huber, William W., 1946
Huddleston, Thielen B., 1930
Hudelson, Clyde W., 1912
Huebner, Dave, 1976
Huff, George A., 1890, 92
Hughes, Henry L., 1920
Huisinga, Larry, 1970, 71, 72
Hull, Walker F., 1908, 09
Humay, Daniel M., 1966
Humbert, Fred H., 1927, 28, 29
Hungate, Eddie, 1985
Huntoon, Harry A., 1901, 02, 03, 04
Hurley, O. Landis, 1940
Hurtte, Frank, 1944
Huston, William E., 1966, 67, 68
Hyinck, Clifton F., 1931

I

Ingle, Walden M., 1938
Ingwerson, Burton A., 1917, 18, 19
Iovino, Vito J., 1956

Lindgren, Justa M., 1898, 99,
  1900, 01
Line, Jerry, 1967
Lingner, Adam, 1979, 80, 81, 82
Litt, Leon B., 1907
Little, Charles D., 1984, 85, 86,
  87
Livas, Steve, 1969
Logeman, Ron, 1976
Lollino, Frank V., 1961, 62
Lonergan, Charles P. A., 1904
Lopez, John, 1979, 80, 81
Lovejoy, Charles E., 1917, 18, 19
Lovelace, Curt, 1987, 88, 89
Lovellette, Lindell J., 1960
Lowe, Kevin, 1974
Lowenthal, Fred, 1898, 99, 1900,
  01
Luhrsen, Paul H., 1952, 53
Lundberg, Albert J., 1937, 38, 39
Lundgren, Carl L., 1899, 1900
Lunn, Robert J., 1945
Lynch, James, 1985, 86
Lynch, Lynn, 1949, 50
Lyons, Thomas E., 1909, 10

M

MacArthur, John E., 1942
Macchione, Rudolph J., 1944
MacLean, Dan, 1979, 80
Macomber, F. B., 1914, 15, 16
Madsen, Olva, 1914
Maechtle, Donald M., 1946, 47,
  48
Maggioli, Archille F., 1946, 47
Major, Fred Jr., 1950
Malinsky, Robert E., 1948
March, Dean, 1974, 76
Marinangel, Jim, 1967
Markland, Jeff, 1986, 87
Marlaire, Arthur G., 1940
Marriner, Lester M., 1925, 26, 27
Marriner, Scott T., 1931
Martignago, Aldo A., 1947, 48,
  49
Martin, Jeffery C., 1984, 86
Martin, Mike, 1980, 81, 82
Martin, Robert W., 1898
Martin, Russel, 1958
Martin, Wesley P., 1938, 39
Masar, Terry, 1969, 70, 71
Mason, Taylor, 1978
Mastrangeli, Al A., 1946, 47, 48
Mathews, C. M., 1900
Mathis, Mark, 1985, 86
Mattiazza, Dominic L., 1941
Mauck, Jeff, 1985

Mauzey, John, 1968, 69
May, Robert D., 1931, 32
Maze (Mazeika), Anthony M,
  1936, 37
McAfee, Floyd H., 1954, 55
McAvoy, Tim, 1979, 80, 81
McBain, Mike, 1983, 84, 85
McBeth, Mike, 1979
McCarren, Larry, 1970, 71, 72
McCarthy, James P., 1941, 42
McCarthy, Tim, 1969, 70
McCartney, Tom, 1972, 73
McCaskill, Arthur, 1964
McCleery, Ben H., 1909
McClellan, Lynn, 1987, 88
McClure, Robert T., 1978, 79
McClure, William E., 1927, 28
McCormick, Olin, 1892, 93
McCormick, Roscoe C., 1898
McCracken, Mac, 1975, 76
McCray, Michael P., 1976, 77
McCullough, Lawrence, 1978, 79
McCullough, Thomas M., 1941
McCullum, Thomas, 1961
McDade, Richard L., 1958, 61
McDonald, James W., 1937, 38
McDonald, Ken, 1979
McDonald, Mark, 1977
McDonald, Phil, 1974, 75, 76
McDonough, Mike, 1967, 68
McGann, David G., 1961
McGann, Mike, 1983
McGarry, Shawn, 1987, 88
McGovern, Edward F., 1943
McGowan, Mark, 1985, 86, 87,
  88
McGregor, John L., 1915, 17
McGrone, Bryan, 1987
McIlwain, Wallace W., 1922, 23,
  24
McIntosh, Hugh, 1969
McKee, James, H., 1895, 96
McKeon, Larry, 1969
McKinley, George H., 1901, 02
McKissic, Dan, 1967, 69
McKnight, Wm. A., 1901, 02, 03
McLane, E. C., 1897, 98, 99
McMillan, Ernest, 1958, 59, 60
McMillen, James W., 1921, 22,
  23
McMillin, Kirk, 1969, 70
McMillin, Troy, 1978, 79, 81
McMillin, Ty, 1972, 73, 74
McMullen, Rolla, 1955, 56
McQuinn, Mike, 1980, 81, 82
Melsek, Daniel, 1976
Menkhausen, Brian, 1986, 87,
  88, 89

Merker, Henry F., 1897
Merriman, John Riley, 1909,
  10, 11
Meyer, John, 1977
Meyers, Curtis, 1980
Meyers, Melvin, 1959, 60
Michel, Chris, 1985, 86
Middleton, George E., 1920
Miles, Joe, 1980, 81, 82, 83
Miller, Bob, 1982, 83, 84
Miller, David H., 1939
Miller, Kenneth R., 1951, 52,
  53
Miller, Richard R., 1952, 55, 56
Miller, Roy A., 1922, 23, 24
Miller, Terry, 1965, 66, 67
Mills, Douglas C., 1961
Mills, Douglas R., 1927, 28, 29
Milosevich, Paul, 1939, 40, 41
Minnes, Mason, 1970, 71, 72
Minor, James R., 1955, 56
Minor, William B., 1962, 63, 64
Mitchell, Bill, 1967
Mitchell, Robert C., 1955, 56,
  57
Mitchem, Rickie, 1975, 76, 77
Mitterwallner, Merwin H., 1925,
  27
Mohr, Albert W. T. Jr., 1918,
  19, 20, 21
Mohr, Scott, 1987, 88
Mongreig, Louis M., 1917
Moore, Craig, 1986, 87
Moore, Paul, 1976
Morgan, Octavus, 1971, 72, 73
Morris, Harold H., 1916
Morris, LaRue, 1936
Morris, Max, 1943
Morscheiser, Jack, 1971
Mosley, Larry, 1980, 81
Moss, Perry L., 1946, 47
Mota, Joseph L., 1961
Mountjoy, Earl L., 1909
Mountz, Robert E. III, 1960, 61
Moynihan, Charles J., 1903,
  04, 05, 06
Muegge, Louis W., 1925, 27
Mueller, Dave, 1963, 64
Mueller, Richard A., 1948, 49,
  50
Mueller, Steven, 1988
Muhl, Clarence A., 1923, 24,
  25
Muhl, Fred L., 1903
Mulchrone, John, 1979, 80
Mulchrone, Pete, 1979, 81, 82
Mullin, Tom, 1972, 73
Munch, Donald, C., 1930

Murnick, Scott, 1987
Murphy, Mike, 1979, 80, 81, 82
Murphy, Patrick, 1960, 61
Murphy, Thomas W., 1951, 52
Murray, Ed., 1973, 74
Murray, Lindley P., 1931

N

Naponic, Robert, 1966, 67, 68
Navarro, Mike, 1970, 71, 72
Neathery, Herbert, 1950, 51, 52
Needham, James, 1891, 92
Nelson, Evert F., 1927
Nelson, Jesse W., 1914, 15
Nelson, Kenneth J., 1934, 35, 36
Nelson, Ralph W., 1956
Nelson, Steve, 1983, 84
Nelson, Steve, 1989
Newell, Richard F., 1960, 61
Nichols, Sidney W., 1917
Nickol, Edgar, 1926, 28
Niedzelski, Clifford T., 1941
Nietupski, Ronald, 1956, 57, 58
Nitschke, Ray E., 1955, 56, 57
Noelke, Robert, 1978, 79
Nordmeyer, Richard J., 1955, 56, 57
Norman, Tim, 1977, 78, 80
Norton, John, 1977
Nosek, Stephen A., 1951, 53, 54
Nowack, Albert J., 1926, 27, 28
Nowak, Bill, 1967, 68

O

O'Bradovich, Edward, 1959, 60
O'Connell, Thomas B., 1951, 52
O'Keefe, Arthur F., 1931
O'Neal, Ronald D., 1961
O'Neill, Dick A., 1931
O'Neill, Robert J., 1939
Oakes, Bernard F., 1922, 23
Offenbecher, Wm., 1956, 57
Olander, Milton M., 1918, 19, 20, 21
Oliver, Chauncy B., 1909, 10, 11
Oliver, Percy L. Jr., 1954, 55, 56
Oman, Steve, 1967, 68
Ormsbee, Terry, 1974, 76

Ornatek, Tony, 1968
Orr, John M., 1944
Osby, Vince, 1982, 83
Osley, Willie, 1970, 71
Ovelman, John W., 1930
Owen, Boyd Wm., 1930
Owens, Isaiah H., 1941, 46, 47

P

Pagakis, Chris N., 1949, 50
Palmer, Harry, 1933
Palmer, Peter, 1952, 53
Palmer, Ralph W., 1943
Pancratz, Kevin, 1975, 76, 77
Panique, Ken, 1971
Parfitt, Alfred W. Jr., 1943
Parker, Quintin, 1986, 88, 89
Parker, Roy S., 1901, 02
Parker, Walter A., 1891, 93
Parola, Jerry F., 1961
Parola, Tony, 1964
Parrilli, Anthony K., 1959, 60, 61
Pasko, Larry, 1956
Pasko, William, 1961, 62, 63
Passmore, Don, 1981, 82, 83, 84
Pater, Matt, 1987, 88
Patrick, Gerald J., 1958, 59
Patterson, John D., 1939
Patterson, Paul L., 1944, 46, 47, 48
Paulson, Wayne, 1963, 64
Pavesic, Ray, 1977
Pawlowski, Jos. G., 1940, 41, 42
Peach, John W., 1976, 77
Peden, Don C., 1920, 21
Pepper, Cam, 1989
Perez, Peter J., 1943
Perez, Richard B., 1956, 57
Perkins, Bernon G., 1931
Perkins, Cecil, 1926, 27
Perkins, Clyde M., 1943, 45
Perrin, Lonnie, 1972, 73, 75
Peters, Forrest I. (Frosty), 1926, 28, 29
Peterson, Mark, 1972, 73, 74
Peterson, Clifford L., 1938, 40
Peterson, Daniel E., 1951
Pethybridge, Frank H., 1914
Petkus, Bob, 1965
Petraitis, Luke, 1989
Pettigrew, James Q., 1906, 07, 08
Petty, Harold O., 1932
Petty, Lawrence O., 1916, 19

Petty, Manley R., 1914, 15, 16
Pezzoli, Phillip A. 1938
Pfeffer, John E., 1892, 93, 94, 95
Pfeifer, Myron P., 1940, 41, 42
Phillips, James E., 1938, 39, 40
Phillips, Jim (Chubby), 1973, 74, 75, 76
Phipps, T. E., 1903
Piatt, Charles L., 1931, 33
Piazza, Sam J., 1948, 49, 50
Pickering, Mike, 1969, 71
Piel, Mike, 1986, 87
Pierce, Jack B., 1945, 47, 48
Pierce, Stephen, 1985, 86
Piggott, Bert C., 1946
Pike, David R., 1962
Pillath, Jerry, 1968
Pillsbury, Arthur L., 1890
Pinckney, Frank L., 1905, 06
Pinder, Cyril C., 1965, 66
Pittman Donald C., 1947
Pitts, R. L., 1902, 03
Pixley, Arthur H., 1893, 94, 95, 96
Plankenhorn, James, 1961, 62, 63
Pleviak, Anthony J., 1966, 67, 68
Plummer, Ashley, 1980, 81
Pnazek, Karl, 1969
Podmajersky, Paul, 1943
Pogue, Harold A., 1913, 14, 15
Pollock, Dino, 1989
Pokorny, Ray, 1976
Polaski, Clarence L., 1936
Popa, Elie C., 1950, 51
Pope, Jean A., 1904
Portman, C. P., 1933, 34
Postmus, Dave, 1987, 88
Potter, Phil Harry, 1916
Powell, Larry D., 1978, 79
Powless, Dave, 1963, 64
Price, Samuel L., 1963, 64, 65
Priebe, Michael, 1978, 79
Primous, Marlon, 1988, 89
Prince, David C., 1911
Prokopis, Alexander, 1944
Pruett, Eugene F., 1913
Prymuski, Robert M., 1946, 47, 48
Pugh, Dwayne, 1982, 83, 84, 85
Purvis, Charles G., 1939

Q

Quade, John C., 1893, 94

HAIL TO THE ORANGE AND BLUE!

Qualls, Mark, 1988
Quinn, Bob, 1969, 71

R

Raddatz, Russ, 1968
Radell, Willard W. Jr., 1965
Railsback, Fay D., 1906, 07, 08
Raklovits, Richard F., 1949, 50
Ralph, Stanley, 1975, 77, 78, 79
Ramshaw, Jerry, 1977, 78
Rebecca, Sam J., 1950, 51
Redmann, Doug, 1967, 68, 69
Reeder, James W., 1937, 38, 39
Reese, Jerrold A., 1984, 86
Reeves, Harley E., 1892
Reichle, Richard W., 1919, 21
Reinhart, Rick, 1973
Reitsch, Henry O., 1920
Reitsch, Robert, 1925, 26, 27
Remein, Robert O., 1982
Renfro, Rick, 1983
Renn, Donald Dean, 1954, 55
Rettinger, Geo. L., 1938, 39
Rhodes, Ora M., 1896
Richards, Edward J., 1922, 23
Richards, James V., 1908, 09
Richie, James K., 1908
Richman, Harry E., 1927, 28
Riehle, John, 1968
Riggs, Thomas J. Jr., 1938, 39, 40
Ringquist, Clarence L., 1928
Roberson, Garvin, 1971, 72, 73
Roberts, Chester C., 1909, 10, 11
Roberts, Clifford, 1958, 59, 60
Roberts, Gilbert J., 1922, 23, 24
Robertson, Robert, 1966, 67
Robinson, Darrell, 1969, 70, 71
Robinson, Olaf E., 1929, 30
Robinson, Roy, 1972, 73, 74
Robison, M. W., 1922
Rodgers, Randy, 1968
Rokusek, Frank E., 1922, 23, 24
Romani, Melvin C., 1959, 60, 61
Rooks, Thomas, 1982, 83, 84, 85
Root, Clark W., 1930
Root, George H., 1893
Rose, Jerry, 1968
Ross, Steve, 1970, 72
Rothgeb, Claude J., 1900, 02, 03, 04
Rotzoll Dan, 1970, 71
Rouse, Eric V., 1976, 77, 78
Roush, Wm. D., 1928, 29
Rowe, Enos M., 1911, 12, 13
Royer, Joseph W., 1892
Rucks, Jim, 1970, 71, 72
Rue, Orlie, 1913, 14

Rump, Charles A., 1905
Rundquist, Elmer T., 1915, 16, 17
Russ, Jerald B., 1945
Russell, Eddie L., 1963, 64, 65
Russell, W. Hunter, 1930, 32
Rutgens, Jos. C., 1958, 59, 60
Ryan, Clement J. Jr., 1955
Ryan, John (Rocky), 1951, 52, 53
Ryan, Mike, 1968, 69
Rykovich, Julius, 1946
Ryles, Richard, 1982
Rylowicz, Robert A., 1950, 51

S

Saban, Joseph P., 1945
Sabino, Daniel, F., 1950, 51, 52
Sabo, John P., 1918, 20, 21
Sajnaj, Chester B., 1943
Samojedny, George, 1969, 71
Santini, Veto, 1969
Saunders, Don, 1964
Sayre, Elvin C., 1934, 35, 36
Scarcelli, Tony, 1980, 81, 83
Schacht, Fred W., 1894, 95, 96
Schalk, Edward A., 1931
Scharbert, Robert D., 1961, 62
Schertz, Thomas, 1986, 87
Schertz, Todd, 1986
Schlosser, Merle J., 1947, 48, 49
Schmidt, Burton J., 1947, 48, 49
Schmidt, Gerald, C., 1967
Schobinger, Eugene, 1912, 13, 14
Schoeller, Julies E., 1905
Schooley, Thomas, 1977
Schneider, Craig, 1986, 87, 88, 89
Schrader, Chas., 1956
Schulte, Rick, 1981, 82, 83, 84
Schultz, Arthur F., 1930
Schultz, Emil G., 1922, 23, 24
Schultz, Ernest W., 1925, 26, 27
Schulz, Larry, 1974, 75, 76
Schumacher, Gregg H., 1962, 63, 64
Schumacher, Henry N., 1930
Schustek, Ivan D., 1931, 32, 33
Sconce, Harvey J., 1894, 95
Scott, Bob, 1975, 76, 77
Scott, John, 1977, 78
Scott, Robert E., 1952
Scott, Tom, 1968, 69, 70
Scully, Mike, 1983, 84, 85, 87
Seamans, Frank L., 1932
Searcy, Todd M., 1984, 85
Sebring, Bob, 1984, 85
Seiler, Otto E., 1909, 10, 11
Seliger, Vernon L., 1946, 47, 48

Senneff, Geo. F., 1912, 13
Serpico, Ralph M., 1943, 44, 45, 46
Sewall, Luke, 1980, 81, 82, 83
Shaffer, Jim, 1989
Shapland, Earl P., 1912
Shattuck, Walt F. Sr., 1890
Shavers, Errol, 1989
Shaw, Kenny, 1979
Shea, Dan, 1980
Sheppard, Lawrence D., 1904
Sherrod, Michael, 1978, 79, 80
Shively, Bernie A., 1924, 25, 26
Shlaudeman, H. R., 1916, 17, 19
Short, Wm. E., 1927
Shular, Hugh M., 1897
Siambekos, Chris, 1986, 89
Siebens, Arthur R., 1913
Siebold, Harry P., 1937, 40
Siegel, Kenneth C., 1944
Siegert, Herbert F., 1946, 47, 48
Siegert, Rudolph, 1954, 55
Siegert, Wayne, 1949, 50
Sigourney, Chris, 1979, 81, 82, 83
Siler, Rich, 1981
Siler, Roderick W., 1901
Silkman, John M., 1912, 13
Simpson, Tim, 1988, 89
Singman, Bruce, 1962
Sinnock, Pomeroy, 1906, 07, 08
Skarda, Edward J., 1936, 37
Skubisz, Joe, 1987, 88
Slater, Wm. F., 1890, 91, 92
Slimmer, Louis F., 1923, 24
Sliva, Oscar, 1969
Smalzer, Joe, 1974, 75
Smerdel, Matthew T., 1942
Smid, Jan, 1952, 53, 54
Smith, Bobby J., 1976
Smith, Charles J., 1944
Smith, Darrell, 1981
Smith, Donald I., 1950
Smith, Eugene R., 1920
Smith, J. Dale, 1956, 57
Smith, James A., 1939, 41, 42
Smith, Kevin, 1975
Smith, M. Rex, 1950, 51, 52
Silva, Dave, 1989
Smith, Marshall F., 1948
Smith, Mick, 1965, 66
Smith, Stuyvesant C., 1919
Smith, Thomas D., 1965, 66
Smith, Willie, 1969

Smock, Walter F., 1900
Snavely, Edwin R., 1931
Snook, John K., 1932, 33
Soebbing, Mark H., 1976
Somlar, Scott, 1980
Sorey, Revie, 1972, 73, 74
Sowa, Nick, 1979
Spiller, John, 1969
Sprague, Stanley R., 1945
Springe, Otto, 1909, 10, 11
Spurgeon, A. Lowell, 1935, 36, 37
Squier, George K., 1914, 15
Squirek, Jack S., 1978, 79, 80, 81
Stahl, Garland, 1899, 1900, 01, 02
Standring, Bob, 1973
Stanley, Tim, 1982, 85
Stapleton, John M., 1959
Starks, Marshall L., 1958, 59, 60
Stasica, Stanley J., 1945
Stauner, Jim, 1974, 75, 76
Steele, James, 1890, 91
Steger, Kurt, 1975, 76, 77
Steger, Russell W., 1946, 47, 48, 49
Steinman, Henry J., 1929
Stellwagen, Joel, 1966
Stephenson, Lewis A., 1901
Sternaman, Edward C., 1916, 17, 19
Sternaman, Joseph T., 1921
Stevens, Don, 1949, 50, 51
Stevens, Lawrence J., 1951, 52
Stevenson, Jeff, 1985
Stewart, Baird E., 1952, 53, 54
Stewart, Charles A., 1905, 06
Stewart, David L., 1957, 58
Stewart, Frank, 1914, 15, 16
Stewart, James R., 1926, 27
Stewart, Lynn, 1962, 63, 64
Stewart, Thomas C., 1946, 47, 48, 49
Stine, Mike, 1983
Stone, Clyde E., 1902
Stone, Richard R., 1965
Stotz, Charles H., 1938
Stotz, James T., 1966
Stotz, Richard A., 1966
Stout, Hiles G., 1954, 55, 56
Stowe, Bob, 1980, 81, 82, 83
Strader, Wayne, 1977, 78, 79, 80
Strauch, Donald J., 1916
Straw, Thomas C., 1931, 32, 33

Streeter, Sean, 1988, 89
Strong, David A., 1936
Studley, Chas. B., 1949, 50, 51
Studwell, Scott, 1973, 75, 76
Stuessy, Dwight T., 1926, 27, 28
Sturrock, Tom, 1968
Sullivan, Bruce E., 1965, 66
Sullivan, Gerry, 1971, 72, 73
Sullivan, John, 1974, 75, 77, 78
Sullivan, Mike, 1974, 75
Summers, W. Michael, 1961, 62, 63
Suppan, Mike, 1974
Surdyk, Forian J., 1937
Sutter, Kenneth F., 1956
Sutton, Archie M., 1962, 63, 64
Swanson, Mark B., 1930
Sweney, Don, 1893, 94, 95, 97
Swienton, Kenneth R., 1952, 53, 54
Swoope, Craig, 1982, 83, 84, 85

T

Tabor, Hubert B., 1921
Tackett, Wm. C., 1892, 93
Tagart, Mark, 1984, 85
Taliaferro, Mike, 1962, 63
Tarnoski, Paul T., 1905
Tarwain, John, 1928
Tate, Albert R., 1948, 49, 50
Tate, Donald E., 1951, 52, 53, 54
Tate, Richard A., 1965, 66, 67
Tate, Wm. L., 1950, 51, 52
Taylor, Carooq, 1977, 80
Taylor, Joseph W., 1904
Taylor, Keith, 1983, 85, 86, 87
Taylor, Randall R., 1976, 77, 78
Teafatiller, Keith G., 1984, 85
Tee, Darrin, 1986, 87
Tee, David, 1982
Theodore, James J., 1934
Theodore, John A., 1935
Thiede, John, 1977, 78
Thomas, Calvin, 1978, 79, 80, 81
Thomas, Ken, 1987, 89
Thomas, Stephen K., 1961
Thomases, Robert, 1938
Thompson, Darryl, 1982, 83
Thompson, Herbert P., 1911
Thorby, Chas. H. J., 1895
Thornton, Bruce, 1975, 76, 77, 78

Thorp, Don, 1980, 81, 82, 83
Tilton, Harry W., 1894
Timko, Craig S., 1965, 66, 67
Timm, Judson A., 1927, 28, 29
Tischler, Matthew, 1935
Tohn, Clarence G., 1943
Tomanek, Emil, 1944
Tomasula, David G., 1965, 66, 67
Tregoning, Wesley W., 1941, 45
Trigger, Jeff C., 1966, 67, 68
Trudeau, Jack, 1983, 84, 85
Trumpy, Bob 1964
Tucker, Derwin, 1975, 76, 77, 78
Tumilty, Richard J., 1941
Tupper, James O., 1913
Turek, Joseph J., 1939, 40
Turnbull, David, 1937
Turner, Elbert, 1988
Turner, Greg, 1986, 87, 88
Turner, Shawn, 1985, 86, 88
Twist, John F., 1908, 09, 10

U

Uecker, Bill, 1972, 73, 74
Ulrich, Chas. Jr., 1949, 50, 51
Umnus, Leonard, 1922, 23, 24
Uremovich, George, 1971, 72, 73
Usher, Darryl, 1983, 84, 85, 87
Utz, George J., 1956, 57

V

Valek, James J., 1945, 46, 47, 48
Valentino, Ralph Rudolph, 1949, 51
Van Dyke, Jos. A., 1932
Van Hook, Forest C., 1906, 07, 08
Van Meter, Vincent J., 1932
VanOrman, Ellsworth G., 1935
Varrige, Tom, 1980, 81, 82
Venegoni, John, 1978, 80, 81
Verduzco, Jason, 1989
Vernasco, Joseph P., 1950, 51
Vernasco, Walter L., 1952, 53, 54
Versen, Walter G., 1944
Vierneisel, Phil, 1973, 74, 75, 76
Vogel, Otto H., 1921
Vohaska, Wm. J., 1948, 49, 50
Volkman, Dean E., 1965, 66, 67